MERCILESS MONEY

My Diary of a Shameful Economy

Written and Illustrated by
Vivien John

MAPLE
PUBLISHERS

MERCILESS MONEY My Diary of a Shameful Economy

Author: Vivien John

First Published in 2025

ISBN 978-1-83538-710-8 (Paperback)
978-1-83538-711-5 (E-Book)

Written and Illustrated by Vivien John

Book Layout by:
Maple Publishers
www.maplepublishers.com

Published by:
Maple Publishers
Fairbourne Drive, Atterbury,
Milton Keynes,
MK10 9RG, UK
www.maplepublishers.com

A CIP catalogue record for this title is available from the British Library.

CONTENTS LIST

An Author's Note

The moment our birth is registered we sign a contract that begins the game of life according to the nation's rules. As citizens, we are expected to contribute physically, legally and economically to an established, yet fallible system with minimal knowledge and agreeable compliance.

Amidst these expectations, I continue to seek the truth. I am one of many who are not prepared to comply with what is said, written and widely accepted without some level of scrutiny. And If this makes us extraordinary (and almost certainly a proverbial pain in the arse), then I am prepared to risk societal acceptance and personal popularity in order to find it.

Aside from the who, how and when, what I really want to know is WHY. Having asked the question, 'why do we still need money?' I have yet to receive a satisfactory answer, hence this book.

To all fellow truth-seekers, don't give up.

The Opening Bit

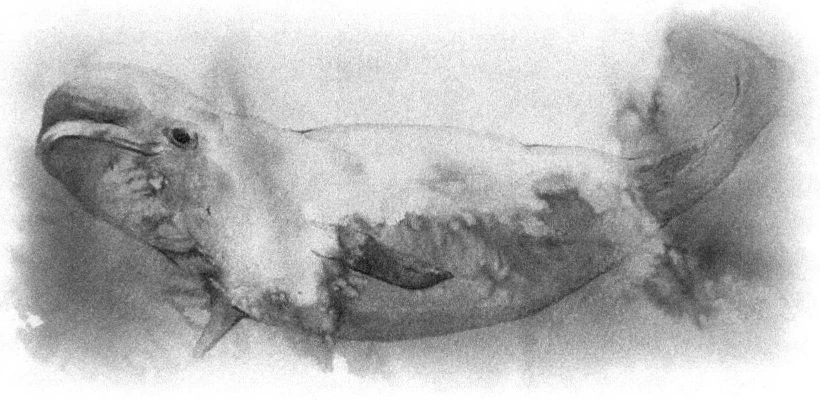

THE GUARDIAN **2nd August 2022**

BP profits triple to £7bn as oil prices surge because of Ukraine war

'BP will hand billions of pounds to shareholders after tripling its profits to nearly £7bn in the second quarter of the year amid high oil prices during Russia's invasion of Ukraine, sparking anger from MPs and campaigners as families struggle in the cost-of-living crisis'

The Situation

As I am drafting this introduction, the morning's news is announcing radical increases in the cost of energy that will triple the cost of household energy bills in less than one year. We are told by Uswitch [1]that households collectively owe £1.3 billion to their energy suppliers, and that 8 million households have no credit balance. Shortly I will be one of them. Added to increasing public anxiety is public anger when learning that the same energy suppliers are announcing exorbitant profits that would clear all this debt two times over. The Eon energy supplier confirmed profits of £3.47 billion in the first 6 months of 2022.

'Oil companies in the UK and beyond have enjoyed booming earnings in recent months on the back of rising energy prices as households around the world have struggled with soaring bills.'[2]

The cost of living has risen to extraordinary levels. The UK Parliament confirms that we are facing:

- the highest rate of inflation since 1982
- an increase in energy prices by 95%
- a significant increase in road fuel prices
- a rise in the cost of agricultural products e.g. wheat.

Many must be asking themselves, how long can this go on? How long can I hold out before I must use up my savings or take out a loan, just to keep my head above water? How long before I seriously consider getting a second job or visiting a foodbank?

It isn't the best of times, that's for sure. When looking back, some will say it felt like the worst. The winds of change blew a gale through the years 2022 to 2024 -

1 Price comparison website that also enables people to switch to a different energy supplier

2 Big oil's quarterly profits hit £50bn as UK braces for even higher energy bills. J.Jolly & M.Sweney. 2022. The Guardian.

astrologists consulted their charts and foresaw a hurricane. The events that unfolded rocked the very foundation upon which we build our lives and our futures - economic stability. This country faced the penalties of soaring costs resulting in a blitz of strikes and protests. For the first time since 1961 the national debt reached 100% of the nation's gross domestic product (GDP). Put simply, we owed more than we could pay off. The nurses, doctors and physiotherapists striked for better pay and working conditions. The train drivers and rail staff; the barristers, the postal workers, teachers, and those that kept our ferries crossing the channel – all fought their corner in an effort to arm themselves against the effects of a stubborn inflation.

The Vision

Several years ago I started to casually consider what would happen if money, or the concept of money, was lifted from our lives, from each and every country, from the earth. What would happen if the financial system simply disappeared, dissolved. What if money was no more - would the world collapse, would we cease to be? Does the absence of money prevent us from sleeping, waking, eating, putting on our clothes and engaging in some sort of function? Why are we assuming that there has to be a monetary system in place for us to continue existing? Why do we need it to thrive?

Ask any parent what they want for their child and they will (most likely) say, 'I just want them to be happy.' What does happiness equate to –comfort and security? Purpose and fulfilment? Peace and acceptance? Love? Whatever the translation, this feeling of happiness is one we chase to the end of our lives. This will never change – we are all always seeking the same emotion, yet we look for it in the shallowest of places. From the moment we are born we are taught to value money; we are persuaded to believe that it holds the key to a successful life. We know at heart that the pleasure money gives us is short-lived. It is transient and insatiable. Yet still we collect and we consume more and more, living in constant fear of judgment or destitution.

'After a certain point, more money doesn't make us happier. Instead, we find ourselves on a hedonic treadmill in which happiness is about matching our level of consumption with our peers, and when they do better and we don't, even if we are better off in absolute terms, we are less happy.'[3]

What is money anyway but a piece of paper, a lump of metal or an electronic digit. Is it token of exchange or a symbol of power? Is it just a sum that fluctuates according to variables beyond our control? Is it a number that rises and falls according

---

3 The Value of Nothing: how to reshape market society and redefine democracy. R.Patel. 2009. Portobello Books

to the politics of the day, a war, or even the weather? Should it be an entitlement or a reward? It is certainly something that limits a person's options and dictates their degree of freedom and comfort. Maybe for some it is a key to a garden of abundance and for others a lock on a prison of hardship. Or is it all these things at different times and for different people?

I find it bizarre that to collect a bag of groceries, I must enter a card into a machine; and if I don't have that card, I will not be able to eat. Why is this one thing, this piece of plastic, paper or metal standing in the way of anything I need, when what I need can be easily had. What is money to us these days? A number that goes up or down according to our activities. We work and the number goes up, we eat and the number goes down. We work again and the number goes up again, we turn on our appliances and the number goes down again, and so it goes on. A number. It's just a number, it isn't real, it's not tangible unless you want it to be. When was the last time you saw your number in physical form or held it in your hand? Have you ever wanted to see all the cash that you own – laid out in front of you? Maybe you are just satisfied that somewhere accessible to you, there is a number that rises more than it falls. Isn't that what we all want?

When did you last pay for something with cash? Thinking back over the last couple of weeks, I put cash in a parking ticket machine (there was no option to use a debit card) and I purchased items at a car boot sale. I recall during the lockdown of 2020 carrying the same £10 note in my purse for months. Instead, I played the numbers game whereby I regularly looked at my finances on a website and watched them fall and rise over the months, much like watching waves ebb and flow on a beach. I observed a predictable pattern that rarely changes, so long as I fulfil my part of the currency contract. I began to wonder, why is this number placing limitations on my life, the lives of my children, my parents, my friends and community? Why is it even there and what would happen if it wasn't? What would change? And if there were changes, why should there be?

But what if I continue to access the goods or services I need to live comfortably. What if I then in turn fulfil my agreed responsibilities to support the needs of others much as I, and as we all do now. For example, I carry on doing the job of my choice whilst collecting my food from a shop and filling my car with petrol without having to present a card or hand over a note. The staff at the shop continue to order the food and stock the shelves. The tanker drivers continue to deliver the fuel to stock the pumps at the petrol station whilst they in turn collect their own weekly food and fuel. No transactions take place. Each taking what they need without the concern that they will have to go without or make do with less.

Whenever I propose this concept in conversation, most respond with the question, 'Won't people take more than they need?' Maybe they would initially until they realised that they could not consume it all or sell it on for profit. There would be no gain to be made, because everything would be available to everyone. Nothing would be free because that implies forfeit of payment. There would be no financial transactions because there would be no money.

This may sound as though I am just going through a rough financial patch and fed up with a system that isn't giving me what I need and what I want. Indeed, virtually all of us are currently going through hard times. It's 2022: an unjust war in Europe threatens our physical and financial security. The virus lingers, threatens and consequently disrupts staffing levels in all areas of production, distribution and essential services. There is a mass movement of people; many leaving their jobs to find alternative employment. Many essential roles (as in the public sector) are not being filled, creating frustration and delay in the provision of services. When I compare the opportunities I had to those of my children I can see there is a financial shortfall. It is reported that that millennials (born between 1981 and 2000) are the first generation to be worse off than their parents.[4] Despite our advancements in equality and technology they still cannot afford to live independently, to own their homes, be free of debt, or work shorter days.

Yet one man's loss is another man's gain.

An Unfair Distribution

I've joined the 99% club. Well, sort of, and mainly out of curiosity. I've had my induction via Zoom and I am now a member of an organisation that firmly believes it has the evidence to prove that the wealth in this country is unevenly distributed. It believes that no amount of economic growth will close the gap. The 99 % represents the population who share only 1% of the world's wealth. The remaining 99% of wealth is enjoyed by just 1% and the gap grows steadily.[5]

'Oligarchs have enormous wealth. They have enormous power. In fact for the 1%, things have never been better. They have their mansions all over the world, their private islands, their expensive art, their yachts, their private jets. Some of them have spaceships that someday may take them to Mars. These oligarchs like the way things

---

4 Millennials will be the first generation to earn less than their parents. J. Myers. 2016. World Economic Forum.

5 99% How We've Been Screwed, and How to Fight Back .M.Thomas. 2020. Apollo.

are going and, with unlimited resources at their disposal will do everything possible to defend what they have and maintain the status quo.'[6]

Whilst the evidence is persuasive, it's the feeling of injustice and powerlessness that is compelling. A feeling that no matter how well this country prospers I am not likely to enjoy or benefit from the financial fallout however many hours I work. I will simply be giving the money back to those whose pockets are already swollen with superfluous abundance.

I was naïve enough to believe that our financial system, be it national or international was a system of fairness and one that manages the concept of greed i.e. fair pay for a fair day's work etc. I am sure this view is shared. It is one that keeps us believing that we need to work hard for what we want and the opportunities that are available to us but must be fought for. Most of us simply accept the pattern of borrowing and paying back so that we can call our home and our goods our own. It is ingrained and unquestioned, even though we seem to be working harder and longer for less return.

When I decided to write this book my research revealed a system that traps people into poverty and debt, increases the divide between the rich and the poor, and is anything but the fair model we have presumed it to be. I have no objection to a financial order that fairly controls the distribution of wealth if it did just that. But it is the unjust, exploitive and often criminal side effects of an unfair currency system that outweighs the benefits that I object to. We send the money up through our labour and our taxes, but we see little of it coming back down.

The more I research the more likely I conclude that the monetary system is very complicated, and I confess I don't understand all its intricacies. What I do see is a conveniently complex system evolved by (predominantly) men to benefit themselves by the control of power and infiltration of governments. They line their pockets with riches they cannot possibly consume within a lifetime and at the expense of the citizens they claim to serve and represent. I liken it to an impenetrable veil, one that allows us to see a shadow of truth, but that resolutely divides the haves and the have-nots. We keep it there through our own complacency, acceptance of defencelessness, and in believing that we are due nothing but must work for everything. It has been said that we now work harder and longer than our medieval counterparts.[7]

---

6 It's OK to be Angry About Capitalism. B. Sanders. 2023. Allen lane (Penguin Group)

7 Do We Work More Than Medieval Peasants? G. Pakalka & A. Noreika. Technology.com

Is money worth keeping when the means by which it is created and shared is deceptive and unjust? You could say that money is not the culprit, it is people who cannot be trusted with it. There is reason to question a system that holds a population to ransom and denies people of their very basic human needs; a system that forces us to make critical choices about the way we allocate our income. For many it is a choice of eating or keeping warm.

My thoughts are the same as they have been for a number of years, but the situation I describe has sparked an urgency to share an ideal. I propose a brave and no doubt controversial alternative to our current arrangement which is not fulfilling my and many others' beliefs of what a fair society should be. I'm not the first to suggest a money-less society but for many the concept of living without financial controls asks a lot of the imagination and faith in the innate goodness of human nature. Yet we are fair and we are good by nature. We are charitable and we have empathy, we just feel powerless.

We Have the Heart

THE GUARDIAN **10th August 2022**

Stranded beluga whale removed from Seine river in France as part of rescue attempt

After nearly six hours of work, the 800-kilogram (1,800-pound) cetacean was lifted from the river by a net and crane at around 4am (0200 GMT) and placed on a barge under the immediate care of a dozen veterinarians

The second item of news this week describes the rescue of a stranded Beluga Whale in the River Seine (NW Paris). The mammoth rescue operation involves over 80 individuals including animal specialists, police and divers. The world is captivated and watches in desperate hope that this one animal can be saved and returned to its natural environment. This reaction proves our instinctive yearning to preserve life, and that we have an intrinsic magnet that draws us to the earth, to nature, to our origins and to each other.

Whilst I may not live long enough to see it come to fruition, I do believe that a world that relies on a monetary system is dissolving. I believe that the generations are leaning more towards a moral and viable society that no longer bases its values on individual wealth, recognition and short-term gain. I believe humanity can and wants to live a harmonious existence where it willingly gives as much as it receives, expresses gratitude when there is abundance and shares its reserves when there is hardship.

It is not my primary intention to dig deep to discredit dysfunctional systems and it hasn't really been necessary. My observations and my conversations together with local and national news items are all evidence of this nation's dire financial ethics and circumstances. They are described in no particular chronological order but refer to notable and less known events that occurred between 2022-24. I have also researched and quoted relevant reports and articles where appropriate and in support of the points I have raised.

We each have personal stories to bring to this deliberation, I have therefore invited the opinions, memories and experiences of a random group of adults from different backgrounds (aged from early 20's to those in retirement) as a representation of the general public. I have referred to them as Research Participants and am grateful for their honest contributions.

I may be accused of not comprehending the complexities of the financial system and some will say my views are too simplistic. But if our system is too complicated to fully understand then it is exclusive. It excludes and therefore disempowers the majority. My aim is to present an idea of an alternative way of living, The change may be incremental, and it may be up to our descendants, our future generations to implement new ideals. But if you believe there can be a better, fairer, more altruistic model on which to base our future and those of our children and grandchildren then please, read on.

PART ONE

The Economic Truth

Chapter One

World Cup Wagers

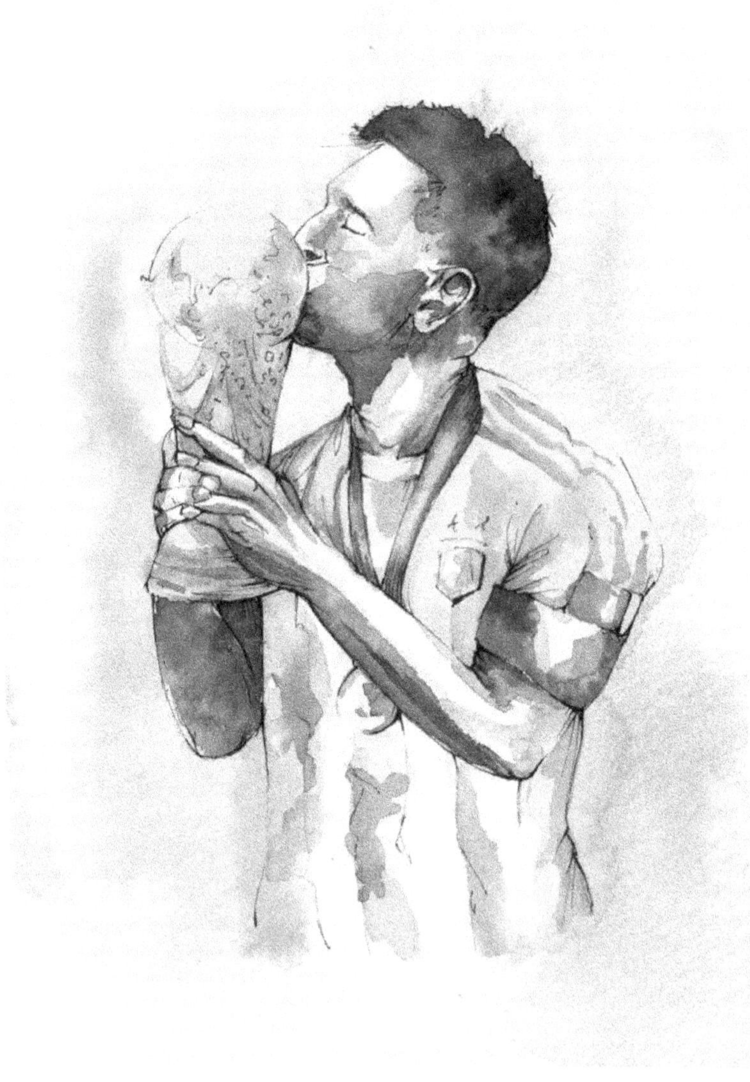

19 September 2022 – It's the day of the Queen's funeral and I've torn myself from the TV to take my aged dog for a walk, the pace of which is not dissimilar to the royal procession. As I make my way out of the village I am hailed down by a group of children looking no older than 10 years, selling small items. These items (hair grips and toys) are of little interest to me, but I join in. Children's ideas and ambitions should be taken seriously. The conversation goes:

Girl: 'would you like to buy something?'

Boy: 'It's for charity.'

Me: 'Which charity?' He looks puzzled and doesn't answer.

Me: 'What have you got for sale?'

Girl: 'Would you like to see a menu?'

She means price list. I love the way young children pick up words and phrases and use them out of context. I read the list crudely written in felt pens and note there are stickers. I love stickers, so I buy some that remind me that *nothing is impossible* (including finishing this book) and that *coffee makes everything better*. I give her 50p as per menu. She asks me if I want my change and tells me to have a nice day. It's a delightful transaction, a simple and innocent adventure into the adult world of free enterprise.

From the moment we are born we enter into a system that will govern our decisions for the rest of our lives. Finances will dictate where and how we live, what we eat, how we are educated and who we have relationships with. We begin working with money the moment we understand how it gets us what we want. We ask for pocket money, we find a part time job, we save it up and we spend it. From a young age, we begin to understand its worth. Like the children I encountered, we consider how much someone would pay in exchange for the goods we can offer and we price them accordingly. Perhaps Napoleon's observation of Britain being a nation of shopkeepers carries some credence.

The use of money has a sinister side, and I will explore that in subsequent chapters, but to add balance there is merit in critiquing the benefits of our financial system, when it is working at its best, when it is fair and serving all individuals and their communities.

Pride and Independence

When I was 12 years old, I lied about my age to work in a vegetable-packing factory in the school holidays. When I told the employers I was 13, nobody questioned my parents or asked for identification documents, and so I was hired.[1] I started work at 8am and finished at 1 or 2pm, repeating the same task over and over, often at least 60 times in one hour. I packed onions, root vegetables and on one occasion, bulbs. The noise prevented any kind of comfortable conversation. The music (barely heard over the din of conveyer belts) was dull and unfamiliar. In winter the small industrial heater did its best, but we were still cold.

It took just one day's work to fully understand the value of an education. How many times had I been reminded that a lack of qualification would lead to 'working in a factory all your life!'. I dismissed the advice as any tender-aged student might, until I experienced for myself the monotony of relentless labour that demanded no application of skill or thought. I'm not implying that the women (almost all were women) who worked in the factory were not educated, but I knew that for them this work was more of a necessity than a choice. Yet aged 12, it was entirely my choice. It gave me the means to become financially independent. I felt a sense of pride and achievement in entering an adult's world on my own and thrilled to be rewarded for my efforts.

In terms of gaining independence, I can see that I was only replacing one dependence with another, albeit a preferable one. Instead of relying on the good will of my parents (whose judgement of my merits changed from one day to the next), I relied instead on a less subjective system of reward that was consistent and appealed to my sense of justice – I had earned it. No longer did I have to suffer the humiliation of having to ask for money and of being either refused or deferred. Hearing "not now, I'm busy" or "I'll think about it", just meant further humiliation in having to ask again at a more convenient time.

I felt immense pride when I received my first pay packet - £5 cash for 3 (short) days' work. When, in later years I ventured into self-employment, I celebrated earning my first £100, and then my first £1000. I felt the same way when I first sold a work of art, provided a commissioned service and when I was promoted to a higher role. The amount of money itself was of little relevance, it was soon spent, but the financial rewards were a reflection of worth and that translates to self-esteem. The children selling their stickers and hair grips will count their pennies at the end of their working day and feel a sense of pride at what they have managed to accomplish.

---

1 The law now allows young people aged 13 to 14 years to work a maximum of 25 hours a week in the school holidays, but employment in factories and industrial sites is forbidden. 2022. GOV.UK

Motivation

For the purposes of balance and perspective I invited a group of willing research participants (RP's) to contribute their knowledge, experience and honest opinions on the various discussions featured in the chapters. Ages range from early 20's to those in retirement. In this case I invited them to vote on which aspect of employment they felt inspired them the most. I asked them to decide between the nature of the work, the people they worked with or the pay they received. Work was favoured most at 38%, then people or the social aspect of the work – 34%, least of all was the money – 28%.

> **Juan:** 'I think the job is the drive, and the money should be a sign of respect that you do your job well. The people come and go in my experience.'
>
> **Claire:** 'I'd love for the money to not matter.'

In 1959 Herzberg published his theory that job satisfaction comes from the intrinsic elements of work, whereas the reasons for dissatisfaction arise when the hygiene factors have been compromised. The illustration may help to explain this. What he's saying is, a pitiful wage will leave you disgruntled, but a great wage alone won't bring you happiness.[2]

Herzberg's Two Factor Theory (1959).

2 Herzberg's Two-Factor Theory. M. Alshmemri et al. 2017. Life Science Journal

In the world of employment do we consider money to be the primary motivator? Research suggests not. Whilst a wage maybe the reason for working and will factor into our choice of job and the numbers of hours a week we will work, pay appears to provide the least stimulus. When I was completing my studies in business management, I conducted research on the employment factors that motivate employees. I interviewed both operational workers and an equal number of managers, asking them each to rate the following factors in terms of importance:

- Pay
- Working conditions and contracts
- Colleagues
- Managers
- The work itself, responsibilities and opportunities

The most revealing conclusions showed that employers overestimated the importance of pay and underestimated what the actual work meant to each individual. Above all, the employees valued their colleagues, followed by the job and a level of responsibility. Pay was the least motivating factor.

Fairness and Reward

I'm recalling a conversation I had with a manager over 30 years ago. I heard that one of my colleagues who did the same job was getting paid more per hour. My anger prompted me to challenge this and so I asked for a few moments of her time. She invited me into her office. "What do you want to see me about?" Plucking up a lot of courage, I responded, "I've heard that M is earning £3.50 an hour." (the current rate for bar work was £3 per hour). I kept quiet, hoping the statement alone will indicate my intention.

"Who told you that?" As she wasn't denying it, I felt encouraged to go on.

"It doesn't matter who told me.... I know." This was somewhat a bluff, as he never actually told me himself, I heard it from someone else.

"Why is he getting more than me? I work just as hard." She didn't deny that it either, she just looked at me and pondered.

The conversation was short and to the point. I don't recall what was said next, but I did receive the same pay increase. I don't even know why he was quietly paid more and at the time I didn't really care, I just remember feeling unappreciated and insulted. Later in the year, when I approached the same manager for holiday pay, she apologised and said that this year the company simply couldn't afford it, and I believed her. I had first hand evidence that explained at least one of the reasons for the shortfall. Whilst on shift with a co-worker, I watched him enter the cash for drinks into the till and put the cash paid for meals directly into his wallet. He was stealing from the company, and therefore to my mind he was denying me my holiday pay. I was angry, only this time I didn't care to be the start of any conflict, so I kept quiet and seethed.

In theory and in principle, money rewards labour. A person works, they get paid; they in turn pay for what they need to live, which in turn rewards the person that provides it. The system of reward can arguably incentivise the individual to work harder, longer or better when monetary recompense is linked to their performance. What is paramount however, is the guarantee of fairness. Nothing in my experience enrages people more than being treated unfairly.

'Fairness of treatment at work is a central determinant of employee well-being, affecting both psychological and physical health risks. Researchers have emphasized two aspects of fairness that are particularly important in accounting for this. The first is fairness in the way decisions are taken. The second is the balance between 'effort and reward'. Fairness at work is also important as a factor likely to affect organisational performance. Employees who feel they are fairly treated are more likely to be committed to their organisations and to trust new management initiatives.'[3]

Now I am working in the public sector my pay follows an agreed structure where there are no secrets as to who earns what. You are paid according to your bracket which aligns to your role and the level of responsibility and accountability it holds. Is this fairer? Yes, in that there is less dispute with the employer as it is a national agenda. A person can only earn more if they apply for a higher role. However, it doesn't stop people comparing their efforts and output with another who earns the same. I hear individuals complaining, "what does he do all day?" "She spends half her day on her phone." "He always takes a longer lunch break." "How come she always get to work from home, and I don't?"

Feeling Secure

Montse. 'To just live from day to day is a feeling that would suffocate me. I need to know that I have savings for any extras that may arise, such as the car breaking down, the boiler, community expenses or the dentist."

3 Fairness at Work in Britain. First Findings from the Skills and Employment Survey. D.Gallie et al. 2017. Cardiff.ac.uk.

I recently read that some billionaire somewhere said they wouldn't feel safe unless they had a billion dollars sitting in the bank. I haven't been able to trace the source, but the statement did prompt me to give the subject of savings more thought.

For as long as I can remember I have saved a sum of money in a building society account for the sake of emergencies. Except for a couple of very lean years, I have managed to maintain a modest balance. Some years were kind and the balance rose and the interest accrued was substantial. More recently the balance has shrunk and the returns in interest are negligible. Nevertheless, it does, and always has, provided a feeling of security and protection from destitution. Whatever happens I feel I will be able to afford the next bill, whether it be repairs to my car, or veterinary fees.

I have no intention of spending this money, I'm not tempted to, in fact I want to add to it for no other reason than to feel more secure. Should I die and it hasn't been spent, then it will have served its purpose – to help me feel safe and to pass this same token of security to my children. Some may consider this a wasted opportunity, and I can empathise as I felt the same way about my parent's savings. When they relocated to a care home, I was staggered by how much money they had accumulated over the years. Initially I was resentful. All I could think of was how much more useful the money could have been for my children in purchasing their own homes. Now I have come to realise that their savings served the same purpose as mine, we just differed on the amounts. It turns out that their readily available reserves equalled the costs for their care up until their house was sold. No more and no less, and less aggravation for me as I avoided the need to negotiate with the local authorities at a time when communication was severely limited.

The amount of savings needed to feel secure- each stalk represents an RP.

The illustration shows the number of RP's specifying the minimum sum they would need in savings to feel financially secure. Each stalk of wheat represents an individual's preference.

Most people would agree that savings are important, even though they contribute little or nothing to the economy. The opinion of how much money is enough differs between individuals, and may relate to earnings, age or experiences. It matters little, as the reason for savings or investment is to keep it intact or to make it grow for the sole purpose of security. It is not a situation, not a state of being, it is a feeling.

A Question of Choice

One day in 2019. Having circled a one-way system in Coventry numerous times, I finally enter the car park I had programmed (clearly unsuccessfully) into the satnav. My next challenge is the Pay to Park machine. I can't fathom why, but to retrieve a ticket is not as simple as feeding the machine a few coins and waiting for it to print and appear. As I become more and more flustered by what should be a simple transaction, a very thin dishevelled man who had been asking visitors for change, comes to my aid. He shows me the sequence to follow and within a few minutes I am able to purchase my ticket. He then asks me if I could spare some change. I look in my purse but I have no coins left, only a £10 note. It only takes a microsecond to calculate that I have worked less than an hour to earn it and will spend even less time squandering it on coffee and cake. So, I gratefully give it to him.

At first he refuses, "No, it's too much!" I explain, "you have no idea how much stress you have saved me. I can now enjoy the rest of my day thanks to you. Please take it." As I leave the car park, I can still hear him voicing his excitement at being able to afford not just one hot meal, but maybe even two in one day.

At the time the encounter left me feeling good, now my thoughts are mixed and I feel a sense of guilt. Why should I have, and he have not? How would I feel worrying about how to afford a meal that day. Do you give money to the homeless, or do you prefer to give them food? Perhaps you prefer not to support them at all. Perhaps you assume that any cash you give will be spent on alcohol or other substances, and you feel bad about contributing to their ill health. I think our thoughts are often tossed between the various possibilities, but it's an interesting debate. Our decisions are usually linked to our values and beliefs regarding causes of homelessness and the effects of begging. I am inclined to agree with the author of an article published in the Guardian:

'No one in their right mind thinks it's a clever scam to sit on a freezing pavement suffering the humiliation of asking people for a few coins. And frankly, there are many people out there who are seriously mentally ill and are chaotically struggling to stay alive.'[4] I agree, what an awful way to make money, a pittance at that.

I favour giving money to the homeless as I believe cash provides choice. Who am I to dictate what it should be spent on or what that person needs. It is no different to giving a teenager a gift token or a banknote when we know that it will most likely be spent on yet another pair of expensive trainers (how many do they need?) in place of an educational book that will help them through their exams. It is acknowledgement of the fundamental freedom and right to choose one's own way of living. It is a gesture of respect.

Just for the Thrill of It

When it comes to gambling money provides the perfect agent for channelling this compulsion.

'Gambling in its variety of forms is a popular pastime in Great Britain, with nearly half of all adults participating in at least one form (including the National Lottery) each month. Most spend small amounts which are similar to or less than spending on other leisure activities and do not report experiencing any harm from gambling.'

'However, around 300,000 people in Great Britain are estimated to be experiencing 'problem gambling', defined as gambling to a degree which compromises, disrupts, or damages family, personal or recreational pursuits, and a further 1.8 million are identified as gambling at elevated levels of risk. Gambling harms, can wreck lives, impact families and communities, and even lead to suicide in extreme cases.'[5]

During the last World Cup my son and I decided to follow our own betting game. We agreed that for every game we would each choose a team to win, and if we concurred on the outcome, we would bet on the score or the goal difference. The betting began at £1 per game and increased to £2 for the second round and quarter finals. The stakes went up to £5 for the semi-finals. By the time the finals arrived, my son was leading by £10. To keep it interesting (and because he loves his mum) he suggested placing our stakes with the bookmakers for an Argentina win, which they did but alas not in full time play. The bookies won in the end, as they always do.

---

4 Should you give homeless people money? T. Courtenay. 2018. The Guardian Newspaper

5 High stakes: gambling reform for the digital age. Department for Culture, Media & Sport. 2023. GOV.UK

Are we gamblers? Not really. It brought a lot of fun and conversation for a short period, and for two people who don't normally watch football, we sat and enjoyed many matches together, particularly the final. It was worth the small expense.

We value money highly, sometimes above all else, so the risk of losing it, albeit small sums, is both exhilarating and devastating. I cannot imagine what else could replace it. Forfeiting time is draining. If we had decided to bet a job, a chore (washing up or cutting the grass for a month) it wouldn't have the same appeal. It would take far too much effort and increase the likelihood of the bet not being honoured. Betting clothing is inappropriate, a body part is drastic, food might have worked - the winner pays for next day's take-away?

'Research outside of the gambling field consistently demonstrates that consumers tend to spend more and are less aware of their expenditure when transacting electronically compared to when using cash. In the online gambling context, there is some evidence that the use of digital payment methods (notably including credit cards) contributes to overspending and problem gambling for some individuals.'[6]

Betting and losing money is worryingly convenient – perilously easy. It is a clean, clear and simple agent for taking a risk; accessible and faceless. The ease with which electronic currency can be used over cash can exacerbate addictions hence new regulations to limit spending and to provide safer gambling systems and environments.

The Ultimate Benchmark

Money gives us both a theoretical and tangible means to compare and to attribute value. We assign our own illogical inconsistent assessment to determine our purchasing decisions. Let's say I visit a supermarket or store to buy amongst other things, a box of cereal. I have a mental limit on how much I intend to pay. When I see the price has risen beyond that limit, I will either decide to look for an alternative or pay extra for the convenience of not having to shop somewhere else. I may even leave empty handed. These amounts may equate to less than £1 but money still provides the standard for me to compare and decide. Ironically, I will fill my car with petrol paying little heed to the cost which could vary up to £5 between petrol stations. I will also pay up to £65 for a pair of comfortable shoes but I won't pay more than £2 for a pair of tweezers. The more I think about it, the more I see how irrational my assessments are, but it's my benchmark – we all have our own.

6 Digital gambling payment methods: harm minimization policy considerations. S. Gainsbury & A. Blaszczynsk., 2020.

Money – a means of exchange, a ticket to prosperity, a cushion, a dare and a yardstick, where did it all begin? When did money move from metal to paper, to plastic and to digit? Moreover, how did it evolve from a simple tool of trade to the complex industry we know it to be today?

Chapter Two

Copper, Nickel, Polymer and Zinc

"It's just money - it's made up. Pieces of paper with pictures on it so we don't have to kill each other just to get something to eat."

[Film: Margin Call, 2011]

Notes and Coins

My brother and I used to collect coins. Having lived in different countries and travelled frequently, we amassed an extensive collection of silver and copper specimens that rewarded us with endless hours of amusement. We made coin rubbings with thin paper and a sharp pencil. We sorted them into size, denomination, country of origin and any other characteristic they could share. We raced them, rolling them deftly off our index finger to see which would go the furthest.

On rainy days we would set up our armies of plastic animals either side of a single bed and hide them under the shelter of upturned books. We chose the largest and heaviest coins as bombs and flicked them over with the aim of destroying each other's armies. The first to crush the other's *general* was the winner. Old English pennies worked the best due to their size and weight.

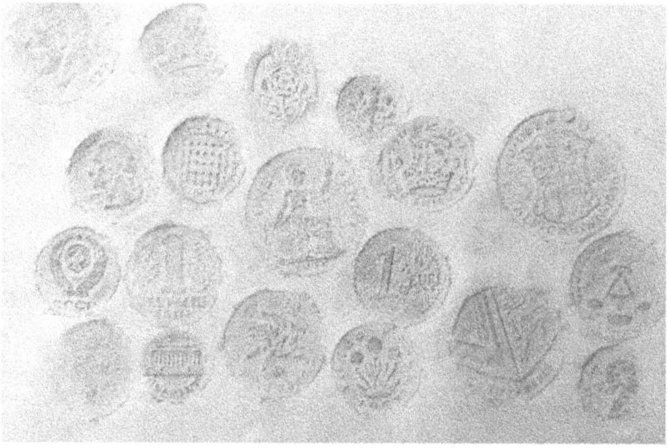

All the coins in our collection were unique in their design, and even their degree of shininess. My favourite was the Moroccan Dirham probably dated around 1965. It was exceptionally shiny, the image was intricate and regal, yet the reverse showed an image of a young monarch, in shirt and tie. I favoured it above all others.

We still use money in its physical form, but we seem to be relying on it less and less. UK notes and coins account for only 3% of the currency in circulation. According to the Bank of England, in June 2022 more than 4.7 billion British bank notes were in circulation, totalling a worth of about £82 billion. The COVID19 pandemic increased the use of credit/debit cards and the contactless method of payment. Apps such as PayPal's Zettle and London-based Fintech SumUp have become increasingly popular for the small trader.

Nevertheless, people still trust cash. It is not rejected when offered as payment, and wisely or not, large amounts stashed away are often relied on as a contingency should things go awry. Whatever the format, human beings have long used currency as a means of exchange, a method of payment, a standard of value, a store of wealth and a unit of account. Communities, societies and nations have been brought together in the process of exchange, of giving and receiving.

Prior to monetary systems, individuals and communities relied on trade to ensure they had what they needed to sustain themselves and their families. I'll give you my fur for your grain, a metal tool for 3 chickens, if you fix my roof I will darn your clothes. Coinage was introduced as early as 700 BC, as an agent that was portable, durable and reflective of its value i.e. the use of precious metal.

Durable

The first coins were hammered. A round or oval piece of metal was struck hard between two dies creating an imprint. As the coins were produced individually, not all were alike. Some of the coins were too valuable for smaller trade, so they were cut into half and sometimes quarters. The original Farthing for example was a literal quarter segment of a silver penny. The Royal Mint attributes its beginnings to the issue of the monogram silver penny during the reign of Alfred the Great (848 – 899 AD) often referred to as the first King of (all) England. There followed a succession of changes and improvements to design.

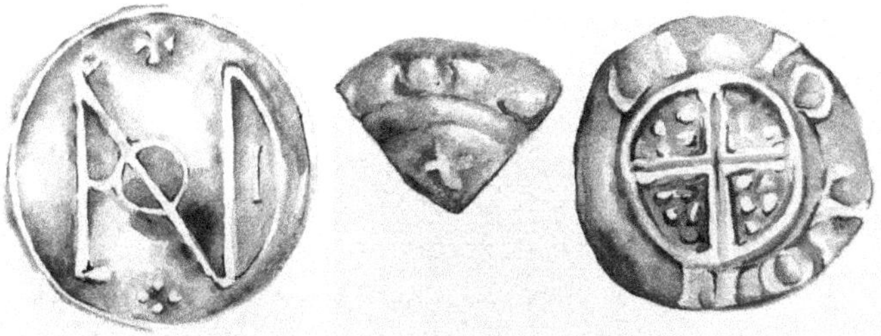

Alfred the Great Penny; Quarter Penny; Silver Cross Penny

When coinage became more widely used it slowly decreased in value[1]. As circulation increased, the Romans were the first to number their coins as denominations. The value of the coin was printed in numbers on the coin and did not need to match its weight in precious metal.

'The basic silver coin of the Roman Empire was the denarius. By decree of Caesar Augustus in 15 BC. It was nearly pure silver, 95–98% and had a fixed weight and value in relationship to the rest of the Roman monetary system. Over the next 270 years, the silver content of the denarius declined gradually and then precipitously to about 2%.'[2]

The smallest denomination of UK currency is the one penny coin. The halfpenny was withdrawn from circulation in 1984 and by all accounts was not missed. Small and easily mislaid, for many this tiny bronze coin was more of a nuisance than an asset. Any further division of the penny is likely to be digital not physical.

Despite its appearance, the current £1 coin contains no silver nor gold. Each coin is made from a combination of copper, nickel and zinc. 'The new £1 features a range of overt and covert security features that, when combined, protects it from increasingly sophisticated counterfeit operations, making it the most secure coin in the world.'[3] The £1 coin is also smaller and lighter than the last version which was replaced in 2017. Some have calculated the current worth in metal to be around 39p, but metals fluctuate in value.

As the world began to connect in the wake of exploration of new lands and the import of exotic goods, coinage allowed people to access merchandise that was not so readily available in their local community. This gave currency a means of unification; a common denominator that everyone recognised. But as merchants amassed more wealth, there needed to be a more practical alternative to transporting cumbersome bags of change.

Portable and Regulated

Whenever I was handed a Scottish pound note as payment for a pint of beer or a packet of crisps it was always accompanied by the words 'it's legal tender!' I checked

---

1 'The UK has the longest history of inflation data, dating to the 1200s in the Middle Ages. Over the almost 1,000 years since, inflation has averaged around 0.9%.' What Do 1,000 Years of Inflation Data Tell Us? B.Hafeez. 2021.

2 The decline and fall of the Roman *Denarius*. A.W. Pense. 1992. Science Direct.

3 The United Kingdom £1 Coin. The Royal Mint

with a manager the first few times I was handed one just to be sure. When I was told they were legitimate, I continued to accept them and gave my colleagues the same assurance. Giving them back as change however proved much more difficult. 'Can you change this for an English one please?' was the usual reaction. This was no disrespect to the Scottish people or the Scottish authorities, it was just that the banknote looked unfamiliar.

Banknotes - money that is printed and issued as a receipt for goods and services. 'In 1694 the Bank of England was established to raise money for King William III's war against France. The Bank started to issue notes in return for deposits. These notes were initially handwritten on Bank paper and signed by one of its cashiers. Today, all British banks carry the chief cashier's signature. After 1696, it was decided not to issue any notes worth less than £50 and since the average income then was less than £20 a year, most people went through life without ever coming into contact with banknotes.'[4]

Banknotes are now made of a thin plastic called polymer, which can accommodate enhanced security features making them harder to counterfeit. Polymer is expected to last two-and-a-half times longer than the old paper notes, as they are resistant to dirt and moisture and therefore less likely to disintegrate. They may survive a washing machine cycle, but they are not completely indestructible.

What is money, what is currency, and what is the difference? 'The terms "money" and "currency" are often used interchangeably. However, several theories suggest they are not identical. According to some theories, money is inherently an intangible concept. Currency, on the other hand, is the physical or tangible manifestation of the intangible concept of money. According to this theory, money cannot be touched or smelled. Currency is the coin, note, object, or physical representation that is presented in the form of money.'[5] I use the words money and currency interchangeably as the quote suggests, mainly to avoid repeating the same word.

For currency to retain its value there must be a limit to how much is in circulation, a regulated supply. When money is scarce its value increases, when money is plentiful it loses its worth. At its worst currency has been rendered entirely useless when printed excessively by the state to combat poverty and recession. Wars are often responsible for the depletion of a nation's resources (including financial, natural and even human) and desperate times call for desperate measures.

---

4 Banknotes: a short history. K. Allen. 2013. The Guardian.

5 The History of Money: Bartering to Banknotes to Bitcoin. A.Beattie. 2024. Investopedia

'After World War I, (Germany) tried to pay its reparations by printing money, and prices went through the roof to the point that in 1923 they were about a trillion times higher than they should have been. People were paying for loaves of bread with entire wheelbarrows full of cash. Money eventually became so useless German citizens used it to light their pipes and stoves.'[6]

The Gold Standard

I'm now looking at the £10 note in my purse which has printed thereon 'I promise to pay the bearer on demand the sum of ten pounds'. Basically, it's an I owe you. But what do I owe you? From the year 1717 anyone taking a bank note to the Bank of England could expect to be reimbursed with the equivalent value in gold. The promise ended in 1931. I can now exchange my banknote with other notes and /or coins totalling the same value, but I can no longer claim gold.

The gold standard refers to a monetary system that directly links a country's currency to the value of gold. Any country that employs the benchmark of a gold standard agrees a fixed value for gold and buys and sells gold for that agreed price.

'In 1834, the United States fixed the price of gold at $20.67 per ounce, where it remained until 1933. Other major countries joined the gold standard in the 1870s. The period from 1880 to 1914 is known as the Classical Gold Standard.'[7] As this produced a somewhat constant method of standardising currency, many countries' economies thrived during this period enjoying exceptional economic growth. There was still fluctuation in the value of precious metals when more entered the system (as in the Californian goldrush), but for the most part the gold standard ensured relative stability. There were also times when the gold standard was abandoned, notably linked to when countries suffered great duress, particularly World War 1 (WW1), the Great Depression and World War 2 (WW2).

After the pending conclusion of WW2, delegates from 44 allied countries met in July 1944 for a conference in Bretton Woods, in the state of New Hampshire. After a month's deliberation they decided to replace the gold standard with US currency. Participating countries agreed to maintain a fixed rate of exchange against the US dollar which in turn was linked to gold. Only the US was permitted to print surplus money as it held the greatest gold reserves. Europe in the meantime was suffering the financial effects of a devastating and costly war. The World Bank and International

---

6 12 Times Currency Was Rendered Almost Worthless (and Why). K Burnside. 2019. Ranker

7 Gold standard. M D. Bordo. Econlib, Macroeconomics, Money and Banking

Monetary Fund (IMF) was established to regulate this system, support economic growth in less developed countries (with a view to maintaining world peace) and to aid countries in crisis. In 1976 this included the British government which was forced to borrow £3.9 billion from the IMF to stabilise the value of the Pound. In effect the Bretton Woods agreement elevated the United States to the most powerful country in the world.

The Bretton Woods system was not a lasting one. Following a period of inflation, unemployment and poor economic growth (again exacerbated by war - Vietnam) the demands on gold reserves were more than the US could satisfy. Therefore in 1971 President Nixon made the decision to detach the US dollar from the Gold Standard rendering no backing for the dollar, except a promise.

Currency that has no tangible backing is referred to as Fiat Money. According to author Richard Daughty[8], no Fiat currency has ever survived; they always return to their intrinsic value of zero. Yes, even the £10 note in my purse will at some point be worthless. Until that date arrives, we save and we store our sterling, be it in notes or accounts, on the assumption that it gives us financial security.

Many believe that precious metals, namely gold and silver, are still the most sustainable and reliable forms of wealth. Gold cannot be printed or duplicated, it is therefore permanent and holds its value. The simplicity of the Gold Standard could anchor the world currency exchange but could also restrict individual governments in extraordinary times. When the country needs to raise money quickly as it did during the pandemic lockdown, will a gold standard system permit this?

Credit and Electronic Currency

Credit - credence – belief. The term originates from Middle French word *crédit* (belief, trust), from the Italian word *credito,* and from Latin *creditum* (a loan, a thing entrusted to another).

Although the concept of credit is ancient, the first formal credit card is said to have originated in 1950 when a wealthy man forgot to bring his wallet out with him and was therefore unable to pay for a business dinner. To make amends Frank McNamara proposed the idea of issuing a small charge card for members like himself that could be presented at their club and be settled at the end of the month – the Diners Club

8 'FIAT is going to die.... it's dead just needing a funeral'. R. Daughty, 2021. Common Sense, YouTube video

Card was born. This, and the American Express card were initially made of cardboard; plastic ones followed less than a decade later.[9]

In 1966, Barclays launched the first UK credit card – Barclaycard. These were sent out to all their customers and later were available upon application. In 1972 the Access credit card brought competition to the UK market and now in 2022, comparison websites are offering a choice of over 20 different providers. Many banking systems are now linked to supermarkets.

Still one of the most popular forms of financial transactions (one can instantly see their appeal), credit/debit cards are light, portable, durable and they are simple to use. When I applied for my first credit card some 40 years ago it didn't take me long to figure out that I could save a whole month's wages by simply paying for everything using my credit card and then pay off the full amount when my next pay cheque came in. By settling in full I incurred no extra charge in interest fees. Had I been astute enough or even paid enough, I could have invested my pay and earned interest, but my personal priorities at that age lay elsewhere.

I still use a credit card for some transactions and (so far) have always been able to pay the balance in full thus incurring no additional interest. Despite the looming hardship our media promises us, I aim to maintain this principle, preferring where possible to go without than pay for borrowing which currently incurs 12.9% interest on purchases and balance transfers (December 2023).

Over 90% of the world's currency is now created, stored and transferred electronically but still maintained by central banks. They are numbers that move around between organisations and individuals, both on a corporate scale and personal level. As most currency is now exchanged electronically, the only thing we need is a reliable and secure online network to conduct financial transactions. It is interesting to read that the Bank of England are making plans to issue a digital currency which they may name Central Bank Digital Currency (CBDC). Digital, because it won't consist of notes and coins, but neither will it be a cryptocurrency like Bitcoin (which is privately issued).

'We are looking at the case for issuing a digital pound. It would not replace cash. A digital pound would be like a digital form of cash – a banknote for the digital era. Like banknotes, it would be issued directly by the Bank of England. You could hold your digital pounds in a digital wallet and spend them in shops or online. A digital pound

9 The History of Credit Cards. J Steele. 2023. Creditcards.com

would be denominated in sterling and its value would be stable, just like banknotes. £10 in digital pounds would always have the same value as a £10 banknote.

If we introduced it, it would not replace cash. We know being able to use cash is important for many people. That's why we will continue to issue it for as long as people want to keep using it. You would simply have even more choice when you make payments. The digital pound would not be a cryptocurrency or crypto-asset. As opposed to cryptocurrencies, which are issued privately, a digital pound would be issued by the Bank of England and be backed by the Government.'[10]

I'm unclear what this will add as we already conduct most of our transactions electronically using our cards, phones and other devices. We would still need a device and a bank account.

Over the course of 24 hours I saw a man pay for goods in cash, and I spoke to a woman who had no need of it. The man took a tenner from a wad of notes in his wallet that must have measured an inch in thickness. The woman needed a cash machine that would dispense £5 notes. She needed to pay someone £15 in cash, and didn't want to be left with a fiver she would never use. So long as we have a monetary system, cash will be a feature of our society for a long time to come.

Cryptocurrency

'Digital, decentralised, no authority' was the attraction of bitcoin when it was initially launched in 2009.[11] The Bitcoin Whitepaper written in 2008 by Satoshi Nakamoto introduced the concept and plan for the first digitalised currency and its implementation, free of banking control and government constraints. Cryptocurrencies do not exist in physical form, and their value is determined by the free market.

Bitcoin, by far the most valuable, is finite; 21 million bitcoins are available of which (to date) 19 million have been mined (purchased). Despite a seemingly limited availability, crypto are readily purchasable as fractions, meaning slices of the crypto pie are available, they simply get smaller. Transactions are peer to peer, secure and only require an internet connection. So, what is the attraction? In 2011 one bitcoin was worth $1. At this very moment (9.20am 23/11/22), its value is $13,919. A remarkable increase, yet this price has dropped significantly in the last year since its peak in November 2021. Websites differ on the highest value of bitcoin; some say nearly

10 The digital pound. The Bank of England.

11 Bitcoin Billionaires. A true story of genius, betrayal and redemption. B Mezrich. 2019. Little Brown Book Group

$69,000 while others report a maximum value of $48,000. Either way the figures show that the value of cryptocurrencies can go up and can also fall. Furthermore, the agencies that facilitate transactions are not regulated and can be unreliable. In the last week in the US, FTX and its affiliates have filed for bankruptcy leaving an estimated 1 million customers and other investors facing potential unredeemable losses.

THE NEW YORK TIMES **11th November 2022**

Embattled Crypto Exchange FTX Files for Bankruptcy

The announcement capped a stunning week that has shocked the crypto industry.

On Friday, FTX announced that it was filing for bankruptcy, capping an extraordinary week of corporate drama that has upended crypto markets, sent shock waves through an industry struggling to gain mainstream credibility and sparked government investigations that could lead to more damaging revelations or even criminal charges.

There are now nearly 20,000 cryptocurrencies in circulation. They range from the highest in value Bitcoin and Ethereum, to those worth a fraction of a cent. Can you spend it? Most certainly if you have an app which links to your crypto wallet, or a crypto card to use for transactions. Having completed a quick search I see that large companies such as Adidas, Nintendo, Burger King, even Clarks shoes will take crypto in exchange for gift cards. For the most part crypto is used as a commodity, something purchased as an investment but not as yet, a tool for daily living.

Quantum Financial System

On the horizon of banking evolution is the concept of quantum money and is best explained here:

'Knowing that improved technologies are necessary to create an infallible system, some banks head towards quantum-based solutions which enable high-speed processing of vast amounts of data. Being able to analyse this data would bring many benefits, such as making more accurate calculations. That, in turn, would result in better decision-making or improving the customer experience by presenting more relevant offers. Quantum banking, based on quantum computing, seems to be a pretty promising alternative for financial management as we know it.'[12]

12 What is Quantum Currency? How Will Quantum Money Affect Finance? I Bartosińska, 2021. Binarapps.

The proposed Quantum Financial System (QFS) aims to centralise the banking of digital currencies. Legislation and protocol have yet to be developed as do the encrypted devices that each account holder will need to process payment. Does this mean we will all have quantum phones? Will we see it soon? "Despite increasing investment in quantum technologies, one of the issues inhibiting quantum computing from advancing more quickly is the lack of quantum technology talent. Until the industry matures, and more opportunities emerge for less technical talent, startups and established companies will be vying for the same limited resources."[13]

Faster, more efficient and more secure, but no mention of whether we will be better off.

Banks

I recall at the age of 18 taking some time to decide which of the big four (major high street banks) I would trust to manage my finances long term. At that time choosing a bank did seem like a lifelong commitment although the choice to move banks was ever present. I chose the National Westminster Bank (NatWest) simply because of the pretty background pictures they printed on their cheques (British birds if I remember correctly). I still bank with NatWest, and now so do both my children.

So long as there is currency, there is banking. Banks have therefore been present in society in one form or another throughout recorded history; their initial and primary responsibility as the issuers and lenders of currency and safe-guarders of wealth. A short educational video for children suggests that the first banks appeared approximately 4000 years ago in the East – Babylon, India and Sumer.[14] Individual lenders then became companies which then evolved into banks. Italy was the focus of trade during the 15th and 16th century Renaissance period and still today harbours the world's oldest working bank - Banca Monte dei Paschi di Siena founded in 1472. The word *bank*, originates from the Italian word *banco* or French word *banque* meaning a bench or money exchange table.

The UK's oldest independent bank was founded by Richard Hoare in 1672. C. Hoare & Co has its head office in Fleet Street and incorporates its own museum.

The two key players in today's UK banking system are the commercial banks, those we see in the high street and the central bank, the Bank of England. In the US the central bank is called the Federal Reserve. We conduct our personal financial

13 Quantum computing and the future of bank tech. R Jackson. 2023. ABA Banking Journal.

14 History Of Banks. Educational Videos for Kids. 2022. YouTube Video. Happy Learning

transactions and run our individual businesses with the commercial banks. These are privately owned organisations whose primary focus is to create profit.

The commercial banks main functions are to:

1. Support their customers to deposit and withdraw monies be they electronic or cash. This includes providing the facilities to enable transactions between accounts, either their own or those belonging to others e.g. pay for goods, services and utilities.

2. Design and provide the hardware to manage transactions e.g., cash machines, credit and debit cards, statements banking apps etc.

3. Loan money. This is the primary and most lucrative purpose for existence - how they generate the most income (see chapter **The Money Tree**).

The Central bank is the banker for the commercial banks and the bank to the government. The Bank of England is owned by the government and carries out a number of responsibilities:

1. To manufacture the nation's cash i.e., bank notes and coins

2. To create central bank reserves (electronic currency lent to and deposited by commercial banks) and to facilitate transactions and settlements between each other.

3. To hold and distribute government finances acquired by taxation and other means.

4. To ensure the integrity of sterling as the country's recognised currency. This also entails managing the rate of inflation by adjusting rates of interest.

5. To protect the nation's financial system including in times of crisis or threat.

Anyone wishing to view these responsibilities in detail can access the Bank of England Acts from the first in 1694 to the most recent updates published 2009.

Also worth mentioning is the World Bank Group (WBG), established in 1944 following the Bretton Woods Conference (see **Gold Standard**), and whose headquarters are based in Washington DC, USA. The aims of its five institutions are to reduce poverty, increase shared prosperity, and promote sustainable development. The WBG claims to be the world's largest source of funding and financial knowledge for developing countries.

The intricacy of the banking system suggests that it is the safest place to store money. Banks are linked to their governments, to other countries, to natural resources, to people and to each other. Banks are secure, they don't go bust - or do they?

Chapter Three

The Money Tree

"You're thinking of this place all wrong. As if I had the money back in a safe. The money's not here! Your money's in Joe's house...right next to yours. And in the Kennedy's house, and Mrs Macklin's house, and a hundred others."

[Film: It's a Wonderful Life, 1946]

I bought my first home, a small two-roomed bedsit in 1983. Following an earlier recession in the early 1980's, house prices (at the lower end) were affordable, and I welcomed a place of my own.

Within 18 months the property had risen in value by almost 60%, partly because it sat at the lowest end of the market. At the time I was encouraged by word on the street that mortgages were easy to come by. You didn't need much of a deposit and only needed to show minimal evidence to prove a sustainable income, and so I sold it and purchased a two-bedroomed home. I recall selling my bedsit instantly and having to act quickly as smaller homes were selling within a day of being advertised. Whilst I entered the property market at a time of economic hardship, I was certain to profit from the boom that followed. That's how it goes - an endless cycle of *boom* to *bust* to *boom* to *bust.*

The Money Tree

How does the money lending system work? Our research participants (RP's) were asked 'which **one** of these answers matches your current understanding?' What do you think?

a. The bank stores my deposits and uses this to generate interest by lending it to others i.e. the money is finite, it just moves about.

b. When I apply for a loan the bank creates a sum of money (a number) in their system and gains the interest as I repay it. On full settlement the original number is deleted.

c. The bank stores my deposits in an account, generates interest and then is able to relend them back to me (with further interest).

Our RP's favour a, the answer is b.

Do banks really make money from nothing? If 97% of money is generated by loans, how are loans created? Do bankers really have access to the mythical money tree? This example may help to clarify.

If I was to ask my bank for a loan of £5000 for home improvements, having agreed, the bank would create two entries in their banking system. £5000 would appear as an asset (what is owed to them) and £5000 would also appear as a liability (what the bank owes me). The bank does not need to find the money in the first instance, the number (in this case £5000) is created in the bank's accounting system. I then use my newly acquired money to purchase the wallpaper, paint from the local DIY superstore, and I pay a decorator to transform my home. The money enters the economy thereby stimulating national economic growth. We can therefore conclude that debt equals growth. By generating more debt the banks receive more interest when the debt is repaid. A bank makes money by collecting interest and therefore making loans. The more loans, the greater the return.

This now raises the question - if banks are not reusing the money deposited with them for further loans, how much of the money that is deposited by customers, does the bank have to hold? Our RPs were asked which one of these answers matches their current understanding:

a. Some of it. The banks are chancing that I and all account holders will not wish to withdraw all our funds at once and certainly not at the same time.

b. All of it. It goes into an account and stays there, where it is available to me when I need it.

c. None of it. The bank just needs to be certain that it has enough capital to ensure a safe and efficient market.

d. All of it in theory, but my actual money moves around as a number and will most likely be used for the bank's own investment or to lend to someone else. It is all available to me if I need to withdraw it.

Few selected answer b. It would be a little naïve to think that a bank's primary function is to secure people's currencies, banks are businesses after all; they provide a service in return for profit. if you have managed to avoid paying them any interest or fees, it's because they are securing only a fraction of your finances and creating wealth with the rest.

The answers for a and d edge closer to the truth and the most popular choice amongst the RPs. I think we all understand that our money is used to fund other projects and investments. It is all still available to us when we need it - so long as we all don't need all of it, all at once. If you have seen the film Mary Poppins, you will have observed in its simplest form how a run on the bank can create a banking crisis.

Young Michael Banks is being persuaded by the bankers to invest his tuppence in a bank account. When he adamantly refuses (because he would rather use it to feed the pigeons), they take it anyway to his cries of "give me back my money!" He is overheard by two customers at the cashier's desk who look up in alarm; "the bank won't give somebody their money". "Well, I'm going to get mine!" "Give me mine too!" says another. There follows a scene of chaos whereby the cashiers are ordered to close their stations and "stop all payments!". It's funny and simplistic but it is also a good illustration of what happens when fear prompts the public to make too many demands on a bank all at one time.

Answer c is the most accurate. Congratulations if you knew that - don't worry if you didn't, I didn't either. Banks do not need to hold any agreed portion of a customer's money so long as they hold enough capital to ensure continuation of a safe and efficient market and are able to withstand any foreseeable problems.

This doesn't mean to say that banks pick from the money tree at random and without question, the element of risk must be assessed. Banks need to be assured that all repayments are a certainty, evidenced by an individual's credit history or secured by assets belonging to said individual e.g. their property, secure employment, or a substantial deposit to cover any default in payments. In whatever way money is lent, loaned, created or however you want to frame it, the contract is a gamble; one that banks accept and encourage whilst observing margins of responsibility. At least that is, until they don't, and in the lead up to 2008 they didn't.

'Well, is this fair?'

'Bubble after bubble
Crisis after crisis
Crime after crime'
[Christian Felber. 2005]

I'm watching a YouTube video that captures the moments when Richard Fuld (final Chairman and CEO of Lehman Bros) was held to account by Chairman Waxman of the US House Oversight and Government reform committee on the causes and effects of Lehman Bros Bankruptcy – 6 October 2008.

Waxman: "Your bank is now bankrupt; our economy is in a state of crisis, but you get to keep 480 million in dollars. I have a very basic question for you, is this fair?"

Richard Fuld does not deny the numbers but avoids answering the question.

"Well Mr. Fuld, there seems to be a breakdown, because you did very well when the company was doing well, and you did very well when the company wasn't doing well. And now your shareholders who owned your company have nothing. They've been wiped out. It seems that the system worked for you, but it didn't seem to work for the rest of the country and the taxpayers are now having to pay up $700 billion to bail out our economy. We can't continue to have a system where Wall Street executives privatise all the gains and then socialise the losses. Accountability needs to be a two-way street. Do you disagree with that?"[1]

Free rein to markets, unregulated banking, reckless risk taking, denial of the chance that it could all go badly wrong. When failure is considered a possibility, placing financial bets to reap financial rewards. Makes for a good movie, doesn't it? For a detailed dramatisation of the events that took place in the lead up to the 2008 financial catastrophe I recommend the documentary Inside Job (currently available on YouTube). You can also watch films The Big Short and Margin Call. Don't expect a happy ending.

For those who would like a quick reminder (no spoiler here, we all know and felt what happened), here is a brief sum-up of the events that sparked a world humanitarian crisis and one where the culprits walked away with their fortunes intact.

To set the scene, we need to be aware that both the US Central Bank (the Federal Reserve) and the chief financial government advisors were mainly former CEOs of the US major banks. They favoured unregulated banking; the freedom for the private banking sector to create financial national growth and not to question how.

By the early 2000's there were several parties involved in the purchasing and backing of mortgage loans:

- **The homebuyers** who requested a loan (mortgage) from local lenders to purchase a property
- **The local lenders** who sold the loans to the investment banks
- **The investment banks** who combined several loans together (which included mortgages) to create packages known as Collateralized Debt Obligations (CDO's), which were then sold to Investors.
- **The investors** who received the repayments, and who engaged **rating agencies** to evaluate the level of risk each loan carried. This in turn determined the interest rate. Investors could be anywhere in the world.
- **The rating agencies** would rate a loan anywhere from a AAA (minimal risk) to BBB- (greatest risk) and everything in between.

With or without hindsight, it doesn't take an expert to see that the more removed one is from the release of money or the contact with the individual on the street, the easier it is to disassociate oneself from the outcomes, be they good or bad. Everyone

---

1 Waxman: I have a basic question for you. Is this fair? N. Pelosi. 2008 www. youtube.com

was keeping an eye on the profit incurred within their own part of the process and bending the numbers in their favour when there was financial gain to be made.

Let's see how that worked out:

- **The homebuyers** requested the loan from local lenders to purchase a property.
- **The local lenders** were not concerned whether a borrower could repay as the risk was passed to the investment banks
- **The investment banks** were even less concerned as the more CDO's they sold the greater the profit they made
- **The rating agencies** rated most CDO's as AAA (low risk) as this is where they made the most money even though many were more realistically of BBB standard (high risk).
- **The investors** took advice from the rating agencies and determined the interest rate which was likely to be unrealistic given the lack of thorough evaluation throughout the chain. The Investors carried the risk and then they insured against it.

Between 2000 and 2003 mortgage loans in the US had quadrupled. There were several who had spotted the unstable bubble (when the cost for an item rises far above the item's true value) and alerted the press, the government and the banking industry. Whilst the warnings went unheeded by the government, the banks decided to hedge their bets by insuring against the very CDO's they were selling. These were known as Credit Default Swaps. It's like me selling you a very dodgy toaster that I'm pretty certain will catch fire, and then I take out an insurance policy for when it does. Sure enough, by 2008 because of the tenuousness on which these mortgages were arranged (a disregard for substantial deposit and lack of a thorough enquiry into income), many homebuyers defaulted on payments. This sent a ripple effect throughout the economy. As the loans collapsed the banks were left with CDO's they couldn't sell, and the banks ran out of cash.

But banks don't actually go bust, do they? Fast forward to 2008:

- March: First to go was Bear Stearns bank. The Federal Reserve steps in to guarantee its bad loans whilst JP Morgan purchases the institution at a meagre cost to avoid bankruptcy.
- July: Henry Paulson (Secretary of the US Treasury) announces a government bailout of the two agencies that hold almost half of the nation's mortgages -

The Federal National Mortgage Association (Fannie Mae) and The Federal Home Loan Mortgage Corporation (Freddie Mac)

- July: IndyMac, an American bank based in California fails and is seized by the United States Federal Deposit Insurance Corporation insuring deposits up to $250,000.
- September: Lehman Brothers Bank declare bankruptcy. No one, neither government nor bank can save it.
- September: The American International Group Inc. (AIG) who sold insurance against Investment losses, is bailed out by the Federal Reserve. AIG took risks by offering unregulated credit default swaps (remember the toaster analogy?) on the basis that the bottom wouldn't fall out of the CDO market, yet it did, and they didn't have enough cash to pay out the claims.
- September: The global economy almost collapses. Investors flee the money market due to losses from Lehman's bankruptcy. They withdraw a record $172 billion from their money market accounts (only about $7 billion is withdrawn during a typical week)[2]

The timeline goes on with the collapse of more banks, government bailouts, bank mergers, stock markets and oil prices plummet. At the same time the price of gold soars, unemployment increases, individuals and families lose their jobs and their homes. The taxpayers pick up the tab.

'Governments enabled the financial sector's binge by promising to be there to pick up the pieces, and they were as good as their word. When the financiers broke the system, the profit that they made from these bad bets remained untouchable. The profit was privatised but the risk was socialised. Their riches have cost the whole world dear, and yet in 2009 the top hedge fund managers have had their third-best year on record.'[3]

'When the dust settled from the collapse, $5 trillion in pension money, real estate value, $401k in savings and bonds had disappeared. 8 million people lost their jobs, 6 million lost their homes. And that was just in the USA.'[4]

---

2 2008 Financial Crisis Timeline Critical Events in the Worst Crisis Since the Depression. K Amadeo 2022. The Balance.

3 The Value of Nothing: how to reshape market society and redefine democracy. R. Patel. 2009. Portobello Books.

4 Film The Big Short. 2015. Paramount Pictures.

THE NEW YORK TIMES **19th March 2023**

Silicon Valley Bank's risky practices were on the Federal Reserve's radar for more than a year — an awareness that proved insufficient to stop the bank's demise.

In 2021, a Fed review of the growing bank found serious weaknesses in how it was handling key risks. Warnings, known as "matters requiring immediate attention," flagged that the firm was doing a bad job of ensuring that it would have enough easy-to-tap cash on hand in the event of trouble. The picture that is emerging is one of a bank whose leaders failed to plan for a realistic future and neglected looming financial and operational problems.

Credit Suisse, which was caught up in the panic that followed Silicon Valley Bank's demise, was taken over by UBS in a hastily arranged deal put together by the Swiss government.

Have the lessons of 2008 been learnt? On consideration of a vote whether to support the government bailout of Credit Suisse in March 2023, Bathazar Glättli, president of the Greens commented, "if climate was a bank the government would have already saved it."

Interest Rates and Inflation

Following the 2008 crisis the UK interest rates plummeted to 0.5% in March 2009 and remained static until August 2016 when they dropped again to 0.25%.

What are interest rates?

- For the lender: the amount charged for borrowing money based on a percentage of the loan
- For the saver: the amount received as a percentage of savings held in an account

When interest rates are low, the lender benefits and the saver doesn't. When interest rates are high it works in reverse. Interest rates are set by the Bank of England to regulate inflation. Commercial banks do not have to follow the Bank of England, but they generally do along with their competitors.

Interest rates act in much the same way as a household thermostat, only in reverse. When the economy is hot (stimulated, overactive) and prices are steadily rising, the Bank of England increases the base rate to control public spending. When the economy is cold (inactive) the base rate is reduced in order to stimulate spending.

At the time of writing the Bank of England confirmed a bank interest rate of 1.75%. In my lifetime the interest rate spiked at 17 % in November 1979, an increase to combat rising wages and the cost of oil. It then fell to a record low of 0.10% in March 2020 during the first pandemic lockdown.

What is inflation?

- Inflation = an expansion of a nation's supply of currency.
- Deflation = a contraction of a nation's supply of currency

The Bank of England have been tracking the value of currency since 1209 and offers a tool on its website entitled '*What would goods and services cost*'. This calculates the value of currency from one date to the next. I enter a figure of £1 in the year 1209 to see how it would compare today. Goods costing £1 in 1209 would now cost £1551.40 in July 2022. The image shows how the value of a single pound has changed over the centuries. Notice the sharp increase in the last 30 years.

What goods and services would cost beginning £1 in 1209

The problem of Inflation is best illustrated by a review of one day's news.

17th August 2022: National news stations confirm a rise in the UK CPI inflation rates to 10.1%, the first time it has reached double figures since 1981. 'The Consumer Prices Index (CPI) is a measure of consumer price inflation produced to international standards and in line with European regulations. The CPI is the inflation measure used in the government's target for inflation'.[5]

5 The rising cost of living in the UK. 2022. Office for National Statistics.

8 am. Sky News: 'Burnley town in Lancashire is one of the hardest hit by the current economic crisis, by suffering one of the highest inflation rates in the country, 2.5% higher than the national average and 3% higher than London.'

A Reporter interviews Pastor Mick Fleming who helps approximately 2000 people per week in a community hub in Burnley:

"It's going through the roof. More and more people can't extend their income, so they are retiring into poverty; more homelessness, people not being able to pay the top ups for their rent. We are seeing the working poor and the retired poor and that's a new dynamic that's growing really quickly. It's largely with food but travelling as well. They haven't got the bus fare to go to the doctor or even to go to work. If we had free travel for all, it would be different it would keep the economy running. But poverty here is unequal access and we are seeing it more and more unequal."

The reason why communities in the North face a higher rate of inflation has to do with a greater consumption of energy and petrol. Houses are less energy efficient and people are more reliant on cars. Income levels are generally lower.[6]

8.30 am. BBC News: Josie Dent, Economist CEBR "We are forecasting inflation to reach 12% before the end of the year, and ultimately that's a problem for the Bank of England which sets the interest rates which have recently increased to 1.75%. We're forecasting them to make them even higher possibly 3% before the end of the year. Inflation is very tricky to control at the moment because the price increases are coming from abroad from energy prices, imported food prices and the invasion of Ukraine. People expect higher prices and so demand higher wages, but wages are falling as most businesses are struggling with these imported prices."

BBC Financial Reporter: "Inflation has not peaked yet. Your energy bills, these businesses, the stress that they are under, these paper-thin margins could get even slimmer. That's at the point at which we might start worrying potentially about unemployment going up, about entering a recession. That's what's been predicted. Even though wages are going up, we are worse off because of inflation."

If Inflation results in the decrease of the nation's value of currency, who or what is the cause? In the current crisis, the UK seems to be pointing the finger mainly at the Russia/Ukraine conflict for the rise in costs of energy, crude oil and food. Other reports suggest Brexit and the after-effects of the pandemic, and others still link it to the 2008 financial crash that affected the world's economy and never really recovered.

---

6 How the cost-of-living crisis is impacting some cities more than others. V. Quinio & G. Rodrigues. 2022. Centre for Cities

When prices are soaring for whatever reason, the logic is to reduce spending by raising interest rates so that the people can afford less, thereby forcing prices to drop. Restricted pay increases can also limit the amount of money in circulation and stimulate deflation. But this strategy can bring further problems and disruption, not to mention financial hardship for the average household.

18th August 2022. Sky News reporting from the picket line on the latest round of strikes at London Euston Station and interviewing RMT General Secretary Mick Lynch who said: "The companies Network Rail and train operators want to cut thousands of jobs in the industry, and we think that will have an impact on safety and our members' future. They want to rip up our conditions of service. The train operating companies are also attacking our pensions and we haven't had a pay deal across the industry for 2-3 years. Our members are feeling the effects of the cost-of-living crisis but are also worried about their futures."

There are several sides to this dispute; the government, the train providers, the union chiefs, the union members (the workers) and the public (including the businesses whose customers rely on public transport). Each is fighting their own corner and trying to limit the financial fallout of change whether it be pounds in the pocket or millions on the spreadsheets.

In days to come 115,000 postal workers and 1900 dock workers will also strike. They claim their employers are making record profits and awarding shareholders the same, whilst they stretch their comparatively miniscule rises in pay which are grossly insufficient to meet the rising cost of living. Even barristers have announced an indefinite, uninterrupted strike to draw attention to the estimated fall in wages of up to 28% since 2006.

The irony is that despite the increase in prices, the goods, the energy, the food and the fuel still exist in ample supply. There is no shortage. No one is disputing availability. We are paying more and more for the same thing. When inflation accelerates, the workforce, the ones responsible for most of the production are the losers. That's you and that's me. Whatever the financial crisis it will always be the poorest who will carry the burden and suffer the most.

In the UK, the mini budget of 23 September 2022 announced several measures to stimulate economic growth and bring confidence to an individual's personal finances. This included the reduction of income tax, lowering the threshold for paying stamp duty and abolishing the highest 45% tax band to those earning over £150,000 pa. In his defence the chancellor stated that high tax rates limit the country's competitiveness and that reducing them are key to overcoming the absence of economic growth. As a final incentive, bankers are no longer restricted in the size of bonuses they can earn. The cap has been removed presumably to incentivise them to increase the level of national household debt.

SKY NEWS **11th April 2023**

Chief Economist, Pierre-Olivier Gourinchas of the International Monetary Fund announced a "**perilous phase" of low economic growth and high financial risk**" and added that there were also more severe risks in prospect.

He said: "We are… entering a perilous phase during which economic growth remains low by historical standards and financial risks have risen, yet inflation has not yet decisively turned the corner"

"Below the surface," he added, "turbulence is building, and the situation is quite fragile, as the recent bout of banking instability reminded us.

"Inflation is much stickier than anticipated even a few months ago. While global inflation has declined, that reflects mostly the sharp reversal in energy and food prices. The fund said that there was now a one-in-four chance of global growth falling below 2% this year, something tantamount to a global recession."

The Labour shadow chancellor likened the newly elected prime minister and chancellor to 'two desperate gamblers in a casino chasing a losing run', and I am inclined to agree. Within hours the value of the pound plummeted to an all-time low, the market lost confidence and mortgage deals were withdrawn. Within days the Bank of England was forced to take remedial action and once again money holds the nation to ransom.

When held to account, those in the business who are heavily invested in the industry offer the same line of defence – it's complicated. This statement is wearing thin. We know it's complicated, conveniently complicated. We know that the same convoluted and impenetrable structure that unites and infects almost every aspect of humanity is assured on the basis that it is complicated. We are warned that if we dare to tamper or dismantle any part of it, the whole system may collapse with calamitous implications. Is that a good enough reason to avoid change?

The Future of Money

'I believe the best investment you can make in your lifetime is your own education.'

[Hidden Secrets of Money episode 1. Mike Maloney]

To say the current monetary system is complex would be an understatement. Banks, borrowing, interest rates and profits are inextricably linked. One bank's eventual demise (as we saw in 2008) can bring down the economy on a global scale. An international crisis, such as war, can create a surge in inflation, but a nation's economy can also be rocked by reckless banking.

In his video series The Hidden Secrets of Money, Mike Maloney's forecast is that a new system of currency will be inevitable. I wonder if that won't simply invite the same problems of greed and corruption that any system of trade attracts when there is an agent such as currency that controls access? Who will create the new systems - the same banks and governments that created the old ones? So long as currency is regarded as the key to unlocking abundance there will be no change in the distribution of wealth. But I do agree with Maloney when he says, "there is a difference now, there's the internet. People are connected all over the world. Information is spreading, and people are getting educated." When people connect, thoughts and concerns are shared, ideas ignite into action and citizens and their like-minded communities are empowered.

In the meantime, we live with and under the cloud of debt - an often-necessary agreement that chains us to our jobs and relationships. Is debt truly an option or is it our only means of living?

Chapter Four

Paid in Full

ALJAZEERA NEWS **26th May 2023**

'The US government will run out of funds to cover its financial obligations by June 5th if the current spending limit of $31.4 trillion is not raised before then.

Congress is tasked with increasing the nation's debt ceiling and Republican legislators have used their majority in the US House of Representatives as leverage to demand cuts to social programmes in exchange for a ceiling increase as a default looms on the horizon.'

No president is going to want to be remembered for defaulting on debt. In 1917 the US introduced a debt ceiling to give the US Treasury more flexibility in managing the country's debt. Instead of constantly asking the treasury for more money, the government and treasury simply agreed on a limit and a means of paying it back. However, since its introduction the debt ceiling has been revised and increased on 78 occasions. Currently the US GDP stands at $20 trillion, with only $20 million left to spend. The interest payments alone are astronomical. With the US dollar seen as the one of the most desirable and reliable assets in the world, the consequences of default will be devasting, even greater than the 2008 fallout. I wonder if this financial cardiac arrest will finally halt a continued escalation of inequity, but I suspect they will issue yet another sticking plaster to put on a system to prolong a slow but certain death.

National Debt

Government debt for the most part is not likely to disturb an individual's night's sleep. It doesn't disturb mine. Yet, we are reminded constantly that government debt is increasing steadily. The latest figures published by the Office for National Statistics (ONS) confirm a gross debt of £2,382.8 billion in 2021, risen from £1,731.0 billion in 2016.

Government debt originated 'In 1694, the first UK debt was issued during the reign of William III. It was offered for sale by a group of traders and merchants, who formed the Bank of England – which acted as banker for the government. By the end of 1694, the government's national debt was £1.2 million'.[1]

On entering WW1 in 1914 the British economy was holding its own comfortably. There had been a long period of peace, national debt stood at £649.8 million and prices were about 1/80th of what they are today. By 1918 they had risen to 1/40th and so had

1 Historical UK National Debt. T Pettinger, 2022. Ecomonichelp.org.

the debt - tenfold.[2] Had the war been financed by taxing the then current generation, maybe the level of borrowing would have had less impact on future generations, but no one could forecast how long the war was going to last despite hopeful speculation. Both the human and financial cost of the war was felt by all those involved, enemies and allies alike. Almost everyone in Europe was much poorer and owed unrealistically large amounts of money to everyone else with little realisation of the improbability of repayment in full. There followed a rise in inflation forcing the British government to suspend the gold standard in 1919 and then finally withdraw from it in 1931.

On the approach to WW2 Britain was a little more prepared in its outlook but again anticipating a shorter campaign. This time the national debt rose from £8 billion at the outset to £25 billion by the end of the war, reaching a peak of 252% of Gross Domestic Product (GDP) in 1946. This was the same year the welfare state commenced with the launch of the National Health Service and National Insurance Acts. Logic would tell us that debt becomes critical when it surpasses 100% GDP, in other words, the country owes more than it earns.

War hasn't been the only catalyst for intense borrowing. In September 2007 the Chancellor, Alistair Darling guaranteed all bank deposits after the news announced the Northern Rock Building Society needed emergency help from the Bank of England. I recall watching images of customers queuing outside branches to withdraw their money. More recently following the outbreak of the Coronavirus the government extended much needed financial support to the public by means of the furlough scheme, the self-employment income support policy and the Eat Out to Help Out arrangement.

Yet here we are as a nation, theoretically further in debt than ever before but individually still going through the same motions of daily living. So does debt matter? Personal debt is finite. It should ideally be paid off within the person's lifetime otherwise the debts they leave will be deducted from their estate (if they have one) and potentially create a problem for the beneficiaries. Collective debt on the other hand can be carried forward by generation after generation after generation. When we inherit the nation's debt, we simply pass it on.

Personal Debt

'You can exact obedience from the population by imposing debt, then they would be forced to work, to obey just to pay it off.'

[Broke: D. Boyle, 2013.]

2 The National Debt; A short history. M Slater, 2018. C.Hurst & Co. publishers

When I was 10 years old living in Holland, my father gave me 2.5 guilders a week for pocket money. Thanks to Holland's progressive culture of music, I was spending all my money on vinyl singles which cost 5 guilders a piece. T.Rex were No.1 in the charts with Hot Love and I had to have it. My friend's elder sister offered to buy it for me, and I agreed to pay her back in 2 instalments (with no interest). When my mother heard a new song coming from my bedroom for the fifth time in one hour, she asked me where it came from. When I told her, she gave me the scolding of my life. She put 5 guilders in my hand with which to settle my debt, and then promptly confiscated the goods. I didn't see the record again for weeks or was it months - It felt like years. My parents were of the generation that looked upon debt as unnecessary, bordering on shameful. If the money wasn't there, then you went without. You lived within your means. When they finally left their home of 45 years and entered full-time care, I was staggered by how much stuff they had stored over that period. On clearing the house it was evident they threw away virtually nothing, everything had a use and a value.

My generation had a more flexible approach to borrowing. Naturally there were mortgages, (how else do you own your own home) but credit cards and use of overdrafts meant we no longer had to wait for something we could not immediately afford. Nowadays it is seen to be advantageous to purposely create a personal credit history as early as possible. Providing proof to lenders that you are a good risk and reliable when it comes to making payments on time, is an asset. A positive credit score will secure larger loans to pay for a car, a wedding or major home improvements.

We are a household of 3 adults and between us we are currently tied to 5 formal credit agreements: 2 phones, 2 cars, and a laptop. To my knowledge none of us make use of overdraft facilities and my credit card balance is minimal. These are not collective agreements, all are individual. They are neither extraordinary nor excessive. I have no idea if they are typical or reflect the national average. I suspect not, as there is (thankfully) no longer a mortgage agreement nor any student loan.

The Office for National Statistics (ONS) updates and publishes all the figures for household debt in Great Britain, but as there are so many different reasons for loans it's difficult to decipher what is an average household amount. It's all circumstantial and dependent on the size of family and age of each member. The ONS have confirmed that the 'total household debt in Great Britain was £1.28 trillion in April 2016 to March 2018, of which £119 billion (9%) was financial debt and £1.16 trillion (91%) was property debt (mortgages and equity release).'[3] A trillion, for those like me who are not

3 Household debt in Great Britain: April 2016 to March 2018. 2019. Office for National Statistics.

sure how much this actually equates to, looks like this – 1,000,000,000,000. In other words, a million million. I wonder how long it will be before the ONS start publishing numbers in quadrillions, a number with 15 zeros (there's no such number as a zillion).

THE GUARDIAN **22nd July 2022**

Downing Street is exploring the idea of trying to tackle the housing crisis with ultra-long mortgages of up to 50 years that could pass between generations, allowing more people to build up equity rather than pay rent.

Mortgage experts said the idea could bring some benefits but flagged problems, including the potential to saddle children with debt, and the fact it would not tackle the fundamental issue of housing supply.

The idea of multi-decade mortgages being transferred between generations is not new and has been pioneered in Japan, where 100-year family mortgages have been offered for some time.'

3rd February 2023. The Chief Executive Officer of Citizens Advice (South Gloucestershire) agreed to speak to me on the subject of debt.

How did you come to work for the Citizens Advice Bureau (CAB)?

"At the time I started volunteering for the CAB I was a single mother with three young children, under 7. I initially approached them for help as my landlord was trying to illegally evict me and my three young children. I've got a bit of a legal background, so they offered me an opportunity to volunteer to work for them. I made my way up from the volunteer to a supervisor to the Operations manager and now I'm the CEO. It's Ingrained in me, our aims and principles and our work ethic - not just around debt, but around discrimination."

Tell me about your observations regarding debt.

"I quite happily helped people write off their debts, although I know there are many who feel very uncomfortable about this and their attitude is very much, 'don't you feel sorry for the banks and the building societies that don't get their money?' My answer to that is 'not one bit!' They shouldn't be lending to people who are on a low income - their tests should have been a lot more rigorous and their lending is irresponsible. They're not going to go under. I don't believe that most people bring debt on themselves. I think people get into debt and they find that they can't get out of it.

Within the last 6 to 9 months, we're seeing people unable to live within their means. It goes very quickly from credit to debt over a very short period. They say we are all three wage packets away from homelessness and that's what tends to happen to people who just live to their means. The interest rates go up, they haven't saved for that rainy day and that's when debts start coming, creeping in and then [the debts] get on top of them and then they can't go any further.

At the moment there is no end to this. It's a long-term problem until energy bills become competitive again, until people can get on to lower tariffs, until people can start gaining control of their bills again. What I'm hoping is going happen is that a lot of people who have never been in this situation will come to us, and we can look at tailored solutions to debt, including insolvency options such as Debt Relief Orders or bankruptcy, especially if they're in rented accommodation. It becomes more complicated if they own their own home.

We're also finding over the last 18 months, that dual income families are also now starting to use food banks, not being able to pay their bills even with two wages coming into the household. It started with carers, and then went on to nurses. When it came to nurses, and that's the career that springs to mind, we first started noticing that their wages weren't going up with inflation; they were falling very much behind. CAB completed an Insights report in 2021 that predicted this was going to happen with the utility bills, and that was before Russia invaded Ukraine. They were very quick this time last year to blame it on Russia. But we had, six months before that, predicted that this was going to happen. Where is it all going to go? I don't know, I despair of it."

Who do you think suffers most?

"People who have disabilities, or those who are on long term sick and have no chance of ever getting a decent job, they're the ones that suffer the most. It's the most vulnerable group where governments like to make savings. For example, every time there is a welfare benefit change, they tend to target the disability benefits and not the pensions, as it may affect the voting."

Is this this biggest problem that CAB have to deal with?

"Absolutely, yes it is. This week alone, we've been asked to go on to three radio shows and give interviews (I have probably done two interviews in the eight years that I've done this CEO job), That's how much we're in demand. I don't know whether you're aware of it, but the Citizens Advice National have done a cover on British Gas and bringing in bailiffs with warrants to force their way into people's homes and install prepayment meters, many of [whom] are vulnerable. And then Monday I did one on the cost of living generally and am due to do one next week as well. It's relentless because they want to know how many people are going to Citizens Advice. The irony is that this time last year we got a 34% funding cut, even though we said to our local authority please don't cut our funding now, there is a cost-of-living crisis coming."

How does the benefit system help people?

"We're one of 61 bureaux throughout the country that help people to claim Universal Credit (UC). The Department of work and Pensions (DWP) have made the application digital, so UC can only be claimed on-line, making the assumption that everybody can claim online, and assuming you can afford a computer, or you can afford Internet.

Every time there's a change they always pick on people with disabilities. This time they took away all the premiums - carers premiums, disability premiums. The welfare benefit system is broken, and it will continue to be so."

If there was something people didn't have to pay for, what do you think it should be?

"We're very lucky we have an NHS service of which I think I am eternally grateful for. Both personally and for other people, people who are on the low enough income will get free prescriptions. I think it's energy at the moment. I certainly think people worry about keeping warm and having to rely on food banks. It's that heat or eat cliché. Or if we can give people fuel vouchers to free them up to spend the money on food and to eat healthily, or fruit and vegetable vouchers!"

The CAB Insights report published September 2020 shortly after the first lockdown predicted:

'The impact of Covid-19 will lead to a recession causing a jobs crisis that will affect women, young people and low-income earners more [OECD Employment Outlook July 2020]. In the short to medium term we expect an increase in demand for employment, welfare benefits and housing advice as those of working age, particularly in the hospitality or retail industries continue to be affected. We expect enquiries around welfare benefits to increase significantly over the next two years as more people find themselves out of work and as the older population grows, both numerically and as a percentage of the total population. As well as the client profiles we are used to seeing, we expect many more enquiries from middle-income earners who have never had to navigate the benefits system before.

The longer-term effect of a national jobs crisis at a local level will be more demand for debt advice as people struggle to meet their regular payments. Citizens Advice estimate that 6 million UK adults have already fallen behind on at least one household bill during the pandemic. That's 9% of the population. We estimate that it would take an average person that we help with debt problems at least 30 months to pay back just their priority debts, assuming that they spent their entire disposable income on repayments each month. 72% of the people we helped with debt advice between March and June 2020 had less than £100 left after paying their essential living costs.' [4]

Three Wage Packets Away

If financial hardship can cause worry and stress to any individual, what more must it do to those already struggling with their mental health. The following excerpt comes from The Roadblock to Recovery published by the Citizens Advice organisation:

'Non-health difficulties commonly involve problems with finances, debts, social security payments, housing, isolation, employment (or the lack of it). They may play a direct role in causing a person's mental health condition, they may exacerbate it, or they may come about as a direct result of their mental health condition. Unfortunately, they frequently create a vicious circle resulting in further and more serious problems. They impede any therapeutic endeavours, have knock-on effects and hamper the chances of an individual getting back on their feet.'[5]

It is said that we are each three wage packets away from homelessness. Is this a cliché or does it hold some truth? Imagining this yourself, how long could you survive without an income before you are forced to take action? Three months, maybe four? Who or what would you approach first? Maybe you would use an approved overdraft agreement or make full use of your credit cards, which will in turn incur penalties for interest and late payments. You may be quick to apply for universal credit which will take a minimum of 5 – 6 weeks to come through. I suspect you will be reluctant to begin a complicated process as you may believe you will resolve the employment issue within a month – 'its ok, I will get a job soon'. But denial can cause delay, and delay creates waste as you learn to adjust. In any case an application process for any kind of benefit can be daunting and exhaustive, why start it if you don't need to. You may prefer to ask friends and family for help instead.

Looking at the most optimistic outcome, let's assume you manage to resume employment, will it match the level of pay you enjoyed prior to the crisis? How long

---

4 Data Trends and Insights 2020. South Gloucester Advice Services. Citizens Advice.

5 Roadblock to Recovery. A.Fairak, 2018. Citizens Advice

would it take you to repay the loans, be they commercial or private? How long would this setback last and how would it affect your lifestyle - what could you no longer afford and where would you have to make savings? More importantly how would it make you feel?

As I value my freedom above all else, debt makes me feel stuck. The lack of money restricts my movements, limits my choices and disconnects opportunities. But if that's the worst feeling I will endure then I am blessed. Looking back to the time when I worked with children for community education, I was taken aside one day and told that one of my young students had lost her father to suicide. I'm glad I was prepared as the student was very emotional, fluctuating between sorrow and defiance. Not a week went past when she didn't express her grief. Sometime later someone mentioned that the primary reason for the suicide was debt. The first time I met the child's mother she was angry. Ending his life did not resolve the problem, rather she had inherited it and more. With 3 children under the age of 8 she was left to manage a stew of hardship, heartache and relentless responsibility. I wonder if grief even got a look-in.

'When recession begins to bite, people lose jobs and default on debt, thus creating an intolerable and psychological strain which can lead to addictions, state dependency and criminality. We pass this onto our children and now we have generational poverty.'[6]

The Research Participants have offered their views and experiences on debt.

Allan: '[Debt is] inevitable in a capitalist society because it acts as power over the consumer. We accept that as the rules of the game. It is now normalised by having mortgages and business loans.

It's very difficult to say if a particular lending situation is good or bad. It could start as good - a country borrows money to build a dam. It is finished [and] the initial repayments are made. The dam helps the economy and then circumstances change and the loan can't be 'serviced'. The country defaults and then it's all downhill...the dam needs repair, can't because there's no money. So, was it all a waste of time?

My rules: I don't borrow as a rule. I did for property as that was the only way to get it and was relieved to pay it all off. I wouldn't do it again in retirement because of the stress of having a burden like that. If I had to borrow it would be from family or very close friends, but only if I had to as it can damage relationships quite badly.'

Mike: 'Debt is a necessary tool these days to living, even if it is a route to self-improvement via a house purchase, but it seems a necessary evil for most families

6 The Social Distance Between Us. D.McGarvey. 2022. Ebury Publishing

just to survive. If carefully managed, it can enhance your life experiences, but if uncontrolled, it can blight your life.

The apparent ease of securing debt, be it credit cards or retail finance, sometimes removes the true value of money. I have seen this in the younger generation, where a new house has to be furnished with new items, furniture etc, whereas a generation ago, (or my generation) second-hand or going without were the only options.'

David: 'The banks want us all in debt. It makes us slaves to them and money (although it should be termed currency) is all debt-based. My advice is to try to stay out of debt entirely, or as much as possible. Paying any interest prolongs the repayment term and increases the amount of 'money' owed in terms of repayment.

My thoughts have broadly been the same through adulthood. Having a mortgage, I didn't take holidays mainly so I could repay sooner. For those people who say that mortgage is one of the lowest interest forms of debt so prolong the repayment period, IT'S STILL DEBT! I could almost feel the yoke being lifted from my shoulders when I [made] the final repayment.'

Claire: 'I used to really dislike debt - I found it to be a hole that once fallen into, was very hard to get out of. However, as I have learned - debt seems to make the world go round, debt is how the economic system seems to function. To me this seems backwards - it creates a feeling of lack and stress. But those feelings are what drives people out to work - so it keeps the economy going.'

Simon: 'Debt for bit things like student loan and a house are basically part of life, now 'normal' and in my opinion good reasons to go into debt. Buying other things on finance are not worthwhile reasons in my opinion. Although if I wanted to get a good kitchen or car and finance them over 3-5 years with everything increasing in price, I may choose to do that. Especially if money in the bank isn't appreciating, I may as well use it whilst it's not gaining or losing value to inflation.'

Carol: 'Debt is something that I find worrying. I have never experienced debt a great deal – I am still a person that uses cash as much as possible, and if I do use a credit card, I endeavour to pay it off as soon as the bill comes in. I feel somewhat forced into using a credit card as a way of paying now as so many outlets and establishments will not accept cash anymore. For instance, if I want to print photos I have to use a credit card. This still leaves me slightly uncomfortable.

Having said all of that there was a time in our family's lives when my husband lost his job. We had 3 children dependent on us and we could not pay the mortgage – the mortgage has always felt the biggest 'debt'. Because it was such a large amount of money that was owed it felt beyond my control, so I learnt to be at peace with and to trust that it would work out.

Now my children are older and in the present climate are struggling to provide all that is necessary for their own children and just keep their heads above water so to speak. I do get concerned for their well-being and would long to be able to help them financially.'

Bob: 'Debt is a useful part of our economy providing it takes place between an ethical lender and a responsible borrower, this view has not changed over the years. Therefore debt is viewed as a positive, by providing opportunity. Based on this viewpoint I personally feel comfortable with debt because I would only borrow a sum within my ability to repay from a responsible source. More than many I have seen the negative effect of individuals borrowing more than they could repay and lenders irresponsibly lending more than could be repaid. Despite this I would still hold the belief that providing both parties are totally responsible, then debt is a necessary part of our economy.'

Edward: 'I almost feel that debt is a part of a life lesson in growing up. When I was single young man I, like many others lived a carefree life of spending just about everything you earned and it wasn't until something in your life changed, and made you realise that there was more to life than having fun. In my case it was finding the girl that I wanted to settle down with, have a family, buy property and most of all live within my means. The only debt I can relate to is having a credit card. My wife and I have two credit card accounts, both have benefits e.g. cash back or points and both accounts are paid off in full every month. So it pays to carry the debt for a month and get a benefit from having the cards. I have no mortgage, no loans and between us we have five pensions. But that has taken 46 years of being sensible, as only now in our twilight years are we cushioned from the issues that come from being in debt.

I have observed debt many times and it has affected me in the past. A small number of my friends, work colleagues and associates have struggled with money issues and I have offered advice and help to point them in the right direction to get help. I have never judged these people, as I have over the years thought to myself how easy it can be to fall into the trap of living beyond your means'

Carmen: 'Just the word 'debt' makes me feel uncomfortable. It has negative connotations and suggests I have outstanding things to pay that I can't manage or are difficult to meet.

I have had the opportunity to see how people around me have acquired many goods and at the same time many debts. They complain about everything they had to pay and how difficult it was having to meet their repayments. New cars, luxury houses, long trips... I have had less, but I think I live a much simpler and more peaceful existence. I do not live beyond my means and I highly value what I have. I don't think I have been less happy than a person with such possessions and a lot of instalment payments or debts. I believe that getting into debt to increase capital, or as an investment, works very rarely. For this to work you have to have good economic foundations. For those of us with simple and more humble family finances, debt is a trap from which it is difficult to get out.'

Eli: 'In the purchase of a house (the infamous mortgage), I think it unfair that due to non-payment the bank keeps it. There should be a system whereby the family will not be left on the street. I thank God that my brothers have been able to pay their mortgages off. The banks, along with the stock market and the multinationals, are thieves - we work for them.'

Nani: 'Debt doesn't change over time. As countries have more opportunities, they owe more and more, especially as governments can change every four years. I don't feel comfortable thinking that I have a debt. I am one of those people that if I want something and I can pay for it instantly, all the better. The moment I had money to pay off the mortgage for our house, I removed it and since then I have been sleeping very peacefully. Now no one can take away our house that we worked so hard for.'

Debt is contagious and addictive. Despite all the comments that express relief of having no debt, the lure of it is strong when the temptation of a better home, or car or life beckons.

31 January 2023. Finally I own my car. The end of a four-year credit agreement confirms it belongs to me and no one else. I am now significantly better off and already considering how I can afford to make home improvements. My first target is to replace the flooring upstairs and I have made some enquiries. Hmm - far more expensive than I thought. But I am told I can spread the payments. I can replace the flooring in all of the rooms immediately by entering into an affordable 12-month credit agreement. Furthermore, if I sign up by tonight (shop closes at 8pm) I can enjoy a greatly reduced price per square metre. I try to imagine the colours I will choose and wonder if I can also throw in a rug for the lounge. After all I don't have to pay for it all at once.

What began as a desire has been replaced by a sense of urgency and panic at the thought of missing out on a saving. I have drawn myself into an economic decision that I now feel powerless to reverse. I look at the clock - it's 7pm, only one hour to go before I lose out. It's been a long day and I'm tired. Outside the weather is cold and wet, and I am reluctant to leave a warm house to return to the store. To be or not to be in debt, that is the question.

The answer is obvious, but it takes a while to land. I don't need to do anything, nothing at all. There is no urgency other than the pressure I put on myself. The sale will resurface a few months down the line as it always does. Why, after all my research and writing would I hand over my personal decision-making power to a retailer and put myself back into debt? How much happier would I be with a new floor anyway? A feeling of relief returns to me and serenity is restored. I won't deny myself new goods, but I will wait until I can confidently and peacefully pay for them in full and call them my own.

It's a different story when it comes to national ownership. What do we own as a collective? Sadly, what is free to us as citizens is all but disappearing – even the moon.

PART TWO

The Human Cost of Currency

Chapter Five

A Moon for Sale

'All these things God created, He put them in our large home, the world, without surrounding them with walls and gates, so that they would be common to all his children.'

[Johannes Ludovicus Vives (1492-1540)]

Our Heritage

19 September 2022. Today is the day of the state funeral of HM Queen Elizabeth II and I am reminded of my heritage. The Queen belonged to me as much as anyone else. I'm not a royalist, having lived my childhood between four different countries I've considered myself European before British. Yet watching the royal ceremonies as I have countless others over the years, at this moment I'm not quite ready to vote for a democratic republic in place of a monarchy, at least not yet - ask me again in a few months and I will most likely have changed my mind. All through my life *they* were there, *it* was there, always in the background and sometimes drawing very close. Like the occasions when Dad was chauffeur to Princess Alexandra and on another occasion, the Duke of Edinburgh. The story goes - she was charming and thanked him personally, he was gruff and didn't say a word.

We pass the story down through the generations and we admire his British Empire Medal awarded to him for his outstanding service. It's not about a small group of privileged individuals, it is about a national institution and tradition that formed part of my upbringing. It's not a matter of feeling pride or admiration, it is about my identity - a part of me from the stamps I licked, the coins I spent and the history homework that brought me closer to its origins.

I felt no urge to cry when the Queen died, but I admit I did when James Bond said his final words in *No Time to Die*. Initially I felt incredulity, a sudden and deep sense of loss and then outrage. It affected me for days, and I know I was not alone. James Bond belongs to not only me, my memories, but to all of Britain and the world. He is part of our childhood, our imagination. We've seen him married, widowed, tortured, return from the brink of alcoholism to save the world numerous times over. I even remember seeing him convincingly scared (in Goldfinger), but not for one moment did I think I would see him die.

According to CNN news, 'the tech giant Amazon, has closed its $8.5 billion deal to acquire MGM, the home of the Bond franchise and one of the most iconic movie studios in Hollywood history'.[1] So James Bond now works for Amazon and

1 Amazon closes $8.5 billion deal to acquire MGM. F.Pallotta, 2022. CNN Business.

Eon Productions have the film production rights. I wonder what their next move will be – will they revive him somehow? Reinvent him? Return to an earlier part of his life? I know 007 will not stay in his grave for long, his legend generates far too much income. He/she will rise again; at this moment I can't imagine how – but we can be certain of an imminent resurrection.

It's not just about the people, the titles and traditions, but also the buildings and monuments. Thankfully most of our major museums and art galleries are free to all, but not our cathedrals nor many of our heritage sites. To enter my nearest cathedral, I will need to pay £9 (children go free). Anyone wishing to tour St Pauls will be charged £20.50 per adult and £9 per child – this will entitle them to an annual pass. A visit to the interior of Westminster Abbey costs £29 per adult and £13 per child. For a family of four travelling in by train wishing to visit either, this is an expensive excursion indeed.

The National Trust are now the caretakers for Stonehenge in Wiltshire; a family ticket costs £17.30. They also care for the ancient stone circle in Avebury, Wiltshire, but can't charge for visiting. The small village of Avebury is situated in the centre of the circle with the A4361 running through it. Limiting access is impossible. They do, however, own the only car park and charge £7 per visit.

Our Libraries

'In an austerity climate, libraries have been targeted as a disposable resource. Spending on libraries in 2009 was at £1 billion, but by 2019 this had declined by 25%. The same decade saw 773 libraries close – one fifth of all in the UK. The Conservatives' assault on public libraries is a deep injustice to all community members, but it's one that disproportionately affects underprivileged children.'[2]

Who hasn't visited a library at one point in their lives? How many of us affectionately view libraries as havens, places of safety and comfort, and a step away from the bustle of life into a world of wonder. I have fond memories of trips to the local library with Dad on Wednesday evenings. It was there that I found one of my favourite books– 101 Dalmatians by Dodie Smith. I read it from cover to cover, over and over again, as many times as the loan would allow. When my children were young, I borrowed numerous books to satisfy their yearning for a story with bright colours, cute animals and paper flaps they could open, close and accidentally tear. In adult years, when I didn't know what I wanted to read, each month I chose a couple of fictional novels by an author whose name began with the letter A and then the following month moved

2 The Quiet Disappearance of Britain's Public Libraries. A.Walton, 2021. Tribune.

onto the letter B and so on. Before we could afford broadband, I took my son to the local library so he could amuse himself for half an hour playing an online game whilst I browsed the shelves. Most recently I have been ordering and borrowing books through the online reserving system – some of which you will find in the bibliography at the back of this book.

Libraries are not just about books. I personally have attended a course on digital art where I created a self-portrait on an iPad, and also experienced the benefits of the Alexander Technique. The image shows some examples of what our local libraries are offering in the month of August 2023.

Activities offered by a local library

Rather than a drain on the public purse, the report Libraries for Living and for Living Better, led by the University of East Anglia, invites a conversation to recognise the overall impact library services can make on various aspects of society. The report estimates that the nation's library services 'can generate social benefits to their communities to a value of at least £3.4bn per year in relation to the three value dimensions. Libraries' return on investment is at least six times the known annual cost of running libraries nationally.' Not least by 'improving the health and well-being of less affluent communities.'[3] The 3 mentioned dimensions are:

3 Libraries for Living and for Living Better; The value and impact of public libraries in the East of England. J. Gordon et al, 2023. University of East Anglia, Creative UEA and Health Economics Consulting.

Digital inclusion. This includes access to online services for leisure, banking, shopping or other necessary applications such as government benefits particularly for those unable to afford their own internet connections. The opportunity to improve one's own IT skills and to access printing services.

Health, wellbeing and independent living. This can include having somewhere to go other than home; reading a newspaper or text in a different and safe location; being near other people, even if no words are spoken; sharing experiences or knowledge by attending courses or information sessions of interest that will further career prospects e.g. improving spoken and written English or learning how best to present oneself at an interview; signposting to services, activities or support groups.

Children's literacy and associated outcomes. Raising children's levels of literacy and uniting parents who may feel isolated in those first few years of raising a child. Complimenting and reinforcing the learning children receive at school such as reading textbooks that support homework or projects.

Sadly, many more libraries only survive when run by volunteers or the local community. They may account for a small percentage, but imminent closure of a treasured resource has spurred communities into action.

Our Land

As a well-deserved break from all the literature on finance (and I do need a break from it), my friend has loaned me the book, The Salt Path[4] whose narrative has surged a variety of emotions in me including outrage, fear, gratitude and despair. The book describes the sequence of events that led to and followed a couple's eviction from their family home in Wales. When a court ruling stripped the couple of their home and livelihood and a health care professional diagnosed a life sentence of pain and eventual suffocation, the couple took what they could carry comfortably on their back and began walking. Despite the obvious challenges of physical exertion, stamina and limited finances, I am saddened and angered most by the practical restrictions this couple have had to face on their travels. It seems there is no common land left for someone who just wants to pitch a tent for the night. Every acre is owned by someone or a body/authority. The land in question may not have been registered with HM Land Registry but there is no such thing as *no man's land.*

As of April 2018, 'Over 85% of the land mass of England and Wales is registered [with the HM Land Registry]. Much of the land owned by the Crown, the aristocracy,

4 The Salt Path. R.Winn, 2018. Penguin Books.

and the Church has not been registered, because it has never been sold'.[5] All land in England and Wales is owned by someone whether it be an individual, a trust, an organisation or an authority even though there may be some uncertainty as to the owner's identity.

How did we get to lose all our land? We never lost it because we never owned it. As the opening quote suggests, the land, the earth, much like the clouds and the rain exists for us all – for all life not just for those in human form. It is a necessity for life and existence. In medieval times all land was considered to be a gift from God and therefore the divine right of kings who ruled the nation. After the arrival of William the Conqueror, the nation's land was divided and loaned to nobles who then loaned the land to knights. They in turn loaned the land to peasants who in return paid the knights with services and goods such as crops. In other words, *land for duty*. This arrangement, known as feudalism, ensured the peasants had a home, a community and a livelihood that was for the most part, sustainable.

Various events then led to the collapse of the feudal system. Knights left their land to join the crusades. Numerous died in battle and never returned. The outbreak of plague claimed the lives of many, weakening the system even more as labour, and therefore produce, became more scarce. When the communities suffered, many left for towns to seek a wage, ensuing a gradual shift from an economy-based trade to one that was based on currency. A transition from feudalism to capitalism.

Whatever common land we shared or made use of was further stripped from our grasp by the enclosure movement that took hold in the eighteenth and nineteenth centuries. Land commonly owned or used by villagers and settlements, or land that was available to the people for grazing their animals, growing their food and collecting plants for medicinal purposes, became enclosed. The erection of walls, fences, and hedges symbolised and enforced private ownership.

What about common land? 'Common land is land subject to rights enjoyed by one or more persons to take or use part of a piece of land or of the produce of a piece of land which is owned by someone else – these rights are referred to as 'rights of common'. Those entitled to exercise such rights were called commoners.'[6] There's no need to feel insulted by the title *commoner* as it gives us our rights, the right to pick apples, blackberries, pears and plums from wayside trees and hedges.

5 Tracing Ownership of Property and Land. L. Conway, 2022. House of Commons Library.

6 Land ownership, use and rights: common lands. National Archives

Our Space

Accepting that the claim to land ownership goes back millennia and would be very difficult to reverse, one would think that somewhere like the moon remains untainted by laws of tenure. Indeed, the Outer Space Treaty which came into force in 1967 stipulates the following principles based on international space law:

- The exploration and use of outer space shall be carried out for the benefit and in the interests of all countries and shall be the province of all mankind
- Outer space shall be free for exploration and use by all States
- Outer space is not subject to national appropriation by claim of sovereignty, by means of use or occupation, or by any other means
- States shall not place nuclear weapons or other weapons of mass destruction in orbit or on celestial bodies or station them in outer space in any other manner
- The Moon and other celestial bodies shall be used exclusively for peaceful purposes
- Astronauts shall be regarded as the envoys of mankind
- States shall be responsible for national space activities whether carried out by governmental or non-governmental entities
- States shall be liable for damage caused by their space objects
- States shall avoid harmful contamination of space and celestial bodies.[7]

The treaty clearly hasn't stopped some from relying on the ignorance of many to sell acres of moon land for as little as £10.31 per acre. For £22, you can choose your location be it anyone of the seas or craters, or even a small patch on the dark side – no discount offered for not being able to see it through the telescope. For £25 Virgin Experience Days promise 'a piece of this history as well as over 4000 square metres of genuine solid land. You'll receive a lunar site map to indicate where your land is located; lunar deeds; and a declaration of ownership. Who knows – one day you might even get to visit your land!'[8]

---

7 Treaty on Principles Governing the Activities of States in the Exploration and Use of Outer Space, including the Moon and Other Celestial Bodies. United Nations Office for Outer Space Affairs.

8 Buy a Piece of the Moon: Own an Acre. Virgin Experience Days.

Upon purchase Virgin will despatch with their welcome letter a Moon Deed, a lunar Site map, Constitution and Bill of Rights, a copy of the original Declaration of Ownership and a document confirming your mineral rights to your land. In case you are doubting Virgin's integrity there is a small reminder that the offer is a novelty gift and Virgin cannot guarantee legal ownership. All prices are as of 23 July 2023 - expect dramatic increases as the state of planet Earth deteriorates.

Our Homes

Losing our homes is most likely to be our biggest fear; having nowhere to live, have shelter, feel safe and call your own. Even though it may not be ours in legal terms, our home is our home. As a family of the Armed Forces, we were continually on the move. By the time I reached 21 years I had lived in 21 different homes in 4 countries and attended 7 different schools (to date, I have moved home 30 times). The experience was challenging but as long as we had each other, we coped remarkably well. The sequence of events formed our memories and influenced our values for years to come. Curiously, I found the British culture hardest to adjust to. Leaving a decimalised system and getting to grips with an imperial one was tough. Aged seven, my first maths lesson required me to add up money – I very quickly burst into tears. How can there be 12 pennies in a shilling? Why are there 20 shillings in a pound? What's a guinea again? When we returned to the UK after a couple of years in Holland, the British had finally changed their system. This time aged eleven, I was amused to see how people were struggling to adapt – I lost count of the times I saw someone peer at the coins in their hand with a degree of frustration and ask, "what's that in old money?"[9]

More than anything I just wanted to settle in a home. Over those years of military life, we followed a constant programme of moving into temporary accommodation until a more permanent one became available, albeit just for 2 years. We found ourselves living in caravans, shacks and once in a haunted mansion. I saw no ghosts, I was too busy trying to keep warm. Waiting for new accommodation was in some ways a blessing as we also had to wait to be registered with a new school and that could take weeks. But once we had moved into our allocated home, there followed the worst period of all – decorating. It could take weeks, even months – constant home improvement. Those were the unsettling days of continuous disorder; newspaper on the floor, wallpaper samples and rolls littering the room, the smell of wet paint, parents doing their best to work together but rarely surviving the course. When the

9 I still hear the term 'old money' used by those who can only ever have known decimalisation, such was the enormity of the change.

house was finished, then it was the turn of the garden – a less disruptive project as it was outside but, nevertheless, more work and more upheaval.

I yearned for inactivity, quiet, stability – even now I always look forward to coming home, even when I'm on holiday. I loathe decorating or the pressure of maintaining an ultra-clean and tidy home. I want to feel undisturbed. How must it feel for those facing eviction with nowhere else to go?

As interest rates climb the likelihood of someone being able to afford a mortgage agreement falls. Although many are protected from the threat of higher payments through fixed-rate interest agreements, as the rates rise the option to buy for first time buyers is becoming out of reach. 'Those born after 1985 are the first UK generation not to enjoy better living conditions than those born 10 years before.'[10]

There is, and always will be, an incessant demand for accommodation – a home. The current economic climate is pushing the rental market to the forefront of demand. As we have already established that demand drives costs, it comes as no surprise to see rental charges soar. The Office for National Statistics have published figures to confirm a rise of private rental prices paid by tenants in England to 5.1% in the 12 months to June 2023, 5.5% in Scotland, 5.8% in Wales, and a whopping 9.6 % in Northern Ireland.[11] The greatest price increases affect newly let properties, whilst existing tenants are more likely to see smaller rises in rental costs. This makes it harder for those to enter the market, such as young people wanting to leave home. For those already in rented digs, let's not forget the rise in all the other costs that come with independent living; council tax, energy bills and water rates to name a few.

What if you can't pay? What if the landlord wants to sell their property or move back in? When our youngest son was only 2 years old our landlord announced he would be moving back into his house (our home) and gave us notice to leave. The generic advice from the council was for families in this situation to wait until the bailiffs arrive. Being forced from a property will put them at the highest risk of homelessness and therefore more eligible for immediate help from the state. If children are involved the family will be given greater priority. That's not an easy thing to do or wait for, and neither of us was willing to risk an uncertain future. We managed to find an alternative home that was owned by an organisation rather than an individual but struggled to find the deposit. These were lean years indeed. We borrowed from the council and paid the sum back over a 12-month period and then .... we decorated!

---

10 Broke – who killed the middle classes? D. Boyle. 2013. Fourth Estate.

11 Index of Private Housing Rental Prices, UK. June 2023. Office for National Statistics.

Nobody should have their home taken away from them, especially those in debt as they are in no position to afford any alternative. Until very recently you could be evicted if your landlord served you one of the following notices under the Housing Act 1988:

- Section 21 enabling landlords to repossess their properties without having to prove the tenant is at fault or broken any agreement.
- Section 8 whereby a tenancy agreement has been broken; this could include tenant rent arrears or anti-social behaviour.

The Renters (Reform) Bill published 17 May 2023, has introduced the abolition of evictions under section 21.[12] This gives tenants more security knowing they cannot be turfed out of their home without landlords providing valid reasons, such as moving back in, selling the house or a mortgage repossession. The Bill will replace fixed-term tenancies with periodic tenancies, which is a rolling occupancy with no specific end date. The potential fallout from this legal amendment is a reduction in rented properties. The full force of the law is likely to take a couple of years to roll out.

During the summer of 2023, as I saw my parents' savings rapidly diminish, I contacted social services to begin the process of claiming state funding for their care. Over the period of almost 3 years, they have spent in excess of £350,000 which included their savings and the sale of their home, to occupy two individual rooms in a local care home. The application triggered a financial and social care assessment which resulted in them both being given 4 weeks' notice to leave their care home in place of somewhere cheaper, one that the council would be prepared to afford.

At the ages of 89 and 93, both frail and one with dementia, I cannot believe that they are still having to move home. The social worker has done their best to secure 24-hour care, but the council department responsible for sourcing support, have limited my parent's financial entitlement. The provision falls far short of what they are now paying – almost 50%. Despite negotiations the present care home and the council cannot agree on fees. The council will not increase the sum they can pay, and the care home will not reduce their fees. My parents are therefore given notice to leave. They are offered alternative accommodation, including one residence whom the Care Quality Commission has rated *inadequate.*[13]

---

12 Parliamentary Bills; The Renters Reform Bill. 2023. UK Parliament, House of Commons.

13 The Care Quality Commission (CQC) inspect all registered health and social care providers including care homes. They rate them against their fundamental standards as either Inadequate, Requires improvement, Good or Outstanding.

We visit a local one and decide it is good enough, but their assessment still falls short by £100 per week each. Even if we could find funds to make up the shortfall, a helpful manager reminds us of an imminent increase of the national minimum wage from April 2024. This in turn will undoubtedly raise the fees to compensate the extra monies they will have to find to pay their staff.[14] The options available to my parents are withering. It's now a choice between somewhere shoddy or somewhere remote.

I know the council are accountable to the taxpayer and I understand care home fees subsidise empty rooms, but where is our duty of care to two very old and vulnerable people, or have we stopped caring? My mother is inconsolable and simply doesn't understand why she is being made to move. The effect on my father is worrying. It has taken him over 18 months to memorise is way to my mother's room less than 20 yards down the corridor. How will he cope in a new environment? Why is there an institutional disregard for all the financial contributions he has made, everything he has saved and worked for? It's a system that professes to be fair, but in this case it is cruel.

Many of our research participants agree that health and social care should be free to all.

Our Health Service

The National Health Service (NHS) has been serving the British public for over 75 years. It is a system that is designed to be free to everyone, irrespective of a person's socio-economic status, or any other factor. We believe we have free entitlement to health care, although we know we pay for it indirectly through our taxes. We frequently accuse governments of trying to privatise our sacred institution and as I explained to my vet (these are the things you talk about whilst cleaning a puppy's ears) it would take a brave (and arguably foolish) government to fully break the mould that was introduced on 5th July 1948 by Labour minister Aneurin Bevan. 'Illness is neither an indulgence for which people have to pay, nor an offence for which they should be penalised, but a misfortune the cost of which should be shared by the community.'[15]

'No society can legitimately call itself civilised if a sick person is denied medical aid because of lack of means.'

[Aneurin Bevan (1897 – 1960)]

---

14 Chancellor announces major increase to National Living Wage. HM Treasury. 2023. GOV.UK

15 The NHS at 70: many happy returns? S.Cook, 2018. British Medical Journal.

You only have to look at the American health system whereby those employed pay for their health through insurances, to appreciate the one we pay for through our taxation.

'The CEOs of top insurance companies each of whom makes 10's of millions a year in compensation, do not perform heart surgery or brain surgery. They don't treat people who are suffering with cancer diabetes or mental illness. They don't keep our children healthy and provide annual checkups. They don't do the research we need to discover the causes of terrible illnesses that afflict millions. They don't build hospitals or clinics or educate medical and nursing students. That's not their job. They're business people - their sole purpose is to make as much money as possible for their stockholders and for themselves - and they do that very well.'[16]

Unsurprisingly the USA lags behind most of Europe in the life expectancy of its citizens. A large proportion are unable to pay the astronomical costs of their prescribed medication to keep them alive. According to Sanders, costs are up to 10 times more than charged in neighbouring Canada. Healthcare is a right, not a commodity.

Despite its current challenges the NHS continues to serve the people of this nation when they are at their most vulnerable and has since inspired many countries to follow the same or similar model. What we don't realise is how much of our treatment is delivered by non-NHS bodies using NHS resources. I may have been a little naïve in my discussions with the vet, as I read a paper from the British Medical Association (BMA) detailing the steady increase in outsourcing of NHS services to Independent Sector Providers (ISP).

'The contribution of ISPs in delivering NHS-funded care has over time rapidly grown from a small base. Our analysis suggests that ISPs provided approximately 386,800 NHS-funded elective episodes in 2020-21 – or approximately 5.2% of all NHS elective activity. This is 258 times the 1,500 episodes (0.02% of all NHS elective activity) delivered by ISPs in 2003-04, the year in which ISTCs (Independent Sector Treatment Centres) were introduced and comparable records began.'[17]

Evidence collated by the BMA confirms an increase in provision of services for routine treatment such as cataract procedures (46%), and knee and hip replacements (29% and 20% respectively).

---

16 It's OK to be Angry About Capitalism. B.Sanders. 2023. Allen lane Penguin Group.

17 Outsourced: the role of the independent sector in the NHS. 2022. British Medical Journal

'Priority must be to increase investment in long-term NHS infrastructure and capacity to prevent further backlogs of care in the future, not to direct that taxpayer-funded investment into the independent sector and ultimately shareholders' pockets.'[18]

SKY NEWS **4th August 2023**

Govt turns to private sector in attempt to cut NHS waiting lists

NHS waiting lists stood at 7.47 million at the end of May - the highest number since records began in 2007. And while the private sector will be operating eight new community diagnostics centres, they will remain free to patients.

This is privatisation through the backdoor. When you are in pain, concerned or possibly frightened, all you want is for someone to help you, to give you relief and hopefully restore you to health. You want accurate professional advice and most of all, you want to be treated with compassion and understanding. The last thing you think about is whether that nurse or doctor really works for the NHS. After all they are still wearing a uniform, may have a stethoscope around their neck and are most certainly working in a hospital.

Having raised suspicions, I do believe that the current government are facing tough decisions as the NHS workforce dwindles and services collapse under the pressure befallen on those who remain. After all, who else is there to pick up the pieces but the private sector? My friend who is an accountant sheds light on this arrangement:

"It's common practice for Medical Consultants to instigate a Consortium, sometimes a partnership, contracted to deliver so many operations per year to the NHS. If those targets are achieved, then the members of the consortium are permitted to use NHS infrastructure to carry out their private operations, with little costs other than perhaps nominal rent. From their private income, they can pay for administrative services relating to the private work; these administrators are [directly] employed by the NHS. There are no commercial costs charged by the NHS for the use of any equipment, and the fees raised can be reimbursed by Insurance companies as well as the patients themselves, some of whom may be from overseas. The consultants may be surgeons or anaesthetists as well as [those practising in] other specialised fields.

Interestingly, about 30 years ago, the private practices generated large profits for these professionals. However more recently, the NHS remuneration and pension contributions now mean that such private practices are really just a top up for a

18 Outsourced: the role of the independent sector in the NHS. 2022. British Medical Journal

consultant working full time in the NHS. Consultants and GPs can choose their level of sessions that they commit to the NHS, the rest can be available for private work. For example, a Harley Street based consultant may carry out only one session in the NHS, and then have the rest devoted to private practice, and that is where the real money is made."

Am I personally concerned whether the treatment comes via an NHS professional or otherwise? Assuming the treatment is safe and effective - probably not. The concern lies in the fees that are demanded to provide services that make up the shortfall. Will an increase in demand drive up the costs of those services? And who is likely to pay – only the taxpayer.

Our Teeth

We have come to accept that not every aspect of our bodies is included in our healthcare entitlement. We pay to be able to see clearly and most of us pay for our medicines – some of which we rely on to stay alive. When asked to name one thing people shouldn't have to pay for, many of our Research Participants chose dental care.

Montse: 'There should be some kind of help that would allow you to wear a beautiful smile without having to forfeit your salary.'

THE GUARDIAN **23rd May 2023**

NHS dentist numbers in England at lowest level in a decade

'A total of 23,577 dentists performed NHS work in the 2022-23 financial year, down 695 on the previous year. That figure is more than 1,100 down on the pre-pandemic numbers.'

'A growing number of dental surgeries do little or no NHS-funded work, with the BDA citing a £billion dental budget that has failed to keep pace with inflation and population growth over the past decade.'

It does seem bizarre that teeth and eyes are excluded from free NHS treatment entitlement (for the majority) after all we are physically attached to them. According to the British Dental Association (BDA) 'The launch of the NHS in 1948 meant, for the first time-ever, that dental care was free at the point of use, dramatically changing people's access to good oral healthcare, their expectations, and their appreciation of looking after their oral health. In the first nine months of its existence NHS dentists provided over 33 million artificial teeth, a figure that would rise to 65.5 million for the year 1950-1951.'[19]

As demand increased (mainly for extractions and fillings), more practising dentists joined the national scheme. This extended the number of people who received treatment yet at the same time incurred an enormous financial expense. Within just 2 years the service payments to dentists were cut 3 times and without any consultation. The service became unsustainable, and by 1951, the NHS found itself reaching the end of its budget. In response the NHS made its first charge for treatment in the form of dentures which led to the resignation of Aneurin Bevan. Soon afterwards other dental treatments followed suit and unsurprisingly demand for services fell.

To this day the number of dentists who can provide NHS treatment is shrinking rapidly. Last month I received a letter from my dental practice advising me that all their practitioners are no longer providing NHS treatment, instead they offered me a payment plan. The treatment as you are no doubt aware was never free, but it was and is subsidised. Whereas before I paid £25.80 for a check-up, (which also included x-rays, a scale and polish if clinically needed), now I will need to pay £49 for an examination and £22 per small x-ray (£39 for large). The scale and polish service is not included, but a 20-minute appointment with a hygienist begins at £58. Montse can enjoy a 'Six-Month-Smile' for £1950.[20]

I know that NHS dental services offer free treatment for those in dire need (those with no money and not registered with a current dentist) but for the rest of us who are among the *those who can pay, should pay,* it's yet another squeeze on an ever-dwindling purse.

Our Water

When asked to think of something that should be free, our Research Participants favoured water. They felt strongly that this was a necessity that no one should have to pay for.

In 1989, the government sold off the management of the nation's water to water and waste water firms for £7.6 billion. Since that time water bills have increased by

19 The Story of NHS Dentistry. British Dental Association

20 Six Month Smiles is an innovative solution for adults who want straighter teeth in just a few months. It is based on a system of braces, which are believed to be the best way to straighten the teeth, but uses clear and tooth-coloured materials that make them almost undetectable. My Dentist.

40% over the rate of inflation and dividends upwards of £13.5 billion have been paid to shareholders. It is interesting to note that England and Wales are the only countries to follow a fully privatised model of water delivery. According to the Shadow chancellor John McDonnell MP, the support for a return to public ownership of water stands at 83 %, higher than for any other utility.[21] We have no choice regarding whether or how we pay for our water, and who can live without it?

In the UK there is only one allocated supplier per residence, and if you inherit a water meter (as I did over 18 years ago) you also inherit the burden of monitoring your consumption. Having a bath has become a luxury, hosepipes are out of the question, and I'm having to think twice about installing a dishwasher. When the plumbers said they would have to drain and refill the whole heating system to correct a fault .... my heart sank.

Thames Water Company which serves nearly 25 % of Britain's population, has just been fined £3.3m for allowing millions of litres of undiluted sewage to pollute two rivers, killing more than 1,400 fish. This is not the first time. Between the years 2017 and 2021 Thames Water was fined £32.4m for a similar act. 'The fine comes as the company faces concerns over its future amid a mounting £14 billion debt.' 'David Black, the Ofwat chief executive, told members of the House of Lords this week that state ownership remained a long way off but acknowledged that Thames Water would probably seek to hike customer bills.'[22] This travesty will also have a significant impact on those whose pensions rely on the owners of Thames Water, located in China, Canada, Middle East and the UK.

The organisation WE OWN IT has published some alarming figures regarding private ownership:

- Since privatisation, £72 billion has gone to shareholders – an average of £2 billion per year.
- The water companies have built up a debt mountain of over £60 billion and used this to finance dividends for shareholders.
- The average pay for a water company CEO is £1.7 million a year.

---

21 Thirty years on, what has water privatisation achieved? M.Roberts. 2019. Chartered Institution of Water and Environmental Management.

22 Thames Water races to secure investor backing ahead of delayed accounts. M.Kleinman. 2023. Sky News

- Our bills have gone up by 40% in real terms since privatisation[23]

The campaigners are urging the public to sign a petition demanding the water company to be taken into public ownership with 3 conditions:

- billpayers are to be protected by law against bailout.
- communities are to be given powers of governance over the implementation of a plan to resolve issues of leaks and clean-ups
- these new arrangements are to be permanent.

When the unpopular rise in energy costs was first announced, DON'T PAY UK urged the British public to demand 'an immediate reversal of the price hikes'[24] and to furthermore boycott their energy bills - a tempting response but one that carries high risks. Who would chance being left with no heat over the winter? It does remind us of how powerless we are when we have no control over the very things we depend on. Water, food, heat, shelter– the necessities required of any organism let alone a human one – all of which are becoming less accessible to us due to increasing costs.

At what point does our economic dial turn from scraping by to hardship, from hardship to poverty, from poverty to irrecoverable destitution? It only takes one more financial demand to tip a precarious balance.

---

23 Lets take back our water. Our Public Services, Water. We Own It.

24 Dontpay.uk website will be shortly closing down.

Chapter Six

A Lavish Ritual

EURO NEWS **5th May 2023**

King Charles Coronation: How much will it cost and who's paying for it?

The majority of experts believe the the coronation will cost approximately between €57 million - €113 million (£50 million to £100 million).

Unlike weddings, which are paid for by the Royal Family, the coronation is a state function hence taxpayers will mostly be footing the bill.

But as the UK suffers a cost-of-living crisis with soaring food and energy prices, and also a wave of industrial action, people on social media have been critical of the Royal Family for organising such a lavish event.

5 May 2023: My mother expresses her disgust at the cost of the King's Coronation, and I too wonder how the rest of the world judges this most extravagant and lavish ritual. Most reporters have estimated the final sum to exceed £100 million. Graham Smith, Chief Executive of the anti-monarch campaign group Republic, expressed his views: "Charles is already king. There is absolutely no need to go through with this expensive pantomime. At a cost of tens of millions of pounds, this pointless piece of theatre is a slap in the face for millions of people struggling with the cost-of-living crisis."[1]

We would be extremely naïve to even imagine that any savings made by either sacrificing the event or scaling it down, would have any impact on anyone's standard of living. The money was found then plucked from the money tree. For any prestigious event, the funds will always show up. Why then, do they not materialise for more worthier causes?

I'm thinking about a local hospital whose roof has been condemned as unsafe beyond the year 2030. The number of support props (poles holding up the building's deteriorating roof) exceeds 3000 and rises monthly. A councillor comments, "It is very disappointing that the government has allocated just £20 million towards the caving-in roof. This is just a sticking plaster, as the full cost of a new roof is £200 million and £679 million for the whole hospital'.[2]

1 Multimillion-pound coronation 'a slap in the face' L. Elston, 2023. The Independent

2 Repair funding for QEH crumbling roof is a 'sticking plaster' patch-up. J.Bates. 2021. Lynn News

This is but one urgent case amongst many for government consideration but also a stark reminder that the taxpayer has no control over where or how their contributions are allocated. We foolishly make the assumption that if monies were not spent on an unnecessary event, we would all feel a financial benefit. Gil Scott-Heron's poem [3]clearly expresses his sense of powerlessness and resentment to a government-funded action that ignores and insults his immediate needs.

Whitey on the Moon Gil Scott-Heron

(Written in response to the moon landing of 1969)

A rat done bit my sister Nell, with Whitey on the moon
Her face and arms began to swell, and Whitey's on the moon

I can't pay no doctor bill, but Whitey's on the moon
Ten years from now I'll be payin' still, while Whitey's on the moon

The man jus' upped my rent las' nigh 'cause Whitey's on the moon
No hot water, no toilets, no lights, but Whitey's on the moon

I wonder why he's uppi' me? 'cause Whitey's on the moon?
I was already payin' 'im fifty a week with Whitey on the moon
Taxes takin' my whole damn check,
Junkies makin' me a nervous wreck,
The price of food is goin' up,
An' as if all that shit wasn't enough

A rat done bit my sister Nell, with Whitey on the moon
Her face an' arm began to swell, but Whitey's on the moon

Was all that money I made las' year for Whitey on the moon?
How come there ain't no money here? Hm! Whitey's on the moon
Y'know I jus' 'bout had my fill of Whitey on the moon
I think I'll sen' these doctor bills,
Airmail special
to Whitey on the moon.

---

3 Whitey On the Moon. Gil Scott-Heron, 1970. (Official Audio) YouTube.

Poverty

'Hunger and poverty is not a shortage of food but a lack of power.
Hunger is a form of violence, particularly between women.
As women are the predominant gatherers, feeders, sellers, they
will often skip meals in favour of feeding their family.'
[The Value of Nothing by R.Patel. 2009]

I am reminded of the living conditions my best friend endured when we were 11 years old. I say endured, but on reflection it was me who had difficulty witnessing the squalor. Her parents had divorced and whilst her father drove about town in a Jaguar, her poor mother (and I mean that literally) struggled to heat and feed a large family most of whom were under the age of 10. The quilts had no covers, the walls lacked paint, in place of carpets there was newspaper, and the stench of urine was inescapable.

What constitutes poverty? According to the Joseph Rowntree Foundation, 'poverty means not being able to heat your home, pay your rent, or buy the essentials for your children. It means waking up every day facing insecurity, uncertainty, and impossible decisions about money. It means facing marginalisation – and even discrimination – because of your financial circumstances'[4]

In that case, I remember being poor. At the time I didn't recognise I was poor, but I do now. I entered a relationship that brought with it debt at a time when I was unemployed, pregnant and mortgage interest rates were rising monthly. The two-bedroomed house was heated by just one small gas fire, and I had to think very carefully about how I would spend my weekly shopping budget of just £5. For the first time I was called in to speak with a concerned bank manager.

I'd like to say I remember those days with affection, but I don't. I felt sadness and embarrassment. A memory that sticks with me is one of leaving the antenatal clinic to walk a mile back to my house carrying heavy shopping, whilst the other mums-to-be jangled their car keys in preparation for a safe and comfortable journey home. My pride and self-pity prevented me from asking for a lift.

Since those days my bank account has occasionally turned pink but thankfully as yet, never back to red. Many of us have lived through hard times including the research participants.

Mike: 'My experience of being poor was in the early 1970's, with a young family, no heating, no bathroom, an outside toilet (a two-seater) - "Bucket and chuck it!" We

---

4 What is Poverty? The Joseph Roundtree Foundation

had only one minimum wage coming in, against very high interest rates and having to resort to using our credit cards. We earnt extra by doing drawings to barter for goods, or sometimes money. We made our clothes, grew vegetables and kept chickens and rabbits which we ate - the so-called *good life*!

In those days you never felt *poor* because of so many others in the same boat. But looking back then yes, we were by today's standards. You just felt positive about it, always thinking and finding ways to overcome your situation, especially for your family. We learnt a lot from parents who had also struggled (especially through the war) but never allowed it to affect their children.'

Montse: 'I personally remember that when I was little at home, we had no heating and we depended on a stove with wheels which we shared, especially when showering. I remember being very cold.

I was not aware of the expense of keeping a family. Just 14 years ago and recently separated, I had to stay in my large house, unable to heat it. With only my salary to depend on, I would arrive home from work and lock myself in my room with my daughter and just a small heater. It was a room with a sink and TV, and it began to be my refuge. It was the best way to stay warm, the rest of the house was 11 degrees.'

Carol: 'In my mid-teens I was living in a bedsit in North London - earning just enough to pay the rent and put money in the meter for utilities, pay my travelling costs and weekly food shop - barely anything left for what is now described as 'disposable income'. I had no choice but to stay in London, that was a lean time indeed.

Years later married with 3 children, my husband lost his job – this was to prove a 3-year wait for a change of direction. Not sure that I felt I was living in poverty, but I was concerned at times. I sensed how much my husband felt the responsibility of looking after the 4 of us, so that affected me. If I struggled with anything it was because my older children (one aged 15, the other 12) were not able to have some of the things that their peers were able to enjoy and take for granted; a school trip away, freedom to shop for latest fashion, a holiday. This period in our family life did not leave any deep scars or negative memories. On the contrary, they both feel it helped them to get a better perspective on life, on what mattered. They have carried this forward into their adult lives.

Bringing it right up to now, I was very pleased to be eligible for my government pension – the security of knowing that I can count on that financial benefit each month. I had not realised how strongly I would feel about this until it actually happened.'

Whilst we may have known poverty at some point in our lives, I suspect few of us can imagine how it feels to be destitute; to own nothing but the clothes we are wearing and whatever we can fit into a carrier bag. We are not likely to have known what it is like to have nowhere certain to sleep, to stay warm, to keep clean or to feel safe, not just for one night but perhaps indefinitely. Perhaps we don't imagine it at all or not often enough. Bob and Carol Thorndike have, not because they were homeless themselves, but because witnessing others endure extreme hardship was not an experience they could ignore. I first met them 25 years ago through a friend and have since followed their integrous commitment to their cause with interest and admiration. The charity they created was local and modest, but touched the lives of many, not least those who were the most destitute and had nowhere else to turn. I therefore dedicate the remainder of this chapter to recounting their tireless efforts in helping those most in need.

The Ebyon Trust

> On seeing a man on a beach hurriedly throwing stranded starfish back into the sea, a passer-by asks why he bothers? 'Millions will perish, what difference does it make anyway?' He threw in one more and said, 'it made a difference to that one.'
>
> [Ebyon Newsletter, November 1999.]

When Bob and Carol Thorndike finally made the decision to bring the Ebyon Trust to a close they drew a line under a charity that had raised hundreds of thousands of pounds for many individuals whose varying needs were both simple yet essential. Allocating every penny to the causes within Ebyon's remit, they supported desperate people, adults and children alike to enjoy some of the most basic necessities, the ones we all take for granted. To end a vital means of support was not an easy decision to make. The need goes on, relentlessly increasing with time and with change. But with no-one to take the reins, the charity closed its books following the pandemic and the onset of Bob and Carol's retirement.

Bob: 'The name Ebyon has its origin in the Aramaic language where it had the meaning of "needy person". The connection and suitability to the charity's work is obvious but it also had the ability to stimulate questions about the title because of the fact it is an unusual name. The Ebyon Trust was first conceived in 1994 following my conversion to Christian faith from which time my conviction was to plan a means of helping the poor and those in dire need. In essence, it was the practical action of faith to support the most vulnerable in society at a time of crisis in their lives. Although the current welfare state system is in many ways a wonderful programme of support, its origin was to cope with limited numbers of people suffering hardship for a limited period. It suffers from the pressure of putting people into categories as case studies without being able to assess individual needs. For this reason, there will always be those who 'fall through the net'. The cost of restructuring it would be immense and unlikely to be funded by any government.'

The aim of the trust was clear - to provide funding to resolve immediate problems and remove a stumbling block for an individual to thrive. Often these requirements were relatively small but critical to the person at a specific point in their lives.

Carol: 'We can have this misconception that people don't want to work, or they've squandered money, or they haven't had opportunities. But if you have spent your life in a care home, if you've never known any love or security, you find it hard to form relationships and you haven't even got much education to go out there into that world. Then in creeps an assumption that 'this is all I'm worth, this is where I should be, this is now my story'.'

The Trust's aim was to encourage the individual to move towards self-reliance and responsibility in the longer term, and by doing so, escape their current predicament and circumstances - a practical expression of compassion. Ebyon never intended to supplement or to replace the welfare system. It was there to fill a gap that prevented someone moving to a greater degree of independence and self-respect.

Carol: 'Bob always hated injustice and hypocrisy in any form. When he became a believer, the first thing that stood out to him was that - the message against injustice. From the beginning to the end of the Bible, it talks about injustice. So, this is a man who grew up with no biblical knowledge, but he opens this book up and what he sees above all is, I hate injustice. You are to look after the poor, and for Bob it couldn't be a clearer expression of a faith than to help the poor. His feeling was, if someone is cold and hungry, you feed them and clothe them, and then tell them what you want to tell them, but first you ensure they are fed and warm. He never felt he had to save the world. His policy was to make a difference for just one person, one person at a time.'

Whilst Bob's vision was doggedly clear and unwavering, Carol took more convincing. With a greater heart for children, her focus was directed elsewhere.

Carol: 'Honestly, I don't know that I particularly ever thought about the poor or the homeless. I'd seen them and I was probably sad, but I never felt it was my role to help them. And yet he saw it immediately. He'd had two or three years without a job, which would have opened up this understanding more. He'd queued with men to receive benefits and he would tell you that everywhere he went, there was someone in need.'

Anyone given the task of setting up a charity will know that there are many conditions and parameters to adhere to if it is to be recognised and registered. It was also necessary to establish boundaries of eligibility for clarity and fairness.

Bob: 'Without a blueprint to follow the main dilemmas were, how would it attract funding, and could we operate and control each part of the work? When deliberating our margins, we considered the following to help us define our criteria for support:

Who were the most vulnerable and where were they located? What help and support was already being offered? Funding from charities was available for larger tangible items but not for smaller essential daily costs such as food or toiletries for a 7-day period. How would a new organisation interface with existing support groups who worked directly on the front line? How could potential fraudulent applications be eradicated? Initially the thought was to interview all applicants, but during the planning process it was obvious that this was not feasible for logistical reasons, therefore the association with intermediaries became the filter screen.

It was clear from the outset that not all aspects of this work could be analysed because there was no existing organisation found (at that time) which matched the criteria proposed. It seems we were unique!'

Guidelines and parameters were finally agreed when Ebyon registered with The Charities Commission. It would be run by two Trustees who shared a common purpose and who were capable of administering the entire function, and the sole purpose would be one of relieving individual deprivation in their local county. Whilst the charity would deliver presentations, literature and participate in useful group meetings, it would solely rely on donations made as a result of public awareness. No formal fundraising was to take place.

Whilst an individual's circumstances required the charity to adopt a degree of flexibility, certain principles were fundamental to ensure that the most desperate groups in society were being supported. The question is how to make the greatest impact with limited financial resources. Funding smaller necessities across as many clients as possible seemed the best way forward.

Requests for support could only come via an intermediary who had full knowledge of the individual's circumstances and could make an assessment on the charity's behalf. They needed to know that Ebyon could not help those who owned property, received income or wanted to pay off debts. The target group were the most destitute whose only aspiration was to survive each day. clients who only owned the clothes they were wearing and carried their personal items in a plastic carrier bag – they were the ones that needed immediate help. The intermediary would then arrange for them to register for the state system which could take up to 5 weeks to process. The Trust's purpose and function was to cover the essential needs for this intervening period. Intermediaries included managers of shelters, refuges and those who supported the local community.

Following a claim, a decision would be reached, and a cheque issued within 24 hours of receiving the application. When a woman runs from a violent partner with nothing more than the clothes she is wearing the response must be immediate and thereon handled by the intermediary.

Carol: 'There was always somebody going between us and the recipient. We rarely knew who it was that we were helping; it was much better to come through somebody else because we trusted them to know the individual and their circumstances and from then on make the referral. The irony was when social services started to ring us up to ask us for money. I mean it was a compliment in a way that they respected us enough to even know about us and what we did.'

Ebyon's first Newsletter- February 1996

I am pleased to report that from donations and covenants, the trust has now supplied funding to three organisations based in the county who care for the homeless, displaced persons and terminally ill children.

Initially The Trust began its work in 1994 to 1995 working for the street homeless and those who used the night shelters in local cities. In 1994 the homeless and vulnerable were a clearly defined group at the bottom of the social ladder, not discussed enough and seldom given the consideration they deserved. It was several years before the government recognised this category and the identity *street homeless* came into being.

Carol: 'The word poverty is relative I suppose to each individual. When I observe those on the street asking/hoping for money, even the smallest amount, I realise my concept of poverty is not the same as theirs. How tough to be on the ground looking up at passers-by, most of whom look away and make no eye contact – and those that do respond do so in a judgemental way, ' I am up here and you are down there – that makes me higher than you.' I learnt from a few years of volunteering in a day centre and night shelter that every person has a different story to tell. It may seem easy to get down to the pavement level hoping for small change holding the hope of a bigger donation, but so much harder getting out of that spiral of living hand to mouth, day to day. Some are there because of chaotic and toxic childhoods, barely adults themselves. Some [have come] from a broken relationship, some have left the armed forces."

Bob: 'As we set out on this journey, our inspirations were to satisfy a demand running into hundreds of thousands of pounds. But we've learned to accept lesser sums and still have been excited on hearing the way in which some of these smaller donations have met individual needs. The gratitude expressed by a young single mother for the gift of a handmade blanket for her newborn baby was a great encouragement. We were equally excited to hear that teenagers at a hostel for runaways were now able to play indoor football because of the Trust providing funding for this project. Although such a modest requirement, the hostel has been searching for these funds for almost two years to undertake this work. Our belief is that the trust should not store up funds, but rather distribute them to those who need support and watch God replenish them.'

The Trust's first donation came from a widow who had her own experience of hardship to draw on. Having fostered children throughout her adult life and adopted four of her own she recognised need, but she also understood gratitude. When Ebyon gave their first talk at a church business meeting she donated £5. Although the Trust did not engage in formal fund raising, they gave talks to small groups and larger organisations such as the Rotary Club and the local American Air Force Base.

Carol: 'I was one of a group of women that met at the Chapel on the base. I had been doing this for a few years and got to know some of them personally. They come to our home, we've made friends with them. I don't know if it's the case now, but they are really encouraged when they move into this area or a new Air Force Base, to put back into the community.'

Word got round and the number of individuals and organisations supporting Ebyon ran into hundreds. Some donated just once, others when they could and some by standing order. There was surprising resistance from some local establishments who held the obstinate view that poverty could not possibly exist in such an affluent area, and from churches who felt that evangelism should precede humanitarianism.

Carol: 'Their response was "I might have helped you if you were giving a Bible tract or verse, because there's nothing evangelistic about what you're doing." Our belief was that God's bigger than that. He doesn't need you to hand out any tracts, that just annoys people. And that's conditional, isn't it? Like, you can have this pair of socks, but you gotta read this verse as well. Well, heck no!'

Ebyon did not purposely store funds yet never had to refuse anyone because the pot was empty. There was always enough to meet eligible demand. I was initially surprised that neither Bob nor Carol felt the need to establish a website. I recall suggesting it myself, but swiftly came to the conclusion that if they've never had to turn anyone down, what would be the point? Clearly the Trust was functioning well enough without it. Running costs were minimal; petrol, printing and postage – all met by the couple's own finances.

Carol: 'We survived ourselves. Bob was given different jobs (usually home maintenance) and we kept going. Sometimes it was a bit month-to-month, never quite knowing how we were going to do it, but we were provided for.'

Ebyon Newsletter - April 1997

On one particularly cold day, a man who had been sleeping outside the previous night came into one of the shelters, lifted a mug of tea to his lips with his hands that were purple. His face was sore and cracked open from the biting wind, yet grateful for the comfort that this hot beverage brought him. Several years ago, he lived a 'normal' life, married with two children till his wife left taking the children with her.

The work diversified relatively quickly. Ebyon began working with refuges for women and children fleeing violence and violation, teenagers missing from home and who were also escaping conflict and abuse. The Trust responded to the needs of the elderly struggling to survive on their pensions. It also supported young children residing in hostels and specialist care centres. On the next rung of the ladder was a very large group of individuals who were surviving but struggling. Typically – two adults with children, living in private rented accommodation, with low paid jobs to sustain them.

Carol: 'What we learned was that generally people wanted to help. People are affected by seeing someone on the street begging. They think, thank God it's not me. But what they don't want to do is approach that person themselves. They're unsure. They're afraid. They're afraid of being rejected just as the person on the street is. So, they are looking for you to do it for them. I'll give you the money for him. And I trust you because you've just told me that 100% of what I give you is going straight to them. That was an important insight.'

Bob: 'In the warmth and comfort of your home where basic necessities are more than met, secure in the love of those around you, consider Ken, who recently shared his story while sipping a mug of tea at one of the day centres. His face kicked almost beyond recognition, swollen black and blue by a group of youngsters. His only crime .... being homeless.'

Ebyon Newsletter - March 1998

(Describing a children's Christmas party)

Elisha's doll stood taller than her - exceeding not only her height but also her expectations - her face said so much. Unlike Liam's face which could not be seen under his new balaclava, but his body language said it all as he jumped around amidst the paper and the excitement.

Bob: 'It is perhaps a logical conclusion to reach that a man without a coat should be grateful for any coat. But it is the man's welfare that matters. Giving a coat which is old or worn, stained or marked signifies to the recipient this is all he is worth. Giving a coat which is new or unmarked signifies care and compassion and allows the recipient to retain what is probably a very low level of dignity and self-respect. The Trust strives to be an example of compassion to those less fortunate and for this reason we do not distribute to any supported organisation or individual, any item which shows wear tear, marks or stains. Understanding behavioural responses within the context of the poor is a slow process, and for us not an academic study but rather an encounter with different situations.'

Carol: 'But there was also another thing that we were adamant about. It was going to be brand new. It was not a second-hand pair of shoes or a second-hand coat because what that is saying to the [recipient], is that's all you're worth. You haven't got a coat, so be pleased with this one. What is apparent when you're in poverty is you have no choice. You have no choice about anything, so you don't have a choice about what colour you like or whether it fits. There were several cases of recipients who were unable to fill in a form because they were wearing someone else's glasses'.

With the best of intentions Ebyon's principles were occasionally compromised. Carol's spontaneous response to a man whose feet were red and sore and clearly in need of socks was to quickly find him a pair – it just so happened that Bob was wearing them at the time! (newsletter August 1996).

Ebyon Newsletter - November 1998

A lady in the local community felt safe as a wife and mother of 4 living a comfortable lifestyle, until her husband died suddenly and tragically leaving numerous debts.

She now feels totally unsafe with insufficient income to meet basic requirements and the despair of seeing her world fall apart - the loss of a husband, house and self-respect.

The individual cases described in the Ebyon newsletters show that regardless of the level of depravity an individual may endure, they will seek to preserve any fraction of self-respect they can. It may hang by a thread but in doing so becomes ever more critical to their well-being.

The newsletter dated September 2002 describes how a friend of the Trust, a hairdresser who earlier this year volunteered her skills for the benefit of people using some of the projects and centres known to the Trust. She describes a predicament: 'I had been talking with a gentleman, Chris. He was ill and not always easy to understand. When I had finished cutting and styling his hair, he asked me how much he owed. I assured him that there was no charge whatsoever. However, after some lengthy discussion, he insisted, "please don't do this. Let me give you something". He emptied his pockets and gave me 50 pence. He gave me all he had."

In 2001 Bob was invited to speak at a local school on the subject of homelessness before a group of children aged 9 to 11 years. Bob was inexperienced at speaking to very young children and felt rather self-conscious dressed as someone homeless. In the event, both were astounded by the children's genuine interest and understanding of the message. They found encouragement that day. In the audience was a child whose handwritten letter clearly expressed the impact and the appreciation of someone so young. This was very touching to read.

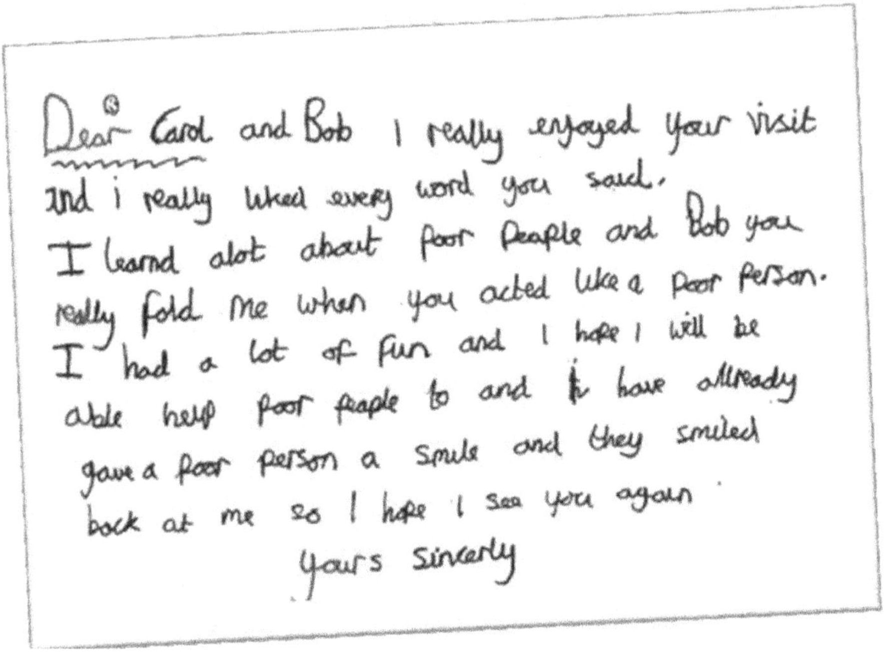

Dear Carol and Bob I really enjoyed your visit
and i really liked every word you said.
I learnd alot about poor People and Bob you
really fold me when you acted like a poor Person.
I had a lot of fun and I hope I will be
able help poor peaple to and I have allready
gave a poor person a smile and they smiled
back at me so I hope I see you again.
Yours sincerly

Letter to Bob and Carol, following school event.

Carol: 'One of the most wonderful stories that we've loved over the years was about a chap who was staying at Jimmy's Night Shelter. He was given the opportunity to choose a new pair of shoes when he'd never had a new pair of shoes in his life. He was very modest when he went to buy them. He was allocated a certain amount of money which he didn't exceed. And then there was a big furore in the dormitory that night because he wouldn't take them off to go to bed.

Bob: 'We are often asked what items are required by the care centres and night shelter; those most requested are cutlery, disposable razors, dog food, dog leads and toiletries.'

Carol: 'One donation we had totally forgotten about came up at a Thanksgiving service. He wouldn't have known we were there or who we were, but he talked about how he'd been given the money for a bike. Two or three years later, he talked about the moment he got this new bike and how it had transformed his life. He was able to get a little job. We could never have foreseen things like that.'

Ebyon Newsletter- August 2004

His grandmother had died, and he wanted to attend her funeral - a return bus fare of £6.50. The Trust provided this plus enough for a drink and a sandwich.

It was considered an important step in the family reconciliation programme.

Ebyon did not seek recognition for its work and sought no public profile for monies received or donated. They made no distinction on the value of each request, whether it be £1000 or 50 pence. Everybody's need is genuinely different, what it takes to meet that need is inconsequential.

Within the pages of the newsletters are many stories and these stories are important. They ignite our imagination and place us in situations we can allow ourselves to envisage without feeling the fear or the pain. But amongst the tragedies are also ones of hope, healing and restoration.

Bob: 'Amongst the realms of despair, there are success stories. Perhaps not ones of great gains and great achievements as some would perceive it, but success nonetheless. One man left a night shelter having spent a long time as a guest there. With an enormous smile he produced from his pocket a key. It was a key to his first room in shared accommodation. He had made the long journey to this point, not alone for it was shared by project workers and others who had walked it with him…but he had arrived.'

Ebyon Newsletter - November 2003

The point of this story is quite simple - she has been given a chance on the route to a stable lifestyle. She has been given a chance. That is the very heart of what the Trust aims to do.

Ebyon Newsletter - August 2004

A man staying at a long-term hostel; a recovering alcoholic who was also a gifted artist was given the opportunity to attend a 2-day painting seminar. Highl motivated by the course he was keen to begin to paint once more with the hope of bringing in additional income.

Carol: 'I can think of a young girl that wanted to start dance and drama school, but you needed to take exams and then you had to buy a certificate. She also needed a leotard. Well that's that if you've got no money, so we gave her money for the exam certificates. We made links with a centre in Peterborough that was working with young adults. There was one chap who was desperate to do hairdressing, but again, even to start an apprenticeship you need a brush and comb etc. They didn't supply them, so we bought a starter kit for him. As time progressed we found we were giving quite a bit of money for birth certificates because you need them to get into the system - it's really crucial.'

A significant part of Ebyon's work was in sponsoring children to take a holiday, often to the coast; an unlikely experience given their difficult circumstances. Not only did the children benefit from a new environment their families also enjoyed a short respite from their responsibilities.

In comparison to others Ebyon was a small trust operating within tight parameters and a small catchment area. Whilst Bob and Carol watched the availability of similar resources and establishments decrease, the human need for immediate help remained relentless. Even the local night shelter began a booking system which required an individual to register with the local council. No longer could the shelter operate under an open-door policy.

Carol: 'You stood there, and you queued and you got a bed. And there weren't too many questions asked. "Put your bottle down, and we do absolutely no drugs here, but come in. You can have a bed, you can have a shower, you can have a hot meal. You need to be out again in the morning, but you can come back tomorrow."'

In 2018 with increasing restrictions imposed by the Charities Commission Ebyon began the process of winding down.

Bob: 'The nature and patterns of deprivation were changing. The volume of deprivation was increasing dramatically in all categories. Linked to this the Charities

Commission would now require a charity to have a minimum of six trustees, each specialising in a different aspect of charitable work such as fund raising, marketing, legalities, finance and planning.'

Ebyon Newsletter- November 2004

A couple of weeks ago we listened to a sermon from a church in Watford in which the preacher said: "If all that we do doesn't help our neighbour in need, then what are we doing?"

That seems to be where we started ten years ago.

Moving closer to retirement, there was no-one to whom they could pass on this responsibility. Towards the end the couple were challenged on their terms and conditions, occasionally accused of bigotry and prejudice in not being willing to extend their geographical boundaries. Bob knew however that the Trust would not be able to sustain high demands from causes beyond the county that were growing in frequency. In conversation with others, both realised that the venture could and maybe should end with them.

It takes a parallel passion and vision to continue in the same vein and this is rarely duplicated in another. When I asked Bob and Carol if Ebyon has been successful they responded, 'absolutely not. There are more people in need than ever before.' But has it changed anything? You would need to ask the man wearing a new pair of boots, the child paddling in surf for the first time, or the family who now have a plaque to commemorate the very short life of their child.

There is more at work here than two people's hard work and determination. There is an energy, one that radiates far wider than can be evidenced by stories, accounts and statistics. An energy that acknowledges an invisible connection, one that unanimously joins us together as members of one human family. A human family occupying one earth, one home and sharing it with ones who are yet more defenceless than ourselves. Who will speak for them?

Bob and Carol Thorndike – The Ebyon Trust

Chapter Seven

Small and Docile

11 June 2023. On a *Sketch n' Wander* morning my friend and I debate the merits and pitfalls of using animals for experimentation. We sit in long grass with our sketch pads fighting off the bugs and suffering the effects of pollen, whilst we casually consider how we both feel about such an emotive subject. I'm prompted to talk about this as Camp Beagle will shortly celebrate a second anniversary of raising public awareness and support for their plight. They have pitched their tents, banners and slogans outside the fences of Marshall Bio Resources. For almost two years they have been protesting against the breeding of beagles for testing laboratories. The conditions in which the dogs are kept are deplorable. Their leaflet entitled Born on Death Row describes their strategy to expose a government-backed animal testing industry that relies on beagle puppies (and other animals) for experimentation. 'Behind closed doors they [the beagles] suffer [nasty things that I won't describe] to meet order deadlines.'[1]

Why beagles? Apparently because they are small, docile and can be housed and cared for using less space and money.

I pass them most days, honk the horn as a mark of solidarity and admire their courage and persistence. Two years have passed since they set up camp, and I wonder how much has changed. Clearly a nuisance to MBR and the police who have to restrain them when the vans loaded with puppies leave the complex, but will their protest reach its ultimate aim to ban animal experimentation? They need 100,000

1 Born on Death Row. Shutdown MBR Acres & Ban Animal Testing. Thecampbeagle.com

signatures on a petition to initiate a debate in parliament. Opinion on whether testing on animals should continue is divisive. One could argue the pros and cons on both sides backed by research that can be interpreted according to how you want to present your case.

My son's dog Ronnie is a 6-year-old beagle, owned and loved since he was just a few weeks old. When Ronnie hears a loud noise he does his best to keep himself safe and finds the darkest and remotest part of the house in which to hide. Usually, he runs to the bathroom and sits in the bath. He can stay there for up to two hours. My son often sits in there with him until Ronnie feels it's safe to come out. If any of us show signs of stress or distress, Ronnie comes immediately to our side placing his head on our lap, under our hand or in the case of my son, places his paws on his shoulders as if to give him a hug. Ronnie is a highly sensitive animal that feels fear, anxiety, as well as joy and excitement, and is quick to sense the same emotions in others.

On 10th February 2023 I said goodbye to my beloved dog Chip of 14 years. Two days previously he had fallen down the whole flight of stairs. Despite the vet confirming good health and movement (he was still walking, eating, sleeping) I could tell by his breathing that he was still suffering. On the morning of the 10th, I heard howling and screaming. Chip had fallen from the settee presumably trying to get to the back door. He lay on the floor shaking and yelping in profuse pain. His body gave out and he gave up his life within minutes. This has been one of the most heart-breaking experiences of my life - four months on and I'm still reliving those traumatic moments.

Animals are sentient beings, meaning they have the capacity to experience sensations and emotions. Dogs feel fear and they feel pain, I am in no doubt that rats and mice do as well. A rodent infected with numerous cancerous cells will surely feel pain that is intense and relentless. When they are in captivity for research purposes there is nowhere for them to run, nowhere to escape to and no place to hide. They cannot exercise their natural survival instincts, nor can they be supported by their own kind. None of this is their choosing.

Animals Used for Testing

The European Partnership for Alternative Approaches to Animal Testing (EPAA) initiated by the European Commission is a private and public partnership. It includes representation from industry and business, regulatory authorities and those who promote animal welfare. Its aim is to replace, reduce and refine the use of animals in chemical research and progress the use of alternative methods and resources. In an EPAA video, Tily Metz of the European Parliament expressed frustration that current practices link more to culture and tradition than science, and that the industry needs 'a change of mentality'.[2] But change incurs costs. It is quicker, cheaper and more efficient to keep using conventional processes. A change in system requires new resources that need to be bought and installed; staff then need to be trained and time is lost in adapting to new methods of research.

In defence, the organisation Understanding Animal Research argue: 'Before pre-clinical animal tests there are a large number of pre-preclinical non-animal tests done on all manner of research tools. These methods are used to remove many potentially toxic, or obviously non-starting drugs from reaching the more expensive animal testing stage – greatly reducing the amount of animal research required for a drug to reach market.'[3]

The organisation's general points for arguing a case for use of animals in research mainly relate to past achievements - what animal testing has done such as the development of important pharmaceuticals and treatment that we all make use of to this day.[4]

But medicine and technology have moved on. I refer to an article written by the Physicians Committee for Responsible Medicine (2017) entitled 'Mice are telling cancer researchers – give it up.' It begins:

'It is widely known that mouse research to study human cancers is fraught with unreliability. Scientists have for decades attempted to replicate human cancer growth and treatment responses in mice by disabling their immune systems and grafting human cell-line based cancers onto them. These studies have notoriously faulty outcomes. In general, cancer animal research has a failure rate of at least 95%, as determined by the results of clinical trials based partly on mouse studies. The few successes are usually clinically irrelevant providing minimal or no real-life value.'

The article ends: 'It's long past time that we take notice of the many ways that mice have shown us that they are not tiny humans. Whether the barriers to this transition (to human-relevant cancer research methods) are research arrogance, career

---

2 EPAA 2019. European Partnership for Alternative Approaches to Animal Testing. European Commission. YouTube Channel

3 Nine out of ten statistics are taken out of context. C. Magee 2013. Understanding Animal Research.

4 40 reasons why we need animals in research. Understanding Animal Research.

and funding considerations or regulatory restrictions, these must be overcome if the abject failure of mouse research for cancer is to be reversed.'[5]

Animal research may well have been reduced but the RSPCA confirm that 'more than 100 million animals are used in research and testing across the world each year, including around four million in the UK. Animals used in scientific procedures can and do experience pain, suffering and distress, which can be severe.'[6] There has been a significant decrease in the use of animals for experimentation in the last decade (apart from the development of the COVID vaccine) but there is still a long way to go.

One of Camp Beagle's youngest supporters has been promoting her own campaign in her local community, and online. Her message to the Prime Minister is emphatic: "I will not stop making a noise." Her own handwritten graphic suggests alternative methods that can be used to substitute animal testing.

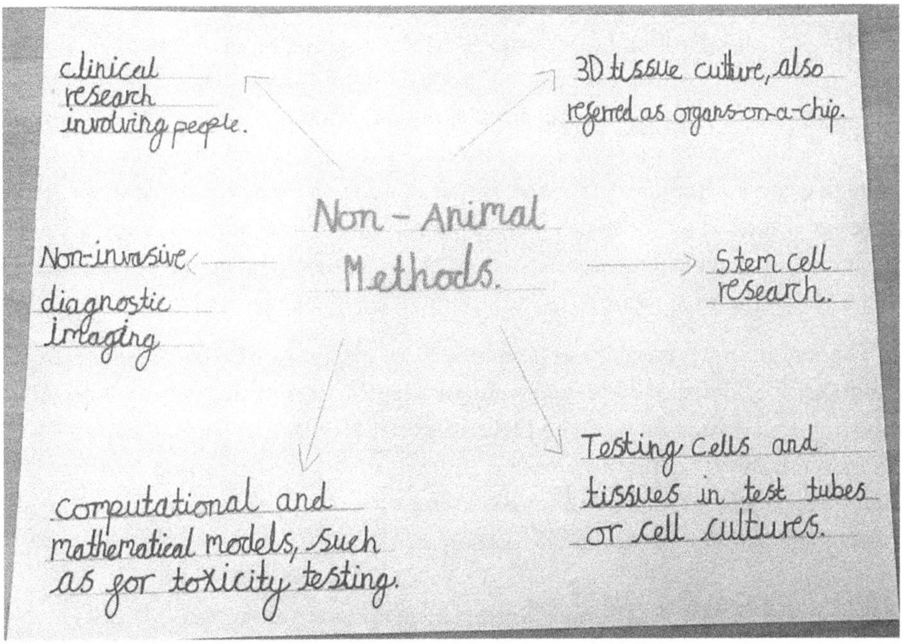

Cheaper, convenient and what has always been done, are not good enough reasons for torturing animals.

---

5 Mice Are Telling Cancer Researchers: Give It Up. 2017. Physicians Committee for Responsible Medicine

6 Animal in Science. RSPCA

5 June 2023. BBC's Panaroma has looked into the use of artificial additives in food and the effect this is having on our health. Whilst watching, I pick up on an interview with a director of a cancer research centre who investigated the effects of the sweetener Aspartame, when given to mice and rats. The results showed that the number of tumours increased when a higher dose was applied. Mice and rats suffering induced cancer and I'm guessing given no pain relief, all for our benefit. To my mind, artificial additives in food are not life sustaining.

THE GUARDIAN **3rd July 2023**

Sunak faces transparency questions over jet travel and Tory donations

Air travel worth £38,500 – used for him and eight staff to attend Conservative events in Scotland and Wales in April – was funded by Balderton Medical Consultants

Labour is also calling for scrutiny of a £50,000 donation from Balderton.

Professor Erik Millstone of University of Sussex reviewed all research and found that there was a link between how research was funded and the conclusions it reached. The studies that exposed harm were funded by non-commercial and independent sources, yet the 'research funded by the makers of aspartame (about 90% of the reassuring studies) were funded by large chemical corporations that manufacture and sell Aspartame.' He concludes, 'So there's a pattern – an expression of a very dangerous bias'.[7]

The programme goes on to describe how the majority of members of the Committee for Toxicology (the independent scientific committee that provides advice to the Food Standards Agency, the Department of Health and Social Care, and other Government Departments) have recent links to the food or chemical Industry. This therefore creates a questionable ethical barrier to safer levels of food production which in turn presents a danger to the UK consumer.

Depressing Statistics

It strikes me as odd that the more advanced we become the harder we seem to work and the sicker we get. How is it that we are fatter, less mobile, poorer, and clearly, far less happy than ever before? Regardless, we keep pursuing the same routes to health and well-being which are evidently having the opposite effect.

---

7 Ultra-Processed Food: A Recipe for Ill Health? Panorama. 2023. bbc.co.uk

The number of antidepressant drugs (AD's) currently prescribed and consumed, is in itself depressing. These are figures published by the Royal Pharmaceutical Society in 2022.

- 14.7% of the population in England (i.e. 56.5 million people) — received at least one prescription item for AD's in 2021/2022 (2021 Census).
- patients aged 17 years and under receiving an AD prescription rose by 9.2% compared with the previous year.
- almost three times as many patients receive prescriptions in the most deprived areas of the country, compared to the least deprived.
- prescribing of AD's in children aged 5–12 years has increased by more than 40% between 2015 and 2021.

'There are complex reasons why prescriptions for antidepressants are rising, which include progress on diagnosis and support for people with depression, changes in dosages, and the range of conditions they are prescribed for'.[8]

Since 1990's when antidepressants were first introduced to the market they were welcomed as an end to misery for many. Characterised as a *miracle drug*, prescriptions have increased at an alarming rate with millions taking them for 5 years or longer. The withdrawal symptoms of AD's can be similar to those of depression and anxiety. They can therefore be mistaken for the original condition returning. This presents a difficult dilemma for doctors when deciding whether to prolong treatment or continue with a plan for withdrawal.

What is most alarming is the flimsy data that the manufacturers submitted for drugs to go to market, and also the inaccurate information published to reassure the consumer and to market the drug. Researchers discovered internal memos revealing the concealment of problematic side effects, until such time that this information was requested by authorities. Withdrawal symptoms were not closely studied, and medicines were licensed before long terms effects were researched.

Joanna Moncrief, Professor of Social cand Critical Psychiatry at University of London stated, 'few trials have lasted longer than six months, none have lasted longer than one year. Anyone taking these drugs for longer than a few weeks is taking part in a huge unregulated experiment to find out the long-term consequences.'[9]

8 Antidepressant prescribing increases by 35% in six years. C. Burns. 2022. The Pharmaceutical Journal

9 The Antidepressant Story. Panorama, 2023. bbc.co.uk

A Cruel Mandate

Incidentally, the manufacturers under scrutiny by investigators are the same ones responsible for the development and marketing of the initial covid vaccines. When European Member of Parliament Rob Roos of the Netherlands (October 2022) questioned Pfizer if they knew whether the Covid vaccine was tested for prevention of transmission before it entered the market, a Pfeizer director confirmed, 'no...... we had to do everything at risk'.[10] Rob Roos summarised in a subsequent statement released on video; 'this removes the entire basis for the COVID passport that led to massive institutional discrimination, as people lost access to essential parts of society. I find this to be shocking even criminal'[11]

THE BRITISH MEDICAL JOURNAL **26th July 2023**

Medical royal colleges receive millions from and drug and medical device companies.

Royal colleges in the UK have received more than £9m in marketing payments from drug and medical devices companies since 2015. The Royal College of Physicians and the Royal College of General Practitioners were the biggest recipients of industry money, the investigation found.

The biggest donor overall was Pfizer, with £1.8m of payments.

"It is deeply disappointing that so many royal colleges negotiate these payments and don't even tell the full and detailed truth about them. Patients need to trust medical institutions that educate or create and implement guidelines which should be based on best available evidence, not lobbying" (Susan Bewley, honorary professor, Kings College London).

In February 2022 carehome.co.uk estimated a loss of 40,000 care home staff following announcement of the cruel mandate based on the belief that the vaccines had been tested to confirm effectiveness in limiting the spread of COVID.[12] 'Revoking

---

10 Pfizer did not know whether Covid vaccine stopped transmission before rollout. European Parliament, 2022. news.com.au YouTube Channel

11 BREAKING: vaccine was never tested on preventing transmission. 2022. Rob Roos YouTube Channel.

12 Government U-turn on mandatory Covid vaccine branded 'a joke' and 'too late' by care homes. S. Learner, 2022. Carehome.co.uk

the Covid-19 vaccination mandate for health and care staff has come "too late" for the thousands of care home workers who already left the sector because of the policy'.[13]

How many drugs and artificial additives must we ingest before we realise the harm they do to our bodies, our mental health, not to mention our quality of life and the planet on which we depend? How many animals must die cruelly and prematurely to support the insatiable human demand for comfort and convenience? How many deep pockets will we line by the digestion of unsafe food and the consumption of unnecessary drugs that are ineffective or even harmful? Our dogged faith in science largely controlled by companies and individuals that would benefit hugely in financial terms, blinds us to the possibility of other treatments and courses of action that are far less harmful and invasive. We are losing the ability to think for ourselves and confidently apply reason to our decisions. We heedlessly entrust our power to organisations and professionals giving no thought to the possibility that their interests and priorities may be different to ours. How long before it's too late.

Money creates distrust. It introduces a fog that can shield us from the true motive behind a request, a campaign, a recommendation or even a mandate. When the truth is not in plain sight, we should pause and consider the conflicts of interest. We can then determine who stands to gain the most and if the decisions they are making on our behalf are in our very best interests. In simple terms – follow the money.

When a handsome, charming representative from the World Wildlife Fund (WWF) asked me to make a donation, he described in detail the perils the rangers faced when they challenged illegal poaching. I was happy listening to his convincing rhetoric (with the added allure of a French accent), until he confirmed that my money would purchase weapons. They in turn would be used by the rangers to protect themselves and the animals they were trying to conserve. I took the time to pause and think - fundraisers can be very persuasive. I had no doubt about the risks the rangers faced and that their job was indeed a perilous one, but what I was being asked to do was to contribute to the purchase and use of more weapons. The thought of my money being used to inflict further injury or harm did not appeal. To me the obvious route to combat the problem of illegal poaching, would be to follow the trail of money, determine who stands to benefit and from what, and then stunt the demand.

---

13 Warning 'many' care workers will not return to jobs despite vaccine rule change. M.Ford, 2022. Nursing Times

A Shark's Tale

My son can say with some confidence that at the age of 6 he killed a shark. I say with *some* confidence - we didn't see it die but it almost certainly could not have survived.

On Sunday afternoons we frequently visited a local shop that specialises in tropical and marine fish, crustaceans and all the other accessories that go with keeping a fish in an unnatural habitat. The aquariums that contain the fish that are for sale, are stacked. There are long ones at the bottom for the larger specimens and those at eye level for the smaller varieties.

One of the long tanks held a single shark. I have no idea whether it was young or fully grown, but it measured about 10 inches in length and swam the length of the 6 ft tank back and forth. It was grey, and sleek like the archetypal image we have of sharks and we imagined it to be highly dangerous.

After an initial wander we would visit the reptiles upstairs before descending to the main shopping area. On this occasion my son was treated to a handful of Smarties (sugar-coated chocolate sweets) from the dispenser and off we went to have one last look and then make our final purchases. As I caught up with my son near the shark tank I noticed in horror that he had fed it a Smartie. The single sweet had landed on the one and only rock, and its coloured sugar-coating had begun to waft upwards leaving the sweet as grey as the shark's skin.

Keeping exotic fish is not easy, keeping them alive and well is even harder. Replicating a square metre of the Amazon River, Lake Victoria or the Indian Ocean in your front room requires constant monitoring of water PH, heat, light and in the case of marine fish, a certain level of salinity. I had no doubt that a single Smartie would cause havoc with the balance and be fatal to its occupant. But who is going to stick their hand in a shark's tank and pick it out?

I'm ashamed to say I did the next best thing and left in haste. I know I should have mentioned the incident to the shop owners, but the damage was done and I did not want to face a monstrous bill. How much is a 10-inch shark worth anyway? I'm searching websites for today's costs and find it all depends on the species. Prices range from £72 to £1100, pre-owned (meaning unwanted) are somewhat cheaper.

If we are going to apportion blame, let's look at the potential culprits. A 6-year-old child is not going to the know the consequences of dropping something into a tank of water and could even be commended for wanting to share his bounty - naturally, I defend my son. Then there's me, his mother. Honestly, I did not imagine this happening therefore I could not have predicted it. I naively assumed the gift of sweets would keep him amused long enough for us all to safely reach the checkout. Then there's the retailers. The tank had no lid, there was no sign saying DON'T FEED THE SHARK. The shop sold the sweets.

The Ornamental Aquatic Trade Association confirm that around four million households in the UK own live fish. This is equivalent to around 14% of the population. They estimate a total spend of over £400 million a year to maintain the hobby of fishkeeping. 'Fish are much more intelligent than most people give them credit for. Fish are sentient. They feel pain subjectively and can suffer'.[14]

And there it is - the point where the world of men, money and goods (in this case confectionary and living sentient beings) collide. We all had a part to play in this tragedy. When we treat living breathing beings as commodities, we create the demand and the retailers respond and advance it.

Demand creates supply; the more people want, the more production increases. When demand is reduced, the supply decreases as there is no more money to be made. Power to make changes lies with the consumer and whilst independent investigations and research are vital in educating the public, it is our complacency, our thoughtless indulgence and sometimes our own desperation that fuels a manipulative and exploitive market.

It was a few months before we returned and immediately noticed the absence of both shark and sweet dispensers.

14 July 2023. Since Chip died, I've missed a four-legged walking companion that can run on ahead of me and run circles in the grass. In the evenings I miss a little warm body snoring quietly on the far side of the settee. I miss the frantic welcome when I come in the door and the unconditional love and affection that comes from

---

14 Why fish welfare matters. 2019. Compassion in World Farming.

a doting animal, and so I have started looking at buying another dog. I have seen an advertisement for a 3- year-old Cockapoo, reasonably local and looking adorable in the photo. She meets my preference for a slightly older dog to bypass the puppy years – endless chewing, weeing and waking up at all hours. My son and I, full of excitement and expectation, book an appointment to see her.

The condition of the dog is appalling. She is shabby and wet, her coat is matted. She cowers in a corner, shaking. I ask questions as to why she is in this condition, and we are told that she has just stepped into her water bowl and doesn't like being wet. I ask why she is being sold, 'she's not an outdoor dog', was the reply. I think back to the photo of her in the ad, sitting outside against a fence and notice a heavy rope attached to her collar. It's been raining outside most of the afternoon, and rightly or wrongly I conclude that she has just been left out in it. The urge to pick her up and take her home, to rescue her and relieve her suffering is instinctive and almost irresistible. My son and I talk alone, he knows how I feel but implores me to "walk away! You have no idea what you are taking on." and reminds me that we haven't even been able to see her stand and walk. Reluctantly I take his advice.

Trawling the ads again I shortlist a litter of schnoodles (schnauzer crossed with a poodle), that are local and affordable. One particular specimen with a white body and chocolate coloured head is particularly eye-catching. Seated on a cushion of silk surrounded by soft pastel fabrics, he looks adorable and well cared for, so I arrange a viewing. This time I take my friend who has kept many dogs. We agree on the way that the puppy must be in optimum health, microchipped and vaccinated.

We arrive at a very small first floor flat whose car port below has been turned into a run for dogs. As we walk upstairs, we are overwhelmed by the noise of barking coming from crates of dogs, two of which are stacked on top of each other, and another on the floor. The TV is on loud and there is clearly no room for any other furniture. Each crate holds over 4 puppies and the other contains 3 dogs, older and boisterous. We can barely make ourselves heard when we ask:

Q: "Have they been vaccinated?"

A: "No" (all puppies should receive their first vaccination by age of 8 weeks)

Q: "Why not?"

A: "It's not a legal requirement. They have been microchipped" (which is a legal requirement).

Q: "Was this done by a vet?"

A: "No, it was done by a dog groomer" (apparently it can be done by any trained professional).

Q: "Where is the mother?"

She pulls out a slightly larger dog that shows no signs of having recently weened pups. Clearly the puppies have not seen a vet since birth and the circumstances she is claiming are dubious and not to be trusted. This time I am feeling more confident about walking away. If I were to buy a dog from these squalid conditions I would be creating demand and in doing so fostering a sordid business.

Animals give of their bodies and their lives for our convenience, for our pleasure and our indulgence, their fate is our choice. But what of humans? Given extraordinary circumstances they too can be driven to make desperate sacrifices.

But I 'm ending on a positive note. She is happy, healthy, just 10 weeks old and equally adorable. We've named her Wynter.

Chapter Eight

Bodies for Commodities

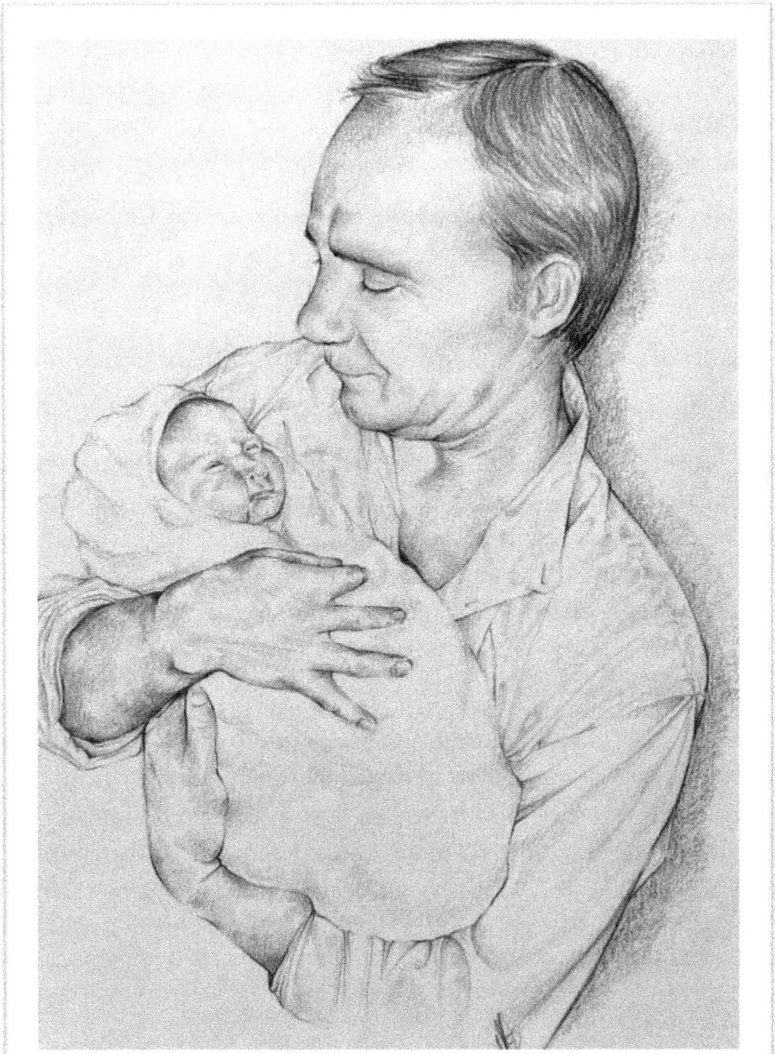

THE TIMES **2nd June 2023**

Italians who arrange surrogate births abroad face criminal prosecution under a new law.

Surrogacy is already illegal in Italy. The new law would make surrogacy a 'universal crime' also punishing people who go abroad to have a child via surrogacy, where it is legal.

The surrogacy industry is very easy to find and access. A quick google search revealed several websites offering surrogacy services advertised in much the same way as any service trying to attract a customer. I find a welcome page that promotes their services: 'We are giving you guarantees and supporting you in every step of the way towards your healthy baby.' The company confirms:

- a choice of 10 clinics in 5 countries (normally six, but Ukraine is suspended due to hostilities)
- Customer reviews
- an offer of 7 packages ranging from €5,300 to a VIP package costing €53,250
- there is no waiting list.

Another agency has photos of their 5 female donors. All appear, young, happy and very attractive. They are given an egg donor number as a means of identification. Each has a brief description of their assets including weight, height, blood type and a little of their personality. For example, egg donor number #241222 -01 is an artistic soul with a flair for creativity, whilst another is purposeful, kind-hearted and always willing to lend a hand. I try the chat function to see if the website is live and am put through to a female consultant.

Surrogacy is when a woman carries and gives birth to a baby on behalf of another person or couple who are unable to have children themselves. There are two types of surrogacy: 'Full surrogacy (also known as host or gestational surrogacy) is when the eggs of the intended mother or donor are used and there is therefore no genetic connection between the baby and the surrogate. Partial surrogacy (also known as straight or traditional surrogacy) involves the surrogate's egg being fertilised with the sperm of the intended father.'[1]

1 Surrogacy. 2023. Human Fertilisation and Embryology Authority

Like Italy, the countries of Spain, Bulgaria, France, Germany, Portugal and Taiwan outlaw all forms of surrogacy including ones where no money changes hands. Italy is now extending this restriction to their citizens when they seek this service abroad. Surrogacy for profit is banned in Canada, Denmark, New Zealand, Brazil, Britain and Australia, but they all allow some forms of altruistic surrogacy, such as the payment of reasonable expenses. The UK government website confirms legality but states, 'if you make a surrogacy agreement it cannot be enforced by the law.... a surrogate will be the child's legal parent at birth.'[2]

In contrast Ukraine was an international surrogacy hub until the Russian invasion. According to some estimates, thousands of babies have been taken abroad by foreigners each year.[3] Yet despite the hostilities Ukraine is still providing surrogacy services, controlling at least 25% of the global market. The Medical Director of a clinic in Ukraine providing surrogacy services, states that he would like to see his business operate as it did before the war, providing approximately 450 babies a year. "We are looking for women from the former soviet republics because, logically, they have to be from poorer places than our clients. I have not met a single woman with a good economic situation who has decided to go through this process out of kindness, because she thinks she has enough children and wants to help someone else who wants them. They do it because they need the money to buy a house, for their children's education. If you have a good life in Europe, you're not going to do it...No one forces these women to do it. They do it freely, and with informed consent.'[4]

'While proponents claim that women freely choose to become surrogates, vulnerable women are often manipulated through the presentation of choice. Potential surrogates are forced to choose between providing for their families through a practice that may violate their moral beliefs or forfeiting a financial opportunity to provide for their families.'[5]

I am sympathetic to the desperate actions of both childless couples and individuals who simply follow their natural instincts to love and nurture a child. Parenthood is both a challenging and incredibly fulfilling experience. Surrogacy has its place and is

---

2 Surrogacy: legal rights of parents and surrogates. GOV.UK

3 Which countries allow commercial surrogacy? A.Laing et al. 2023. Reuters

4 Ukraine's baby factories rake in record profits amid chaos of war. J. Loffredo, 2023. The Greyzone.

5 Lessons from Ukraine: Shifting International Surrogacy Policy to Protect Women and Children. E.Lamberton. 2020. Journal of Public and International Affairs. Princeton University.

best conducted as an open and regulated provision. One cannot ignore however the equally desperate plight of women who go through the maternal processes because of their equally desperate situation. Women are exploited because they feel they have no other choice but to give of themselves and their bodies to feed, house and clothe their own families. When women find themselves in these situations they put themselves at great risk, emotionally and physically.

A Very Risky Business

"I'm having to take on clients I'd rather not see [and] offer riskier, more emotionally draining services"

[The Lancet Public Health. February 2023.]

At the London Assembly in 2012, Andrew Boff, leader of the Conservative group boldly confirmed; "There is a group in London who are at least 12 times more likely to be murdered than the national average. Approximately three quarters of those within this category will also be subjected to violence, assault and rape. However, this group often distrusts the police and are much less willing to report crimes against them than the national average."

Peter Sutcliffe the Yorkshire Ripper, initially targeted prostitutes. As lone night workers they were easy prey. One of his victims 42-year-old Emily Jackson, had reluctantly entered into prostitution to save her husband's business. Finding themselves in desperate need of money she used the van of their family roofing company to engage in sex work as a means of making ends meet. Her murder was brutal and gratuitous. Recent documentaries[6] and dramatisations[7] describing the crimes of the Yorkshire Ripper in the 1970's, have unveiled the lack of choice women had when employment was scarce and they were in need of a reliable income.

If we think we have progressed since 1970 and that resorting to prostitution is now rarely necessary, we should think again. The Independent reported 'increasing numbers of women turning to sex work for the first time as the pandemic pushed people into "desperate poverty'.[8]

---

6 The Yorkshire Ripper Files; a very British crime story. First aired 25 March 2019. bbc.co.uk

7 The Long Shadow. First aired 25 September 2023. itv.com

8 Growing numbers of women turning to sex work as Covid crisis pushes them into 'desperate poverty'. M. Oppenheim, 2021. Independent.

A study carried out by Leeds University focussed on 240 sex workers, including women, men and transgender people who had willingly chosen to enter the sex industry (and had not been coerced or trafficked). 'Of those surveyed, 172 (71%) had previously worked in health, social care, education, childcare or charities, with one respondent saying she could not keep up her mortgage repayments while earning £50 a day as an NHS care assistant.' A majority exceeding 97% of those who took part had qualifications GCSE and above, with 38% having achieved an undergraduate degree and 17% a postgraduate degree.[9]

UK sex workers have the highest murder rate compared to women in other occupations. Research conducted in 2021 reported, '42% of street-based sex workers had experienced violence from the police and that women of colour and migrant sex workers are disproportionally targeted'.[10] When asked if they would like to leave prostitution, 90% of women say YES.[11]

Hunger Crime

'I'll be all around' in the dark. I'll be everywhere — wherever you look.
Wherever they's a fight so hungry people can eat, I'll be there.'
[The Grapes of Wrath, John Steinbeck.]

Astrologists who read the alignment of planets with constellations, observe that the current star charts echo those of the time of the French Revolution and the American War of Independence. When I recall learning about these turbulent periods in history as a child, I was instantly grateful that I lived in a peaceful society where clean hot water poured freely from taps, and no one was at risk of having their head chopped off.

One of my favourite Novels is a Tale of Two Cities by Charles Dickens which is set during the time of the French Revolution. He begins chapter 5 with a vivid description of how the hungry people of Paris briefly escape their misery when a cask of wine is dropped and broken, spilling its entire contents over the rough cobbles. As the wine rapidly disperses in rivulets collecting mud and grime on the way, the citizens swiftly jump to life to catch the precious liquid. Those first on the scene cup their hands to scoop and sip what they can, whilst others soak their garments to squeeze it

---

9 Most sex workers have had jobs in health, education or charities – survey. D.Taylor. 2015. The Guardian.

10 Facts about sex work. English Collective of Prostitutes.

11 Prostitution – The Facts. Streetlight UK.

out into the mouths of their starving children. When it has all but disappeared, they suck, lick and chomp on the rotten splinters of the shattered cask.

My mother can recall hunger. Although she was only a small child during the Spanish civil war, she remembers 1940 as 'el año del hambre', (the year of hunger) that followed the end of the civil war. This was a time of intense strife when food became scarce. The conflict had disrupted the agricultural processes and harvesting, as farmers were not exempt from slaughter. 'It has been estimated that in the period 1939-1944 alone 200,000 people died directly or indirectly from starvation.'[12] She says that although she was very young, she has not forgotten the hunger pains she and her family endured. They were the fortunate ones who were allocated a daily ration of bread as her father held a superior position in La Guardia Civil (civil guard). Others were not so lucky.

We are not at war, there is no shortage of food in this country, but for many having enough to eat is still a problem. '"I'm not overdramatising at all when I say we've got starving, hungry, sad, worried children committing crimes so their families can eat," said Sharon White, the chief executive of the School and Public Health Nurses Association'.[13]

An article in the Big Issue dated 15 September 2023, reports a 24% national increase in shoplifting on the previous year. Whilst retailers are asking for harsher punishments to deter the crime, the reporter provides examples of how the current economic climate is forcing people to take desperate measures. He quotes Laurence Guiness of the Childhood Trust; "One young man, 15, told me he stole formula for his baby sister to help his mother out. He complained he had to go further and further away from his home because the local shops knew him. He said some of the security guards turned a blind eye because they lived on the same estate as him.... with increasing levels of hunger, homelessness and debt driven by inflation and spiralling rents, we are rapidly going backwards as a society".[14]

12 The silenced famine of the Spanish post-war period finds a voice in new exhibition. 2022 The Conversation.

13 Hungry children are committing crimes so their families can eat. N. Hinde. 2023. Huffington Post.

14 Would you prosecute a child for stealing baby formula? Shoplifting's rise amid cost-of-living crisis. I.McRae, 2023. Big Issue.

Desperate Measures

THE NEW YORK TIMES **23rd June 2023**

5 Deaths at Sea Gripped the World. Hundreds of Others Got a Shrug.

On one vessel, five people died on a very expensive excursion that was supposed to return them to the lives they knew. On the other, perhaps 500 people died just days earlier on a squalid and perilous voyage, fleeing poverty and violence in search of new lives.

Those who know I am writing this book have been asking me this week, for my opinion concerning the loss of the Titan submersible that imploded sometime between June 18th and 22nd 2023. You may have followed the news story that described the rescue mission led by the United States Coast Guard, the US Navy and the Canadian Coast Guard. They engaged in a united effort to save 5 individuals who each had paid for a place on a commercial dive to view the remains of the Titanic. The company Ocean Gate charged $250,000 per head for the experience, and on this occasion none survived.

Whilst I was taking time to answer, the enquirers quickly came back with the observation that far less media coverage was allocated to the sinking of the fishing vessel that was loaded with over 700 migrants, of which more than 200 died.

"I understand why the submersible captured attention: It's exciting, unprecedented, obviously connected to the most famous shipwreck in history," said Ms. Sunderland, of Human Rights Watch. "I don't think it was wrong to make every effort to save them. What I would like is to see no effort spared to save the black and brown people drowning in the Mediterranean. Instead, European states are doing everything they can to avoid rescue".[15]

Since they started collating records in 2014 the Missing Migrants Project confirm **27,629** recorded deaths in the Mediterranean and **56,849** worldwide.[16] Each of those individuals also paid a comparably substantial amount of money to escape death of a different kind. How much is charged is difficult to research as there are many routes and operators, but most reporters estimate the fare to cost several thousand Euros per

15 5 Deaths at Sea Gripped the World. Hundreds of Others Got a Shrug. R. Pérez-Peña, 2023. The New York Times.

16 Since writing this paragraph in July 2023 the number has now risen to 28, 248 numbers missing in the Mediterranean and 59, 837 missing worldwide (November 2023). Missing Migrants Project.

person. Migrant smuggling is a very lucrative business. Earnings run into billions of euros. You can be sure that when people put themselves at this kind of risk, they are undeniably desperate.

I'd like to have shared a personal story, but I am grateful I don't have one. I've known poverty, but not hunger that was out of my control, nor have I been so desperate as to have to break the law. I could go on to describe human trafficking, the market for human organs, or the exploitation of children, but that would be gratuitous and unnecessary. To me, these are our horror stories. They are more worrying than the corruption of those who occupy the seats of higher authorities, or the celebrities who dodge their taxes or the conflicts of financial interest amongst those who would represent us. They are the result of an unfair system that cares nothing for the people who do their best to survive within it.

Where money can be generated, there can be doubt and suspicion regarding motive and best interests. Where there is no money involved, there is no gain and therefore there is less cause for crime, corruption or desperate acts. Living in a society without money won't necessarily purge us of all exploitation and abuse, but it surely must reduce it. To change nothing is to allow all these practices to thrive and therefore prolong the suffering and deaths of many. In this advanced age of knowledge and sophistication, no one should have to make these miserable choices just to exist.

Apathy, complacency and ignorance are our biggest enemies. They propel a dysfunctional and imbalanced economy that robs its primary contributors of their energy, their dignity and their safety. When will we acknowledge and accept that we are neither more or less than each other, that we are related and connected, and that we are all entitled? We need to leave this cold and merciless path of division and walk the road of unity.

It's time to wake up.

PART THREE

An Overdue Awakening

Chapter Nine

Division, Unity & Choice

The Traitor's Castle

'Everything can be taken from a man but one thing: the last of the human freedoms—to choose one's attitude in any given set of circumstances, to choose one's own way.'

[Viktor Frankl.]

29th November 2022. The BBC have launched a new reality TV series called The Traitors and I watch the first episode. I normally avoid reality TV shows, they don't appeal to me and I am determined to feel negative and critical about this one. I believe it will provide a perfect example of how our media likes to divide us by pitting one person against another, and what better way than to devise a scheme whereby no one knows who they can trust.

The game plan goes like this - 22 strangers share a Scottish castle for a period of 12 episodes and undergo a series of challenges and missions. The players are encouraged to work as a team but are warned that amongst them are up to 3 traitors whose goal is to pick off contestants one by one and in doing so, increase their own chances of winning the final prize of up to £120k. The viewers know who the traitors are, but the contestants do not. At the end of each day the group try to identify a traitor amongst them and collectively vote to send him /her home. Their selection is more often wrong than right, and they frequently send home a *faithful* comrade. Later after everyone has retired, the traitors meet in darkness to decide which player poses the greatest risk to their exposure and murders them before the following morning. They are not murdered - they are sent a message and hence retire from the game.

I am determined to hate this programme. I want to feel outraged by the manipulation of an audience that invites it to revel in other people's insecurities, anger and fear. I see this so many times in other reality programmes which is why I avoid them. Contestants are put in situations that exploit their weaknesses, where they are reduced to the basest of emotions and then encouraged to criticise each other's best efforts. It's a gladiatorial spectacle where the viewer then revels in the aftermath of humiliation.

Back to the story. As the situation within the castle intensifies, the paranoia builds. Nobody knows who to trust. There are tears of insecurity, insults and accusations wound delicate egos, and the players are bewildered every waking moment. I am riveted and watch all 12 episodes. I can see how the players have been picked for their diversity but also for the drama they will bring to the screen. Do I shout at the TV screen? Of course I do – how can they miss the obvious clues!

I'm not sure if the ending was choreographed but the final episode was a textbook showdown between three faithful contestants and one traitor. The turncoat was ruthless. He played his part with conviction and without mercy, having betrayed two of his own with little hesitation - but he didn't win. Despite his meticulous planning and convincing performance, in the final few minutes he lost – and he lost graciously and congratulated the winners. Each of the final 3 faithfuls claimed a share of the £101,050 prize pot.

I am surprised at the measure of torment many of the players endured during what, after all, was just a game. I witnessed a genuine longing for friendship and trust. Certainly, people were in it for themselves; not just hoping to win the jackpot but also trying to preserve their integrity and their reputation as an honest and trustworthy person in the eyes of the nation. They craved a community with stability, one in which they felt safe to contribute without falling under suspicion. Those wrongly accused felt the pain of rejection deeply. I confess I started watching the programme to justify a bias but by the last episode I felt encouraged. I know in each of us there is innate goodness and spirit that will reveal itself and shine more brightly as circumstances darken. We may not recognise it consciously, but instinctively we know we are all connected, we are here for each other.

Knowing your Onions

How can we find truth? It's not going to conveniently land in our laps via the 6 o'clock news, that's for certain. Conflict attracts viewers, scandal sells newspapers, and controversy feeds our social media, all of which provide a space for companies to sell their produce and services.

We joke that television only reports bad news, yet a continual torrent of discouraging communication steadily erodes our trust, our feeling of certainty and our safety. Everyday the news reports alarming facts and more often than not, seeks to lay the blame at the feet of the government in power. It then invites the opposition to boost the attack with carefully chosen words and facts they have pulled from an isolated moment in history where the data supports their criticism and damnation. The nation watches, and a sense of uncertainty and insecurity raises the levels of individual fear and anger. We are being taught to view others with suspicion and distrust. We become divided. In this state we (the public) are more manageable, compliant and we are easier to control. How then do we get to the truth?

I have always sought the truth - to hear it, believe it and to speak it. Yet the more I seek it the more it escapes me. I have come to realise that there are several truths and each individual's truth is viewed through their own personal lens. How we distinguish the facts and then represent them differs from person to person as I found when I placed a vase of dead yet attractive branches on a table in the new office's meditation room. There are no windows so I thought a token of nature would help provide a helpful ambiance to support stillness and connection to nature. At least this was my intention. When I proudly shared this with a colleague, they informed me that dead leaves are bad karma. I quickly removed them, horrified that my unforgiveable ignorance should cause offence and worse still bring in some dark entity during a meditation. On reflection (and a good deal of research), I realised I had allowed myself to be influenced by someone else's confident belief and higher work ranking, nothing more. Their truth, not mine.

The truth is elusive and arguably subjective. That sounds like a contradiction as many truths that present themselves at the same time can appear to conflict depending on how the information is perceived, interpreted, and more importantly, depending on what is overlooked or conveniently left out. When we seek confirmation of *our* truth, we will eventually find it, even when we bypass the opposing facts and perspectives during our search. We are constantly bombarded with information that is manipulative and we manipulate others in return. The less we filter, the greater we expose ourselves and even worse, base our decisions on information that is imbalanced and that can only claim a fraction of accuracy.

The book 'We are the 99%'[1] draws the reader's attention to the issue of truth and the stages at which it evolves from the absolute truth to falsehood. The figure below is an interpretation of Thomas's Spectrum of Reliability, running left to right in terms of reliability of information. I have added a further onion at the end which represents speculation. Speculation is not even forecasting. A forecast (such as the weather) bases its findings and subsequent predictions on proven scientific methods that have yielded consistent results.

1 99% - How We've Been Screwed, and How to Fight Back. M.Thomas. 2020. Apollo.

Variation of Thomas's Spectrum of Reliability (2019).

Speculation on the other hand, is different. According to the Oxford Dictionary it is 'the forming of a theory or conjecture without firm evidence.' When used flippantly and with the aim to threaten or scare people, it becomes irresponsible and dangerous. Watch any news item and judge for yourself how much of what you hear falls into this group.

AL JAZEERA **24th February 2023**

One year into Russian invasion, Ukraine's Zelenskyy vows victory

President Volodymyr Zelenskyy says the beginning of the Russian invasion was 'the longest day of our lives'.

Ukraine's leader has pledged to push for victory in 2023 as Ukrainians marked the sombre anniversary of the Russian invasion, while Moscow told the world to accept 'the realities' of its war.

As the war between Russia and the Ukraine reaches its first anniversary on 24th February 2023, reports confirm that Russia's arsenal is depleting rapidly and is now looking to China for its support and provision of ammunition. Before I even finish my breakfast there is talk of fears that such a move will potentially spark a third world war. When these words are uttered by a senior official, they become headline news and unwarranted anxieties can spread rapidly, as if this outcome is inevitable. But it is only speculation.

'President Joe Biden said on Monday the threat of Russian President Vladimir Putin using tactical nuclear weapons is "real", days after denouncing Russia's deployment of such weapons in Belarus.'[2] The word 'nuclear' is enough to shake anyone's sense of safety regardless of their proximity to either country. But this is not a certainty, this is still just speculation.

Let's look at any random news item. On 7th August 2023, the Guardian published the following headline: 'Up to 500 asylum seekers could be on Bibby Stockholm barge by end of week, says minister.' Where does this statement sit in the spectrum of reliability? Definitely under distortion as 'up to 500' could mean any number, even just one. Also falsehood - as nothing yet has transpired. Finally speculation in the words 'could be' in that it quotes the opinion of a single person. Yet I have no doubt that it will ignite a surge of angry protest. It is provocative.[3]

Let's pick another, and I am trying to be fair by highlighting the first headline I come across. This time Sky News publish online:

SKY NEWS **7th August 2023**

UK scientists have begun developing vaccines as an insurance against a new pandemic caused by an unknown "Disease X".

The work is being carried out at the government's high-security Porton Down laboratory by a team of more than 200 scientists. They have drawn up a threat list of animal viruses that are capable of infecting humans and could in future spread rapidly around the world.

Which of them will break through and trigger the next pandemic is unknown, which is why it's referred to only as "Disease X".

The article begins with the truth, as the work has begun and has been evidenced by the journalist firsthand. The facts then become less clear. The viruses are only a

---

2 Biden says threat of Putin using tactical nuclear weapons is 'real'. T Hunnicutt & N Bose. 2023. Reuters.

3 By 7 November 2023 around 70 asylum seekers were living on the barge, and the number of permissible residents was reduced to 425 to meet fire safety assessments. 'Bibby Stockholm migrant barge 'to cost more per head than hotels' despite Home Office pledge to cut bill.' H. Bancroft. 2023. The Independent

threat, not a certainty. Any one of the viruses maybe capable of making us ill, but it is not definite. There is nothing to say whether a disease is likely or imminent, what it is, how many people it will affect (if at all) and what the symptoms will be. When I read further, one of the Professors, Dame Jenny Harries, head of the UK Health Security Agency, clarifies: "What we're trying to do here is ensure that we prepare so that if we have a new Disease X, a new pathogen, we have done as much of that work in advance as possible."

But if like many, you just read the headlines to keep abreast of national and international news, you could convince yourself that we are facing a new pandemic in the very near future. You may feel alarmed and share your worries with your family, friends and colleagues who in turn share the story maybe in person or maybe on social media. Yet there is no pandemic, there is no disease, and no risk has been identified. Nothing much to report in terms of headline news – just a group of scientists in a laboratory doing their job.

Is speculation a bad thing, should we be avoiding any news that forecasts developments that may or may not transpire? Not necessarily. This morning's article on the front page of Euronews.com website entitled; 'The end of the road for fast fashion? The EU hopes so'[4], is an alert. Much like the one relating to Disease X, it is a warning. In this case the journalist highlights the consequences of the excessive manufacturing of cheap clothes in terms of waste and greenhouse gas emissions. So, what is the difference between the two articles? The difference is simply our own discernment. Our evaluation of the validity of the information presented to us. How do I feel about it? Should I be worried? Do I want to look into it more deeply? Do I even want to take action?

Despite the outrage at the time, we should be grateful to Labour aide Jo Moore whose memo a "good day to bury bad news" was discovered on the day of the September 11th attacks in 2001. Would it otherwise have occurred to us that news of importance can be played down when the public is distracted by a greater crisis.

'A rather cynical tradition has developed in Westminster in recent years in which, in the final days and hours before MPs leave Parliament for recess, the government releases a deluge of reports, statistics, and statements in an apparently deliberate attempt to bury them.'[5] I wonder how many more smokescreens have been publicised

---

4 The end of the road for fast fashion? The EU hopes so. S. O'Donoghue. 2023. Euronews. culture

5 Is there ever a 'good day to bury bad news'? Seven times politicians have tried. D.O'Donoghue. 2020. Press and Journal

to take our attention away from a more pressing development. Have any been fabricated? Do I believe we are regularly exposed to fake news? Absolutely. Fake news need not be entirely fake to involve some kind of fabrication or manipulation. It can be subtle. You may have noticed that filmed newsreels are played back to the viewer on a loop. During a report the same shot is played repeatedly, on a loop without a break to support the length of the news report – not an untruth, but somewhat deceptive, nevertheless.

'The universe of "fake news" is much larger than simply false news stories. Some stories may have a nugget of truth but lack any contextualizing details. They may not include any verifiable facts or sources. Some stories may include basic verifiable facts, but are written using language that is deliberately inflammatory, leaves out pertinent details or only presents one viewpoint.'[6]

The use of satire and parody to ridicule a situation or individual can leave the viewer believing they are stupid unless they think along the same lines or draw the same conclusions - much like the Emperor's new clothes. The use of music or colour are powerfully evocative and can manipulate an emotional response. Once as part of a group, I watched a video that was shown to promote a charitable plea. The film showed a derelict place, where children looked nervously at the camera from behind dilapidated walls as if they were living in the midst of a devastating war. It was initially filmed in black and white to sombre music which denoted oppression, sadness and poverty. There then followed the charitable intervention. In this case, Christmas shoeboxes filled with essential goodies were given to the children. The music swiftly changed to a lighter and faster tempo, colour flooded the screen, and the children laughed with excitement. Suddenly they looked happy, healthy and cared for. The message was clear – your donation, and only your donation will make a difference to this child's life. What concerned me most was that everyone watching the film with me that day was oblivious to the tactics that were used to influence them. The sudden change of music, colour or mood went unnoticed.

I have seen a very interesting video on the lesser-known workings of the economy punctuated by short violent visuals of police in riot gear and barking dogs. There was no relevance in adding the footage to the video. Although the information was

---

6 "Fake News," Lies and Propaganda: How to Sort Fact from Fiction. Research Guide. University of Michigan Library.

controversial, there were no riots to speak of. Clearly it was added to spark anger in the viewer.[7]

Several newscasters have thankfully denounced a viral video of a Japanese billboard blaring the slogan, 'Stop War, Stop Zelensky' as fake. It was indeed an edited video of a harmless one 'posted two years ago, viewed eight million times on YouTube, showing someone walking around Shibuya, among the busiest and most popular neighbourhoods in Tokyo.'[8] The more outrageous, the more controversial, the more viewings. More viewings and *likes* result in more money and to hell with the consequences.

Although we have a right to truthful information, our right to believe and to think for ourselves is of greater value in helping us to detect the facts, evaluate the importance or relevance of the data and to find a more balanced perspective. In recognising a third party's interest, we can become more alert to exaggeration, distortion and speculation and how these are used to attract a consumer, or to simply fill space and time. By looking more keenly at what is claimed we can decide how we want to respond to the information presented to us. We can check-in with ourselves – how is this making me feel? Am I feeling frightened and if so, is my fear justified? Will this affect my daily life and routine, or do I need to change my plans? How does this sit with my core values and beliefs? Do I need to re-evaluate? This right of discernment ultimately assists us all to paint the world we want to live in.

Our Fears

'I will not allow anyone to walk in my mind with dirty feet.'

[Ghandi]

I sometimes wonder what I could have achieved had I been less fearful. Had I known that I would make it this far, I wonder if I would have made different decisions. If I knew that I would have a home, a family, an income that would secure the heat and food to live safely, in relative comfort, would I have lived with greater authenticity?

Would I have cared a little less about fitting in and more about who and what brings me joy? Fear is our biggest obstacle. Given that we no longer need to defend ourselves against enemy tribes, search for food and water and escape dangerous

---

7 97% Owned: The Cruel Truth Behind Money Credit and Financial Crisis. Business Documentary from 2012 ENDEVR Documentary, 2020. YouTube.com

8 Fact Check: Did Tokyo Billboard Show 'Stop War, Stop Zelensky'? T. Norton. 2023. Newsweek.

predators, why are we still living so cautiously? Why are we taught to see the world as a bad and dangerous place? Why do we immediately assume that anything or anyone being or acting differently, is a threat to our security.

As I queued up at traffic lights early one morning on the way to work, I witnessed the driver in front of me open his car door and throw up. He vomited, shut the car door and drove away when the lights turned green. It took me by surprise, and I mentioned it to at least a couple of colleagues during the day. Their immediate comment was "he was drunk," and voiced with a degree of disgust. I found this very sad to hear. It was 8.30 am and he was driving, I had assumed he was unwell. The reactions suggested to me that when a person shows unusual behaviour, we will think the worst of them. Drunkenness, laziness, greed, selfishness and stupidity, for most seem to be the obvious explanations for a range of disagreeable behaviours. We seem to have developed an irrational tendency to feel at odds with our fellow man, to be suspicious of his or her actions and motives. Why can't compassion, understanding and charity be our first thought?

What we fail to recognise is that all negative behaviour including our rash judgements are somewhere, somehow, rooted in fear- ultimately the fear of dying. We are taught to criticise and condemn others, but we are hardest on ourselves. As an experienced coach I can say with no reservations that the main reason people request this kind of support is because they doubt themselves. They distrust their intuition and underestimate their capabilities. They think everyone can see them for the fraud that they think they are. Yet curiously when I ask them what they think they can do to improve, they are hard pushed to think of anything they aren't already doing. When I ask, 'who can do your job better than you'? They can't pick out a single colleague. When I ask for the evidence that their work, attitude or approach is being scrutinised and found wanting – there is none to be found.

29th July 2023. Two Jehovah's witnesses call at my door this morning. I don't mind engaging with them as they are always courteous and friendly and can generally sense when it's the right time to offer you a leaflet and politely withdraw. I always find it awkward to fully express my thoughts when I'm standing on the doorstep with a tea towel in my hand, but today I don't mind. Jackie and Sarah ask me if I have ever wondered what God thinks about the world today and all the awful things going on within it. Having first clarified a definition of *God*, I ask them what their experience of the world has been this morning - what awful things have they seen and what horrible people have they met? They admit that the morning has been very pleasant. That's not to say they don't occasionally face hostility, but in fairness that is to be expected by any cold caller who is trying to sell you salvation on the doorstep - it isn't even a home improvement. But today has been very pleasant indeed, and that's my experience of most days too.

Most of the conflict I encounter is between frustrated parents and their equally frustrated children, or partners bickering in supermarkets. I'm trying to recall the last adult dispute I witnessed firsthand. It was last week, on a busy roundabout whereby one vehicle did not make his intent clear enough for the other and a lot of noise ensued. The sound of shouting and beeping of horns was unsettling but soon subsided. Given the limited space we share and the pressure to achieve what is asked of us, it's not surprising we occasionally collide.

My experience is that people are kind, courteous and extremely helpful. They like to be needed and they like to give often much more than they like to receive. They become angry and frustrated when their stability is threatened, or their expectations are not being met. If something, anything gets in the way of their means of survival they will react, possibly in a controlled manner to begin with and then with more ferocity as the situation worsens. It is important to recognise this because every action, whether you perceive it to be helpful or destructive, is fuelled by positive intent. I'm shouting because I need someone to hear me. I'm angry because I feel I have been treated unfairly. I'm swearing because I don't seem to be getting my message across any other way. I'm throwing up because I have a stomach bug.

Our outlook of the world and our attitude to our fellow citizens can be the difference between living with peace or living in a constant state of tension. Trusting our senses, deciphering our observations, applying a little thought and intuition to each situation can change our perspective and bring about a more harmonious and empathic outcome. It can be as simple as asking, in this situation what is my best thought?

We can compare our outlook to living in a block of flats of say 50 floors. Some of us would prefer to live on the ground floor where there's a quick escape route should disaster occur. The view is of concrete and litter and the noise of traffic is relentless. The windows are grimy, our vision is clouded but we feel safe. A few floors higher we escape some of the noise, but we can see through the windows to the flats across the road and those who live there can see us too. Maybe we become preoccupied with what they are doing, and we become more conscious of what they can see in us too, so we hide or put on our very best appearance. In the middle floors we are interacting with our neighbours regularly, on the stairs, in the lift, in their homes. We enjoy a lighter mix of community and activity. Higher up we can still hear sounds from our neighbours to the left, right and above us but the disturbance on the ground, in the street is no longer audible. The view is clearer and the light coming in through the windows brightens up the room. In the uppermost floors we can only hear the wind and see the mountains in the distance. We see the sun rise in the morning and we see the stars at night. We experience a full spectrum of natural colour and beauty and the air is tranquil. At the very top there are no windows, nothing to protect us from the elements. We feel free, we suffer no fear and we live by our senses. The truth is inescapable.[9]

We will need a healthy range of outlooks to support a new system. We will need those who have vision, those that see risk. We will need communicators and realists and we will need to trust that despite the consequences we proceed with good intentions.

Tension limits creativity, it pulls you into the point where you feel safest. When people are tense, they are more compliant and readily accept any kind of support offered them. Yet tragedy, when it strikes also unites us. It did during the pandemic, the Queen's funeral and the countless other minor local disasters that we are faced with during the course of our lives. This is heartening and hopeful. It means that when we are faced with strife, we will stand together in support of one another. We will be allied.

EURO NEWS (video) **8th August 2023**

Georgia – Rescue operation continues after deadly landslide.

At least 18 people confirmed dead and 16 are missing after a powerful landslide last Thursday in a mountainous region of Georgia. Around 400 police, emergency units, firefighters and volunteers are involved in the rescue operation. Local residents have rallied to help.

"*You see how everybody's mobilised. Everybody comes here and wants to be a part of it, so it's a huge motivation to see that people are coming. You want to come as well and do something for everybody*" (a volunteer)

Our Responses

Do you believe we are powerless to make changes that extend beyond our own lives and those of our families? Do you think we readily accept our fate, our position

9 A concept borrowed from the following excerpt: '*Now what is the vision from the high floor? The view is unobscured by fear. The view is not a fearful view. It is a mastery. You see what is before you, you know what it is and you are in agreement with truth. You do not judge from the view and in fact the view does not allow judgment. That was left on the lower floor.*' The Book of Knowing and Worth. P. Selig. 2013. TarcherPerigee (Penguin Group).

in society and freely hand over our control to elected powers and authorities, even when their integrity and interests are questionable? We may feel outrage and complain openly, but on the whole do you consider anything we do to be inconsequential, that we are helpless to make any kind of impact on a grander scale? Is this our fate or is this our choice?

FRANCE 24 NEWS **6th June 2023**

French left, labour unions stage new day of protests against pension reform

Hundreds of thousands of people are expected to take to the streets across France for what will be the fourteenth day of demonstrations since January to oppose the reform

Macron signed in April the bill to raise the pension age to 64 from 62 after the government used a controversial but legal mechanism to avoid a vote in parliament that it risked losing.

I confess to a cynical laugh when I saw the French protesting against a rise in the age of retirement. Retiring at 64 would be very much welcomed in the UK. 'The Pensions Act 2014 brought forward the increase to 67 to between 2026 and 2028.'[10] We've been paying national insurance contributions up the age of 65 for decades, now the UK retirement age has increased and we will have to work a further 2 years. I don't recall us making a fuss, I don't recall any major protests. Why did we not oppose this increase, how did we let this creep up on us with no public resistance? A further review will decide whether the age should be increased to 68 from 2044 onwards. You can be sure a legal amendment will emerge and the retirement age will edge its way to 70. We will be given ample notice probably when we are in our 40's, when retirement seems a long way off and not worth worrying about.

To say there have been no protests is not strictly true as thousands of women born in the 1950s, (specifically 1954) who expected to receive their pension at 60, voiced their anger when they discovered that their state pension age had increased by up to six years in line with equality laws.

When our livelihood is not threatened, when our plans go undisturbed, when life for the most part mirrors the conditions that are important to us, we become complacent. All is well, or at least for the most part, I can't complain, things could

10 State Pension age Review 2023. Policy paper. 2023. GOV.UK

be worse, I'll get over it. Is this complacency or apathy? Apathy is a lack of interest or concern whereas complacency is a feeling of smug satisfaction that deters a person to do, or to be better. Either way, they both point to an attitude of inertia and a lack of conviction – making do, accepting our lot.

What about futility? Despite his left-wing politics my brother refuses to vote as he doesn't see the point.[11] He lives modestly in one of the most affluent areas of London and is resigned to living in a conservative constituency with no change in sight. Voting for labour is simply futile. I argue... pardon me, I debate the issue strongly. If everyone felt like that, well of course there won't be a change. Even if there is little hope of a revolution, every vote, every voice is important. At the very least it offers the opposing party encouragement to keep going. I can see how he has become despondent. Since the seat was introduced in 1997 it has been a safe haven for 3 different conservative politicians, until abolished in 2010 and replaced by two seats - Kensington and Chelsea & Fulham. Now they have another safe conservative seat - two for the price of one.

Kensington did briefly vote in a labour MP, Emma Dent-Goad in the 2017 election, just days before the Grenfell fire. Curiously days prior to the labour victory, actor /comedian John Cleese expressed a similar tone of surrender when he tweeted: 'People are asking me how I shall vote. I shan't. I live in Chelsea and Kensington, so under our present system my vote is utterly worthless'.[12]

What does it take to stir us? In the case of elections, 'two distinct, dynamic emotional responses play influential roles during election campaigns. Anxiety and enthusiasm. Anxiety responding to threat and novelty stimulates attention towards the campaign and political learning and discourages reliance on habitual cues for voting. Enthusiasm powerfully influences candidate preferences and stimulates interest and involvement in the campaign.'[13]

Enthusiasm for sure, and not just for politics. In the first few weeks of the pandemic lockdown there was a surge of creativity and support. Many volunteered their time to help their communities and to distribute essential items. I remember Captain Tom (Sir Thomas Moore) who appeared on our TV screens in 2020 when he raised money

---

11 My brother reminds me that he does now vote, and in fact voted for the Labour MP labour MP, Emma Dent-Goad in the 2017 election.

12 8:08 am • 21 May 2017 @JohnCleese. Twitter.

13 Anxiety, Enthusiasm and the Vote: *The emotional underpinnings of learning and involvement during presidential campaigns.* G. Marcus & M Mackuen. 1993. American Political Science Review Vol, 87. No 3

for the NHS by walking 100 lengths of his garden – he was 99 years old. His initial goal was to raise £1,000 by his 100th birthday, but once the media had made him into a household hero, he attracted over 1.5 million individual donations totalling over £30 million. His positive determination inspired many to follow suit. Former Wales rugby captain Ryan Jones ran a marathon in his garden. Max Woosey aged 10, began camping out in a tent in his back garden to raise money for the hospice who cared for his friend. He only came in for schooling, shower and a hot meal.

The stories are visionary and wholly inclusive. The energy of one person's feat stimulates many into supporting them or doing something likewise. We watch and listen, we cheer, we donate or simply talk about it - we want to be part of it. Enthusiasm tries - it isn't perfect, but it does its best. It runs with an idea, fuelled by a belief that touches a heart, someone's heart, many hearts, runs and runs until it is torn down by critics, expires or is forgotten.

Does anxiety stir us? Without a doubt. People come together and move mountains when they or those closest to them face threats to their security and to their welfare. A quick search on Eventbrite lists various protests occurring in London over the months of August and September 2023.

Friday, 11th August - Support Iran's Revolution! (London, Manchester, Berlin, Sydney, Everywhere) 'Following the death of a 22-year-old woman in Iran, Mahsa Amini, at the hands of the 'Morality Police' for not covering up her hair properly, the women of Iran have taken to streets to demand their freedom.'

Wednesday, 16th August - Justice For Windrush Generations Rally @ Hse of Commons Wed 19 August 17:30. 'Justice for Windrush Generations rally seeking justice for those impacted by the Home Office's hostility.'

Saturday, 23rd September - National Rejoin March II - 'A national gathering to show the strength of support for the UK to pivot back towards a closer relationship with the EU.'

3rd March 2023. Our local museum, a very small one is hosting an (even smaller) exhibition commemorating the levellers of 1647. The movement concerned radical supporters of parliament who demanded that sovereign power should be 'transferred to House of Commons and that government should be decentralized to local communities. They put forward a programme of economic reform in the interests of small property holders—complete equality before the law, the abolition of trading monopolies, the reopening of enclosed land…the abolition of tithes and complete freedom of religious worship and organisation'.[14] While the protestors were unsuccessful, their demands have materialised albeit a few hundred years later.

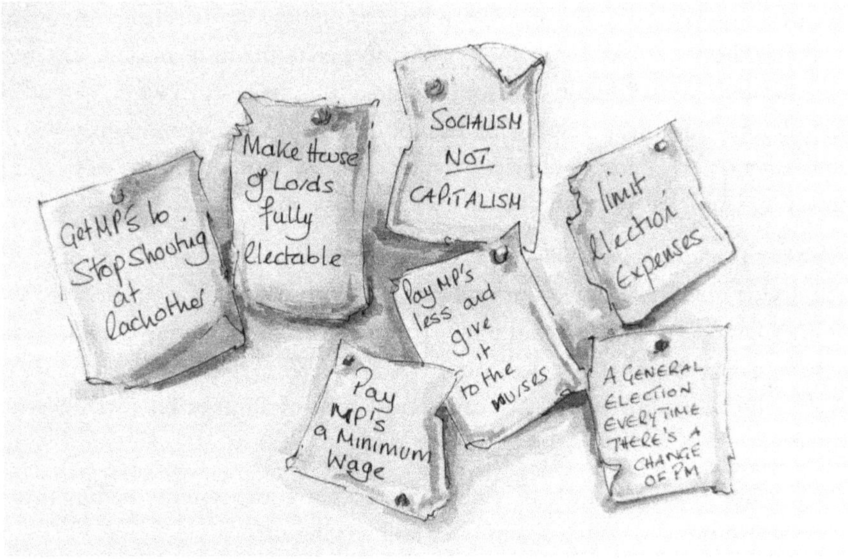

A pinboard put up by the museum invites visitors to display their own protestations.

I would have been proud to be called a leveller; one whose aim is to flatten the pyramid of privilege.

There was no delay when people's protests brought a swift and successful end to the poll tax introduced in 1990 by Margaret Thatcher's government. 'A rally of 200,000 people in London in opposition to the move turned into a riot, with 113 people injured and 339 arrests. The riots contributed to Thatcher's resignation, and the poll tax was abandoned by her successor, John Major.'[15]

There was no complacency or apathy when NHS staff abandoned their posts on several occasions to strike for better pay and conditions. Their passion and determination resulted in an offer of a one-off payment of £1,655-£3,789, and a wage rise of 5% for the lowest paid and 10.4% for the nurses, midwives and other colleagues contracted on similar pay scales.[16] The strikes of NHS junior doctors, senior doctors and consultants continue for a better settlement than the one currently on offer. They

14 Leveler. English History. The Editors of Encyclopaedia. 2022. Britannica.

15 9 Famous Moments in British Protest History. Oxford Royale.

16 NHS pay deal 2023. April 2023. Unison The Public Service Union

are demanding a 35% pay increase. I suspect they will be striking for some time to come.

We have choices. Some we make with little thought as we drift from one situation to another, others we make with more awareness. The menu of options can be and often is, limited. We habitually feel we have no alternative but to work, to look after our families, to commit to responsibilities, but in truth we subconsciously weigh up the consequences of taking an alternative direction and choose the safer option. There are however, decisions we can make with a conscious mind.

We can consciously choose how we perceive our circumstances and our experiences. We can decide how we wish to communicate and with whom. We can elect the values on which we base our actions, and our reactions. We can make purposeful decisions about how, when and where we utilise our resources. We can choose the ways we want to employ and direct our energy. We can choose how we limit or how we liberate our imagination.

We just need to look a little harder, a little deeper at the systems we buy into, the contracts we commit to - and ask, are they still serving us?

Chapter Ten

The 100th Monkey

Since the pandemic my life has changed, I don't need to travel anywhere, I work almost entirely from home. The technological resources that were developed to support remote working have been an indisputable game-changer. I know there are many like me who are working more flexibly, enjoying a much-needed balance in their lives, and wondering why we didn't do this sooner. Why did we put up with traffic queues and noisy offices for so long? I occasionally miss the buzz of catching up with colleagues and seeing the different faces, but I don't miss searching for a car parking space, negotiating a spare hot desk, a shortage of meetings rooms and the inescapable heat generated by the energy of bodies and machines.

Our new offices designed and arranged for us in October 2019 now stand almost empty. The abundance of desks, meeting rooms and the one for meditation are freely available. When I visit, I am always amused at what I see. People sitting back-to-back in silence, each staring at a screen and I wonder what has become of us. What use are our legs other than to walk to and from our vehicles. We now factor in health consciously and with purpose, planning how we will fit in a nutritious meal and exercise. Time restraints have led to eating conveniently and mobility is provided by a year's subscription to the local gym – there is no time, productivity has taken priority.

The relatively recent science of Human Factors is useful in explaining why people don't meet expectations or why they make the same errors time and time again. It looks at the fit between a task or environment and the innate human tendencies in all areas of life - and it is most welcome. Why do we continue to fight against what is inherently human? Our daily lives are bizarre compared to how we were physically and mentally designed to function. Where we would have expected our evolution to lead us to a life of balance, fulfilment and abundance, we work harder than ever and for less reward. When we fail to meet this expectation, we are made to feel inadequate and underserving. We punish ourselves and we punish each other.

Let's Waste Time

What is wrong with working less? What's so bad about spending time doing little, even nothing? When did we forget that outside of our paid jobs we still work. We cook, we shop, we clean, we tend and repair our homes, we nurture our families, we care for those who need extra help and we support our communities. Why is this not considered work just because we don't get paid for it?

'The laziness lie has tried to convince us that our desires for rest and relaxation make us terrible people. It's made us believe that having no motivation is shameful and must be avoided at all costs. In reality our feelings of tiredness and idleness can save us by signalling to us that we are desperately in need of some down-time. When we stop fearing laziness we can find time to reflect and recharge, to reconnect with the people and hobbies that we love, to move through the world at a more intentional peaceful pace. Wasting time is a basic human need. Once we accept that, we can stop fearing our inner laziness and begin to build healthy happy well-balanced lives'.[1]

I don't believe in coincidences, I do believe in synchronicities. Things appear at the right time for a reason. And so it came as no surprise yesterday when I had two separate conversations about time management. One colleague apologised for speaking with a croaky voice, she was clearly run down and tired. She confessed to working all hours without a break and feeling the need to respond to every communication within a matter of minutes. She doesn't turn down any favours or requests and as a result accumulates more work than is actually hers to do. I imagine she is not enjoying her fuller than full-time job. I (kindly) remind her, "the organisation is running on your free time. You don't get paid for your break, yet you are working through it. In essence you are working for nothing. We look after our children and our families for nothing. We tend our homes and our gardens for nothing – let's not start working for our employer – for nothing.' The second conversation came about when a colleague wanted advice on how to deter a staff member from working all hours – again unpaid.

Have you ever calculated a 12-year old's working hours? At our local secondary school, a child starts their working day at 8.30am and finishes at 3.15pm. Like adults they are entitled to a morning break of 20 minutes, and just 20 minutes for lunch; that's only 10 minutes more than my daily entitlement. When they return home, most are likely to have homework which can take anything up to 2 hours to complete (not to mention a parent's free time as well). If they are required to complete chores, let's be reasonable and add just another 15 minutes, their working day can be as long as 8 hours – without the addition of any paid work they can undertake from aged 13 onwards. It doesn't leave much time for play, being outdoors, hobbies and interests, getting together with friends or simply relaxing in front of a screen.

Here are some telling facts. Finland's education system is heralded as one of the finest and their children start school aged 7 years. They spend no more than 20 hours a week in school and complete the only mandatory exam when they reach 16. 'Students in Finland usually start school anywhere from 9:00 – 9:45 AM. Research has shown that early start times are detrimental to students' well-being, health, and maturation. Finnish schools start the day later and usually end by 2:00 – 2:45 PM. They have longer class periods and much longer breaks in between. The overall system isn't there to ram and cram information to their students, but to create an environment

1 Laziness Does Not Exist. D. Price. 2021. Atria Books

of holistic learning'.[2] Finland have topped the World Happiness Report for the sixth year in a row.

> SIX FACTORS - Income, health, having someone to count on, having a sense of freedom to make key life decisions, generosity, and the absence of corruption, all play strong roles in supporting life evaluations.
>
> [World Happiness Report, 2023]

We are not lazy, we are tired. The constant drive for productivity is relentless, higher targets, longer hours for less reward. I hear it constantly from colleagues, "I'm tired", "I feel overwhelmed", "there's never enough time."

Where I work the requests for a 9-day fortnight are becoming more popular. Staff want more free time – 2 days at the end of a working week is not enough. They need time to manage all the other functions it takes to just keep a family and a home, or to book a dentist or doctor's appointment which are generally unavailable Saturdays and Sundays. Many would like to reduce their hours but are frightened of sacrificing their pension entitlement.

SKY NEWS **26th September 2023**

Workplace absences have risen to an average of 7.8 days per year

They have reached their highest level in a decade up from 5.8 pre-pandemic

The UK have run a pilot scheme inviting 61 companies to trial a 32-hour working week for 6 months in June 2022. Staff would work less hours by eliminating one working day in the week and receiving the same full time pay. To date 56 companies plan to continue beyond the trial and implement a permanent change. The research was carried out by the University of Cambridge and Boston College. Their findings included a fall of the number of sick days by about 66% and a reported reduction in stress.[3]

---

2 10 reasons why Finland's education system is the best in the world. M. Colagrossi. 2018. World Economic Forum.

3 The results are in - The UK's four-day week pilot. K.Lewis et al. 2023. Autonomy Research Ltd.

SKY NEWS **21st February 2023**

Major breakthrough: Most firms say they'll stick with a four-day working week after successful trial.

The number of sick days taken by staff in the trial fell by around two-thirds, while almost two in five said they were less stressed.

According to CEO Mark Downs productivity has increased, and Sky News report a 'a decline in the number of sick days taken during the period of the trial. Before the trial, on average, each person would take four or five sick days per year - that's down to less than two.' I listened to the researchers in person, as they presented their findings at a workforce exhibition I attended in London – the argument for reducing working hours is compelling. They confirm the following benefits:

- An increase in performance and productivity (targets are still being met and exceeded)
- An improvement in employee's wellbeing including their sleep and mental health
- A reduction in carbon footprint – mileage dropped by a third
- Employees spend more time with their children and families
- A surge in creativity and innovation
- Absenteeism down by 70%

Between 2015-19 Iceland conducted its own pilot of this kind involving 2500 employees. Such was the success that it led to a significant change in working conditions with almost 90% of the working population now reducing their working hours or making significant changes to their working week. Germany's average working week is 34.2 hours and their trade unions are looking to reduce this further. Spain, Portugal, Canada, Scotland are all looking into introducing similar pilot schemes. 'Belgium became the first country in Europe to legislate for a four-day week.'[4]

As my own organisation is struggling to recruit, I have suggested the introduction of a four-day week which in fairness was not immediately dismissed, but one I doubt will be taken seriously. If it is ignored it will be a shame as the longer-term economic benefits are substantial. Happy employees make for a productive and loyal workforce.

---

4 The Four-day week - which countries have embraced it and how is it going so far? 2023. Euro News

More time equals less stress therefore less illness, which translates into more working hours, and consequently alleviates the stress placed on our health services. We are a public sector service and therefore under greater scrutiny and we are averse to public criticism. You have to ask, what are the real barriers to this change? Fear I suspect, fear of failure and humiliation.

No Money = Less profit = Less Work

Imagine a world where there is no money, no forms of payment and consider all the kinds of employment that would cease to exist. Employment whose sole purpose is to generate profit and whose service or product adds little or no value to a consumer's well-being, would most likely disappear. Insurance companies, recruitment agencies, manufacturers of non-essential goods, producers of processed and fast food, high fashion and perfume brands, bankers, stockbrokers, building societies.... I'm sure you can think of many more. Let's also assume that there is enough food to feed every person on the planet (several authorities verify this) and enough energy for every home or shelter, including energy from renewable sources. Think of how many hours of labour this would free up. So long as everyone had access to what they needed for a comfortable life, how many hours would we have to work to maintain essential services? Three days a week, maybe two?

I asked our Research Participants (RPs) – 'if your livelihood did not depend on money, how many hours a week would you be prepared to work?' Looking at their responses, the minimum is 20 hours (four hours a day), the maximum 46 hours, an overall average of 31 hours. It doesn't sound like a particularly lazy choice to me. Given the greater degree of flexibility this arrangement may bring, many said they would choose to swap around, engage in different activities, meet different people and learn new trades. A few said they would prefer to stay with one group, in one place, doing one trade so long as it was enjoyable. Some said they would prefer to begin later in the day. Some would spread their hours over several days, others would condense them. Consider this too – the more people who engage in work, the easier the work becomes and arguably the more pleasurable.

You may remember I described working in a factory when I was 12 years old. The best shifts were when we packed Spanish onions. We worked 3 to a station, weighing and packing with no noisy conveyer belts or machinery to drown conversation. There were always 2 onions to a pack so very little concentration required, and plenty of opportunity to chat at the same time. The hours passed quickly and pleasurably.

Maybe we should look at work differently. Instead of working hours, we are given work tasks, a caseload or a specific responsibility. We choose to complete them at our convenience given our resources and deadlines – this surely sounds like a more trusting and adult model for employment. Assuming some people function better early morning whilst others find the peak of their energy later in the day, we may see an increase in production and accuracy to boot. This system may not suit every type of work but is certainly conducive to certain projects.

Given the time and resources to live in peace, comfort and safety and to have the time to do what I love most (walking, painting, writing), I would be happy doing most jobs but would most likely lean to those that offer the best intrinsic rewards – helping others. I attempted to identify the work that would be most essential for us all to live well.

- Technology (maintenance and development)
- Transport (production and maintenance and distribution)
- Construction
- Civil engineering
- Indoor maintenance
- Production of food/farming
- Social care
- Childcare
- Healthcare
- Animal support
- Environmental maintenance
- Exchange of goods/resources
- Allocation of employment
- Recycling and waste
- Energy
- Security
- Communication
- Education

When the RPs were asked to select which of these they would readily engage with at a local scale, all but one was selected. We can therefore be reassured that there is something for everyone, or rather everyone is willing to contribute to something that will support their families and communities.

Employment currently rewards those who are most accountable, those who have the greatest knowledge and those who are highly skilled. We seem to hold knowledge in high regard. Watch any afternoon quiz show and you will find that questions of general knowledge are used to filter out contestants and unlock an opportunity to win a prize. It all seems to be about what we know and what we do, very little is said about who we are. I stopped watching a certain quiz show when I noticed that those who had an interesting or unusual job received more attention from the hosts than those in administrative or caring roles. And should their employment or hobby involve music in some way then they were made to feel extremely special. Either you know something, or you don't, why should it define who you are or rate you as being more worthy than another? The TV competition Mastermind is merely a mastery of memory, nothing more.

So, when it comes to hard work, who should we applaud the most? The scholar who has applied inherent intelligence and aptitude to study for hours on end and put an eloquent pen to paper, or the pot washer who toils and sweats in a hot and greasy kitchen for 8 hours at a time. Who deserves the greater pay? The registered manager of a care home, responsible for finance, recruitment, and people management, or the self-employed child minder, who is solely responsible for the children in their care?

You might say we all face the same choices, and I would agree up to a point, but it takes everyone's contribution to keep the societal engine in motion. We need every single person to make our world and to keep it turning. It doesn't matter what we do, and how little or how much we do it, we are all worthy and entitled to a decent standard of living free of worry and lack. Ending an unfair financial reward system will finally level the proverbial playing field and give us what we rightly deserve.

Curious and Caring

Does this mean the end of careers? Not at all. Where there is an acute focus there is mastery. We need uncompromised expertise to move humanity to a better world. We need those who have a life calling to explore something that is of importance to them, in depth, and that will benefit all of humanity. Whether it be based in physics, physiology, astronomy, botany, those who specialise will inch us forward, perhaps with even greater speed once the hurdles of financial restrictions and temptations have been removed.

Will an absence of monetary gain lessen a person's passion for a subject? Will it quash the appetite for curiosity and dull the challenges that follow? Will we lose our scientists, philosophers and physicians? History says not. Did Galileo stop publishing his controversial theories on the solar system when threatened by the Spanish inquisition? Did Darwin retract his theories in the face of hostile criticism? Did sports presenter David Icke not willingly sacrifice his livelihood and reputation when speaking on a popular TV chat show, openly and honestly describing what he believed to be true? Whether you align with emerging theories or you don't, we are indebted to those who dare to lift their heads above the parapet at their own personal and professional expense. Mankind is curious and curiosity is crucial for our development. Curiosity will continue to thrive when money does not.

Naturally the RPs aired their own trepidations concerning how a new system would work, here are a few:

"Peoples attitude, motivation and selfishness in their chosen role."

"We are selfish by nature, and we hurt each other."

"Selfishness and self-centred living and outlook."

"People are greedy."

Ironically when the RPs offered their opinions around the barriers to a moneyless society most mentioned the aspect of human selfishness, yet when asked if this judgment applied to them, they disagreed. We are suspicious of others but trust ourselves. And not because we are in denial, but because we have been conditioned to view the world with distrust.

Did I also mention that we are a nation of volunteers, mostly informal. When have you offered to do something for someone at no charge? Maybe you took care of someone's child or pet or their home for a short period, did a little shopping, or responded swiftly to someone who needed help. Perhaps you offered but it just wasn't taken up at the time. Have you found something valuable and returned it to the owner - have you willingly shared food or money when someone found themselves without? I have no doubt it was recently, perhaps this week, when you showed compassion to another with no expectation of return then thought no more of it. Moreover, has someone responded to your needs in a similar way?

'There is much evidence (experimental and others) that helping behaviour increases the well-being of the individual helper. This is especially true when the helping behaviour is voluntary and mainly motivated by concern for the person being helped. Other evidence shows that when people's well-being increases, they can become more altruistic. In particular when people's well-being rises through experiencing altruistic help, they become more likely to help others, creating a virtuous spiral.'[5]

In the World Giving Index 2023 the UK is ranked 3rd in the world for donating the most money and 17th across the 3 charitable practices which are helping a stranger,

5 Executive Summary, World Happiness Report. J. Helliwell et al. 2023.

giving money or volunteering time. Indonesia came top, largely due to their cultural and religious traditions.[6]

I find this information hugely encouraging, it shows we are a compassionate nation of people. We give willingly to those we don't know and to causes we have no control over. When the cause is critical e.g volunteering during the pandemic or supporting the plight of the Ukranians, we step up our support and place faith in others to do the right thing on our behalf. The CAF UK Giving Report of 2023 confirms:

- £12.7 billion given to charity in 2022 (up £2 billion on previous year)
- People are donating more, rather than there being an increase in donors
- The proportion of people volunteering has declined
- The most popular cause remains animal welfare
- The amount donated per month averages £60
- 53 % consider charities to be trustworthy (a small increase)[7]

Remember, we already live with other people's greed and selfishness. It's already here, perhaps it will always be present somewhere in someone. The proposal of a moneyless society will not eradicate vice and attitudes that only work for personal gain, but it may lessen the impact. Where there is no money to be made, and everyone has what they need, greed may fade. When the selfish few witness the selfless actions of others, they may be inspired to follow their example. When a noble movement gathers momentum, everyone wants to be a part of it. We only have to reach Critical Mass.

100 Monkeys

Critical Mass is best described as the point when a period of slow change suddenly accelerates (goes viral) and then becomes accepted and adopted by the majority – the tipping point, and it all began with monkeys.

The story goes that a study conducted in 1952 observed a young female Macaque monkey who lived on a Japanese Island, washing her food before she ate it. She appeared to be irritated by the dirt she found on her sweet potatoes (who wouldn't), so she decided to wash her food in water to avoid the taste of grit. Her family observed her behaviour and began to copy it, as did her friends and the neighbouring troops.

6 World Giving Index 2023. Global trends in generosity. Charities Aid Foundation (CAF).

7 UK Giving Report 2023. Charities Aid Foundation (CAF).

The tipping point for all monkeys came when the 100th Monkey adopted the new routine. Monkey 100 became critical mass.[8] You might think critical mass is equal to a majority i.e. 51%, but studies and opinion range from 10 – 30% which is very encouraging and certainly more achievable.

People's choices and values that have led to national change have affected the way we eat, live and even the way we talk. Our choice of foods, our lifestyles, the language we use including the discriminatory words that are no longer acceptable, all began somewhere with someone before reaching mass consensus and approval. Think of the increased demand for free range eggs and the condemnation of white veal. Our employment conditions have changed too. The right to request flexible working from day 1 of employment will shortly become law. 'This means from your first day of work, you can ask your employer for changes to how long, when and where you work.'[9] Furthermore, you no longer need to convince your employer of the reasons for your request. If they refuse, they need to justify their decision.

The thought of creating new laws and challenging institutions may seem out of reach and beyond a single reader's capability, but when each individual makes a better choice, voices their thoughts, lives by their values, there follows a shift. Their words influence, their actions inspire, their energy emanates and society is stirred. Thus begins change.

We can begin by looking at how we manage our resources.

---

8 The 100th monkey effect explained -A story about influence. 100monkey.co.uk

9 The law on flexible work is changing - here's what your employer needs to do. A.Arkwright. 2023. TUC.

Chapter Eleven

When the Bin Pongs

BLOOMBERG NEWS **24th May 2023**

Nearly 1.3 billion tons of food is wasted around the world every year

A shocking $1 trillion of food value lost and wasted. When food makes its way to landfill it creates methane, a greenhouse gas that will rise the temperature of the planet. It is also taking waste to be making this waste. So, you're wasting chemicals that you put in, the water you paid for, the energy you use and wasting the labour. A series of inefficiencies from a financial perspective.

My local Council has increased my annual council tax by another £11 a month. I don't think this comes as a surprise to anyone, council tax has increased annually for everyone since it was introduced back in April 1993. But when the council announced that they will soon be refusing to collect garden waste unless I pay an additional £50 a year, I was staggered. Furthermore, they will no longer accept discarded food as part of this service. They did before but they won't now. What will this mean to those who cannot afford the additional expense? Will they be filling their cars with cut grass to take to their local recycling centre or maybe they will just dump it? What will they do with their leftover food? Presumably put it into their general waste bin and increase how much waste goes into landfill. An additional £50 a year might not seem much, but if you add it to the increased costs of energy, water, insurances, food and anything else they want to throw at us, then everyday living starts to become even more uncomfortable and unaffordable.

The Trouble with Tat

'Human Beings have always been susceptible to the illusion that the abundance of material goods is the route to happiness; advertising merely exploits this susceptibility and alienation enhances it.'

[R. Van de Weyer]

There is no denying our throw-away society, capitalism and ecology do not work well together. Goods and resources are readily available in abundance and often cheaply purchased to the detriment of our earth. Consider the quantity of superfluous paraphernalia that we send to landfill – an unwanted Secret Santa toy, confetti, balloons, badges and tiaras in celebration of a momentous birthday; novelty gifts that prompt a giggle and nothing more; merchandise – tote bags, pens, stress balls, freebies that we cannot resist and never put to use. Objects that have given us microseconds of pleasure, are carelessly discarded, disposed of and buried intact for centuries to come. In the case of plastic, 20 – 500 years depending on its structure whilst some estimate it would take up to a million years for Pyrex to decompose.

Whilst laws are introduced to strengthen the responsibility of manufacturers regarding waste and the use of recycled materials, as a nation we have a lot of catching up to do. 'The UK will become the biggest electronic waste producer in Europe per capita by 2024 with each individual responsible on average for 23.9kg of e-waste per person [per year]'. The consequences of e-waste are the discarding of precious metals to landfill. These precious resources are finite and vital for the production of 'essential technology such as wind turbines, solar panels, artificial joints and pacemakers.'[1]

EURO NEWS **6th August 2023**

The end of the road for fast fashion? The EU hopes so

It is estimated that the fashion industry is one of the world's greatest polluters, responsible for about 20% of the planet's wastewater and around 10% of the world's greenhouse gas emissions.

The very fact that a China-based giant is able to add a staggering 6000 new pieces to its website on a daily basis suggests that the concept of fast fashion is going nowhere fast.

A study completed by Labfresh names the UK as the 4th largest textile waste producer in Europe. The average consumer spends a staggering £980 on new clothes and throws away an average of 3.1 Kg of textiles every year. Broken down; 0.3 Kg is recycled, 0.4 Kg is reused, 0.8 is incinerated and the remaining 1.7 Kg goes to landfill.[2] We give or throw clothes away because we either get bored with them, feel we need to look different or up to date, or maybe we grow in size. With the exception of socks and footwear, we rarely throw clothes away because they wear out.

My aim is not to shame but to inform. It's a two-way contract. Manufacturers produce goods to meet demand. Admittedly, they can create demand with the temptation of new innovating products - buy *bigger*, buy *better* and buy *the latest*, but only if we as the consumer respond in the way they want us to. Our decisions of where

1 UK on track to become Europe's biggest e-waste contributor. K. Molly. 2021. Resource.co

2 The Fashion Waste Index. Labfresh.

to place our cash carries immense power and therefore responsibility. Currently we eat, wear, buy and discard to excess.

Nothing Leaves the Earth

21 December 2022. Work is quiet so my colleagues and I have a clear out of the storeroom. We discover over 100 folders that are no longer required as the documentation is now shared and stored electronically. They need to go. As we start to load them into the skip a thought occurs to me. I contact the supplier who sold them to us some 8 years ago and ask if he wants them back. Fortunately, he is still trading and arrives within a couple of hours to rescue the stock. We also find several sealed packs of disposable plastic stirrers (single-use plastics are harmful to wildlife and waterways). We debate the best way to dispose of them – should we use them up, donate them to a charity such as a shelter? We decide the wisest thing to do would be to leave them where they are - sealed and safe.[3]

I was once reminded that nothing ever leaves the planet. It's a disturbing reminder that when we irresponsibly discard our rubbish, we endanger animal life. If we follow the guidelines to responsibly dispose of it, we pollute our soil or ship our problem to another part of the world with less resources to deal with it safely and reliably. When we burn it, we release toxins and pollutants into the atmosphere for us all to inhale. In his Rubbish Book, James Piper assures us that everything can be recycled. Whether it actually is recycled all comes down to the thing that dictates so many of our issues – money[4].

Allegedly first introduced in April 1970 during the first Earth Day, The Waste Hierarchy lists in order of preference the 3 stages of waste management – reduce, reuse, recycle. I have added a further two to make the full list of choices complete.

---

3 Bans and restrictions on a range of polluting single-use plastic items came into force on Sunday 1 October 2023.

4 The Rubbish Book: A Complete Guide to Recycling. J. Piper. 2022. Unbound.

The Waste Hierarchy

Resist – Put simply resisting is making the decision not to buy or use. It is saying no, either to yourself or to the individual /organisation that is tempting you to purchase something. In my case do I really need yet another long-sleeved black t-shirt as I already have 4 at home? What's the point of buying a gadget when the one I have still functions perfectly well? Using the benchmark theory that all our actions and decisions are based on how we want to feel, I ask myself, will this item noticeably improve my life or level of happiness, peace or fulfilment, and if so, for how long? When I imagine I have a new carpet in the bedroom, what is the strength of feeling this invokes compared to the feeling of having another financial commitment? In this case, I would rather be less in debt. You may consider your own personal test.

Reduce – We could all consume a lot less of everything.

Water: bathing, washing clothes, use of appliances – dishwashers, hosepipes, dare I suggest flushing (!) if you have a water meter you've probably already made an adjustment.

Detergents: similarly for washing body, hair, clothes, utensils and surfaces. Even if the suggestion of reducing the frequency is too much of a challenge, we can certainly reduce the quantity used at any one time.

Food is UK's biggest contributor to landfill. Having a dog means surplus food is rarely a problem, in fact my choice of menu has improved as I consider her nutritional needs as well as our own. All other organic waste goes into my new compost bin. Wasting food used to be considered immoral as we were reminded of those who did not have enough. But now the choice of food on shelves has increased. Fast food is readily available /affordable, and portions have multiplied.

Energy: how many appliances do we leave on standby? How many do we charge every day? how many rooms do we heat when we only occupy one at any time? We rely heavily on electricity and gas to keep us warm, fed and entertained.

Fuel – 'Road traffic data suggests that daily road traffic levels in January to March 2022 are similar levels to pre-pandemic traffic'.[5] I'm not disputing this statement, but I am finding it hard to believe. Looking at my own organisation, many more of us no longer travel to sites or even visit our offices. Pre-Covid, I travelled several times a week; usually a 100-mile round trip, but occasionally this stretched to 200 miles. For the last 3 years I could count the journeys I have made for work on one hand, and I am not alone. Being confined to our homes showed us an alternative way to work, one that relied on technology and not an engine. The savings in terms of fuel, time and stress are immeasurable and not just to me, but to my friends and colleagues.

Reuse – the condition for inanimate objects to share this house is usefulness. If something doesn't serve a purpose, then it goes out – see reject. The most obvious ways to reuse unwanted items include cutting up old, discarded clothes to use as dusters, filling the compost bin with grass cuttings, cardboard, peelings etc and using unrecyclable plastic bags for picking up dog waste. I also smash up chipped plates to use them as an alternative to gravel or aggregate. Pistachio nut shells line the soil in plant pots. I spread eggshells amongst newly growing plants to deter slugs (with variable degrees of success). I collect empty glass jars to store the fat from pans to

5 Impact of the Coronavirus (COVID-19) pandemic on flow weighting for congestion data. 2023. GOV UK.

prevent it from clogging sinks. I've no doubt you have your own methods of reusing items rather than discarding them.

Recycle – We have 3 council bins outside our house –the blue one stores materials that can be recycled, the green one for garden waste and the grey one for everything else. We can visit the local recycling centre which is a 10-minute drive away, and of course donate items that can be used again to charity shops. I would say that our unrecyclable waste in the last 10 years has been reduced to one swing bin bagful a week.

This does take effort and some knowledge. Pill boxes for example, you can recycle the cardboard exterior and the inner information leaflet, but the blister pack is made up of mixed materials and should go to landfill. If any member of your family frequently enjoys a Macdonald's meal the paper bag is ideal for wrapping and discarding leftovers. The council won't accept the biodegradable green bags that you can line food caddies. Recycling companies found that they decomposed much more slowly than the food, which in turn slowed the recycling process down, and as a result incurs greater costs.[6]

Foil needs to be discarded in a big enough shape to be detected by the automated recycling sorters. The size of a tennis ball is ideal. Plastics, cardboards and foil trays etc, must be cleaned of any food residue otherwise they are considered contaminated, and must go into the landfill bin. 'Although black plastic makes up 15% of all plastic recyclables (largely single-use food containers), the vast majority is not recycled because the infrared technology used by recycling facilities to sort plastics cannot "see" the colour black. As a result of this failure, most black plastic items end up in our landfills, incinerators, oceans and rivers after just a single use.'[7]

Wish cycling - We often throw waste into the recycling bin hoping that there will be a use for it at the other end. What actually happens is that we unknowingly contaminate other items which henceforth become unrecyclable – we do more damage than good. It's tempting to throw a large cardboard pizza box into the recycling bin, but the remnants of melted cheese stuck to the inside of the lid, means it will be discarded. The same goes for take away boxes and toothpaste tubes.

Juice boxes and soup cartons may appear to be a shiny cardboard, but the material also includes plastic. Crisp packets and chocolate bar wrappers are made of mixed

6 December 2023. Residents have been informed that from April 2024 they must either pay an additional £50 for removal of green waste or find a way of disposing of it themselves.

7 Why Black Plastic Is Bad News. Beyond Plastics.

materials all of which are too difficult or costly to separate – they also will go to landfill. There's a lot we don't know about what we can recycle and what we can't, and most of *the what* we can't is all down to the recycling industry, the costs incurred and a demand for the end product. If there is no market, the materials accumulate and will most likely end up in the ground or in the sea.

Reject - The end of the line. Nowhere else to go. What's in my kitchen bin?

(You can read and sing along to the tune of My Favourite Things from the musical The Sound of Music.)

Soiled puppy training pads, unrecyclable plastic

torn chocolate wrappers and bits of elastic

Blister packs, kitchen roll, tissues soaked in snot

This is my rubbish that's waiting to rot

When the bin pongs

When the maggots hatch

What is there to do?

I simply remember my recycling tips

And curse the bloody council too!

We should recognise that everything we do is a choice and therefore comes with a responsibility. Every action has a consequence, not just to ourselves but also others. Are we really here just to make as much money as we can, consume beyond our need, accumulate and discard as if there are no repercussions. Is that what life is all about? If it isn't, why are we living it as though it is?

Priceless and Free

"Rain- the most important currency in the world"

[Film: This Beautiful Fantastic]

16 August 2022. It hasn't rained here for weeks. The grass, what's left of it, is as yellow as the harvested fields of wheat. The ground is hard, cracked open and the occasional water holes and gullies that our wild animals depend on are all dried up. The trees and bushes are digging deep to extract what moisture they can to survive, and dead leaves carpet the ground prematurely but without the splendour of autumn tones. Every morning and evening the sparrows, starlings and crows flock to the bird baths to bathe and to our dog's bowl to drink, even the wasps take sips. The water is chlorinated as the water butt has run dry, but they don't seem to mind.

The sun and the rain are free to all, but at times like these we know they are priceless. It doesn't take a science-fiction movie to remind us that in future times we maybe trading fuel, clean water or natural food as a commodity. Yet we are also reminded that it needn't be a conclusion to humanity's occupation of the earth.

One year later…

16 August 2023. Some would say it's been a dismal summer. We enjoyed a warm and sunny June, but so far, July and August have been a washout. Yet I'm immensely grateful. Part of my family, who live in the south of Spain, are suffering temperatures of 40 degrees upwards, a level of heat that is breaking all records. In parts of Hawaii, wildfires have claimed the homes and lives of over 100 residents with many more missing and unaccounted for.

You can protect yourself from the cold with central heating, by wearing warmer clothes, but heat is inescapable, particularly at night. I remember last year and am now reading my post of the same day in 2022. Thankfully the grass is green, the blackberries are ripening, the wild animals have access to plenty of fresh water and I get to sleep at night. It doesn't take much for us to be reminded of our frailty, our vulnerability and what we should value above all.

THE GUARDIAN **12th April 2023**

A pair of trainers worn by NBA star Michael Jordan have sold for $2.2m

setting a record price at auction for game-worn sports footwear, Sotheby's announced.

I pick up a stone from the ground. It is unique. Its colour and shape are inimitable, nowhere is there another one like it. It has occupied the earth for millions, maybe billions of years, older than any ancient or prehistoric artefact. If it could speak it could tell us a thousand stories. It's uses are many - construction, tools, weapons, ornaments. Yet in its natural state and in commercial terms, it is worthless.

I ask our research participants what they value most. Some chose a family heirloom or tradition – something symbolic of a memory, a person, or a place.

Mike: 'We have just come back from holiday - the first day of arrival saw one of our bags being lost - the main thing that made us sad was not the clothes etc but a "stuffy" (a soft toy), that had been with us on so many trips around the world and had become part of our family - we named him Thursford and he could say things that we couldn't!'

Nani: 'My Father meant a lot to me. I learned many things from him about all crafts, he always found a solution for any setback. I wear his wedding ring soldered on my wedding ring. Perhaps it is the reason why the personal and the material are very balanced. The personal because you lose the loved one, and the material because when you don't have them, you have an object that makes you remember them.'

Carmen: 'Little things. I highly value those objects that remind me of good times because they make me feel happy again. From a photograph... to a beach stone, a jar with sand, a garment or a jade pendant from my grandmother, even a fragrance or a landscape.'

Juan: 'The only material that I like to keep are family photos, it is the living memory and what lasts - just that!'

Allan: 'One of the things I collect are cassette tapes that I listen to. One of them was recorded at his home by a friend in our early twenties. It's not much to listen to, just him fooling about with his younger brother on a piano but as he committed suicide a few years later it becomes very poignant'.

For others, functionality is important - tools that make our life easier, more efficient, that do our work for us and frees our time and energy.

Sandro: 'My phone is valuable because it allows me to stay in contact, have any information to hand anywhere, and I can play Peggle (casual video game) on the go.'

Allan: 'Washing machine – without it, the hassle is unimaginable. Same with the cooker.'

Something we admire that may contribute little functionality but makes us feel good and in some cases can be considered an investment – like a painting, a handcrafted ceramic or even crystals.

Edward: 'About 16 years ago I started collecting high end watches, and over the years I have collected more, when I've saved enough pennies. What started as something for me, has now turned into a substantial collection, that will be divided between my children sometime after my demise, or maybe earlier. What I didn't realise when I started collecting was how the value of such items would increase over the years, which then made my collection turn to limited edition wrist watches and antique pocket watches, specifically those released by the Swiss watch-making market. What makes it valuable to me is the fact that these items are not produced on a production line, they are built / assembled by a craftsman or woman, who produce something of beauty, that is practical, that doesn't require a battery, that will still be ticking away for many years to come.'

Not everything of value is tangible, solid or can be sold.

Eli: information - The important objects for me are books, because they inform and instruct me. Another would be television, with the cultural and informative programs, mainly it gives me a lot of company. Also, Google and social media, which is an open library, with infinite videos and information. I'm hooked, and it gives me pleasure.'

Isabel: 'Time - the most important are the moments that we spend at home with the family and friends. The meals we make, the laughter we have after dinner, playing board games, chatting on my patio on summer nights with children, grandchildren, sons and daughters-in-law.'

Dawn: 'Time - we can be time rich and cash poor or vice versa. It's hard to have both because most of us are too busy working. For example, if I don't have the cash to do up my home, I will need the time to do it myself. Waste it or use it wisely even if we save a bit of it, whatever. You can't hold it back, the older we get the faster it passes.'

If, as we say, we do not value money above all else, then there must be a better way of using it and living with it. A moneyless society may not be on the immediate horizon, but there are alternatives to our current system, ones that are more aligned to our values and our principles.

Chapter Twelve

The Lewes Pound

"We have it in our power to build the world anew."
[Thomas Paine, Lewes Resident 1768 - 1774]

A Conscious Approach

'The acquisition of wealth is no longer the driving force in our lives, we work to better ourselves and the rest of humanity.'

[Captain Jean Luc Picard; Star Trek, the Next Generation.]

Changing a complex system that influences our every move, every decision that we make on a daily basis must be gradual and incremental to ensure stability and permanence. My enquiries and observations have unearthed many initiatives that have taken steps to clean up capitalism and tip the balance of financial power in favour of the needs of the individual and their local environment.

The term Conscious Capitalism, originally created by John Mackey and Raj Sisodia explains; 'when we operate with higher purpose, stakeholder orientation, conscious leadership and conscious culture, we elevate humanity through business.'[1]

We are becoming more conscious. We owe much to our change of attitude to Generation Z (those born between 1995 and 2010) who seem to show the most concern for the well-being of Earth and themselves. When making a purchase they are less sensitive to price, preferring to focus on quality and sustainability. In doing so, they help us all make better choices. There is no doubt that advances in technology have enabled them to search more easily for what they want to match what they value.[2]

'Set up in 1987, The Body Shop's Community Fair Trade programme has set the gold standard for ethical business trading for decades, not just in beauty but across all sectors. The Body Shop [became] the first global beauty brand to achieve vegan status on all of its products. Its refill scheme saw the brand roll out refill stations in 720 of its stores in a bid to cut down plastic waste.'[3] The body shop was also one of the first brands to confirm none of their products had been tested on animals.

It's not just about the materials used, or the waste that is incurred, a conscious organisation will also be judged by the way it treats its employees and customers. In return for better working conditions, employees are more likely to be loyal and go the extra mile for their employer in difficult times.

---

1 Conscious Capitalism; Liberating the Heroic Spirit of Business. By J. Mackey & R. Sisodia. 2014. Havard Business Review Press

2 Gen Z cares about sustainability more than anyone else – and is starting to make others feel the same. J. Wood, 2022. World Economic Forum.

3 The Body Shop is everything a beauty brand *should* be, and its demise would have devastating consequences. S. Lawlor. 2024. Marie Claire.

Being responsive to shared values can be costly in the short term but if companies want to maintain a customer's loyalty, then they need to think longer into the future and wider into the impact of their processes. In the longer term a reputable consciously oriented business can 'operate with lower gross margin [whilst] enjoying a great deal of saving on marketing or new employees, hiring and training costs and on administrative and legal costs'.[4] For some companies it's a bold move, particularly when profits are the single motivating factor for existence. The larger the company the greater expectation of shareholders.

A Good Bank

A banker's incentive is to make money. For there to be money, there must also be debt, and therein lies the conflict. Banks strive for profit at society's expense.

Christian Felber, founder of the Economy for the Common Good (ECG) poses the question, 'What if the common good was the goal of the economy? Recognising that the economy is distancing itself more and more to aspects such as ethics, feelings, democracy and nature'. He asks – 'what if all future economic systems focussed their activities on fair distribution, were linked to ecology, and upheld the values of human dignity and social justice?'[5]

Felber's TED talk (partly given whilst standing on his head) outlines the 5 motivations for any bank wishing to serve the common good that could stand as a common charter:

1. Convert local savings into loans for local sustainable businesses.
2. There would be no distribution of profits with owners.
3. Savers would not earn interest (as interest widens the gap between those who can save and those who cannot)
4. Banks base their lending decisions on the ethical consequences of all investments. For example, who will it benefit, who may it harm, what is the environmental impact?
5. All loans applications are transparent so that investors can decide or vote on which to approve based on the previous motives.

'Freedom takes on a deeper meaning. Not only can people shape their own lives, but also collectively design the economic, financial and commercial order. People are

---

4 Conscious Capitalism. P. Mackendy. Academia. edu

5 What if the common good was the goal of the economy? C. Felber. 2015. TED Talks YouTube video.

freed from the unhealthy compulsion to constantly consume, accumulate capital and grow economically.'[6]

The ECG follows the value of the common good becoming the goal of the economy. The strategies are long term and the chase for economic growth shrinks. Businesses are freed from the pressure of achieving the highest possible return for the instant benefit of shareholders, and democratic decision-making is restored. As I type the words – freedom and restoration - I can already feel my body relaxing.

One of Felber's opening statements accurately defines money as not an end, but a means to an end. My concern is that so long as money is the means, it is a key, it is a gateway which in turn means it is still a barrier to many. For others it will be chased, manipulated and exploited until the end is no longer in sight, and then money becomes the end. The common good matrix provides a detailed framework on the conditions for the development of fairer financial activities and organisations.

COMMON GOOD MATRIX 5.0

VALUE / STAKEHOLDER	HUMAN DIGNITY	SOLIDARITY AND SOCIAL JUSTICE	ENVIRONMENTAL SUSTAINABILITY	TRANSPARENCY AND CO-DETERMINATION
A: SUPPLIERS	**A1** Human dignity in the supply chain	**A2** Solidarity and social justice in the supply chain	**A3** Environmental sustainability in the supply chain	**A4** Transparency and co-determination in the supply chain
B: OWNERS, EQUITY- AND FINANCIAL SERVICE PROVIDERS	**B1** Ethical position in relation to financial resources	**B2** Social position in relation to financial resources	**B3** Use of funds in relation to social and environmental impacts	**B4** Ownership and co-determination
C: EMPLOYEES, INCLUDING CO-WORKING EMPLOYERS	**C1** Human dignity in the workplace and working environment	**C2** Self-determined working arrangements	**C3** Environmentally-friendly behaviour of staff	**C4** Co-determination and transparency within the organisation
D: CUSTOMERS AND OTHER COMPANIES	**D1** Ethical customer relations	**D2** Cooperation and solidarity with other companies	**D3** Impact on the environment of the use and disposal of products and services	**D4** Customer participation and product transparency
E: SOCIAL ENVIRONMENT	**E1** Purpose of products and services and their effects on society	**E2** Contribution to the community	**E3** Reduction of environmental impact	**E4** Social co-determination and transparency

The Common Good Matrix.[7]

6 Vision and Values. 2019. Economy for the common good.

7 The common good matrix. Economy for the common good.

Bring Back Gold

With the increase in instability of the Pound Stirling and the US Dollar, many are promoting the purchase of precious metals as a dependable investment. In a recent video titled 'Stocks, Bonds and Real Estate to Implode' (2022), Mike Maloney is adamant that the existing fiat currency is 'something that causes pain and poverty' and that a return to the Gold Standard would increase 'our level of prosperity' and we would see a 'whole lot less war and it would be a very, very different world. People, I think, would be living longer lives. Everything's cleaner, less child labour problems.'

Just as a reminder, up until 1971 gold backed all currencies. Why gold? Gold is relatively rare. It is durable - it does not erode and it cannot be forged. It can only be mined so the amount in circulation tends to stay under control. It is also tangible. Unlike crypto currencies, you can feel it, you can hold it, it exists in the material world. Gold is not particularly portable therefore currencies are issued as a substitution. Fiat currency (which followed after the gold standard was dissolved) is backed by nothing but good will and a promise. It can be manipulated, devalued and (as economic history has shown) it is volatile. In time of high inflation when the pound loses its value, investors convert their cash holdings into gold as a means of protecting their assets. Gold therefore offers credibility, authenticity and stability. Or does it?

Although gold offers a financial protection and a guard in times of high inflation, there is no guarantee that the value of gold will not drop at times of greater financial stability. Gold is mined in over 40 countries with China producing the most tonnage accounting for 10.5% of global production.[8] At today's price (October 2022), a gram of gold is worth £46.91. Sold as a small bar it measures 14.7 mm x 8.9 mm and is purchasable from around £62.

I can't help wondering what would have happened if we had still been tied to gold during the 2008 financial crash or the pandemic lockdown. Would the government have been so readily able to bail out banks or provide (for some) a lifesaving furlough scheme? Would the central banks hands be tied when they most need to support a nation in crisis? Does stability result in inflexibility?

Keeping it Local

I had no idea credit unions existed until I started exploring alternatives to high street banking. According to the Bank of England there are 390 registered credit

8 10 Largest Producers of Gold by Country. D. Belder, 2023. Investing News Network.

unions in the UK supporting 1.9 million members and the number seems to be increasing annually. Credit unions run on a non-profit basis. Their chief aim is to offer financial support to their local communities by providing credit at a fair interest rate. The money you place with a credit union is assured by the Financial Services Compensation Scheme as it is with banks and building societies. Whether a credit union will provide all your banking needs very much depends on the ones that are available to you.

So why would you choose to use one in place of a high street bank? If I wanted to join a credit union, my nearest is situated in a neighbouring county over 57 miles from my home. I am eligible to join as I live in one of the 4 counties it supports. The piggy bank illustration compares the products and services in comparison with those offered by high street banks.

My local credit union is run by eight elected volunteers who make up the board of directors and six full and part-time employed staff who are responsible for administration and development. I called them to ask questions on how the credit union works for its members and whether or not it can fulfil someone's entire banking needs. The answer is - not quite, and definitely not on its own.

The opportunities the credit union provides to the under privileged is unquestionably principled. People who have no assets to speak of, or who have been rejected by the usual financial institutions can now apply for support within their local community, but the services offered are limited. The gaps that would make this an inclusive service are plugged by an associated agency and come at an additional cost. Do credit unions attract new members? I was told that although new members join, others leave too after paying off their loans, and that the credit union is restricted by its terms of reference and in this case, the geographical area it supports.

It's a familiar dilemma which reminds us that ethics comes at a cost. Do I choose an alternative that reflects my values but will create more inconvenience, or do I opt for the faster and more inclusive option? After all, why make life harder than it already is?

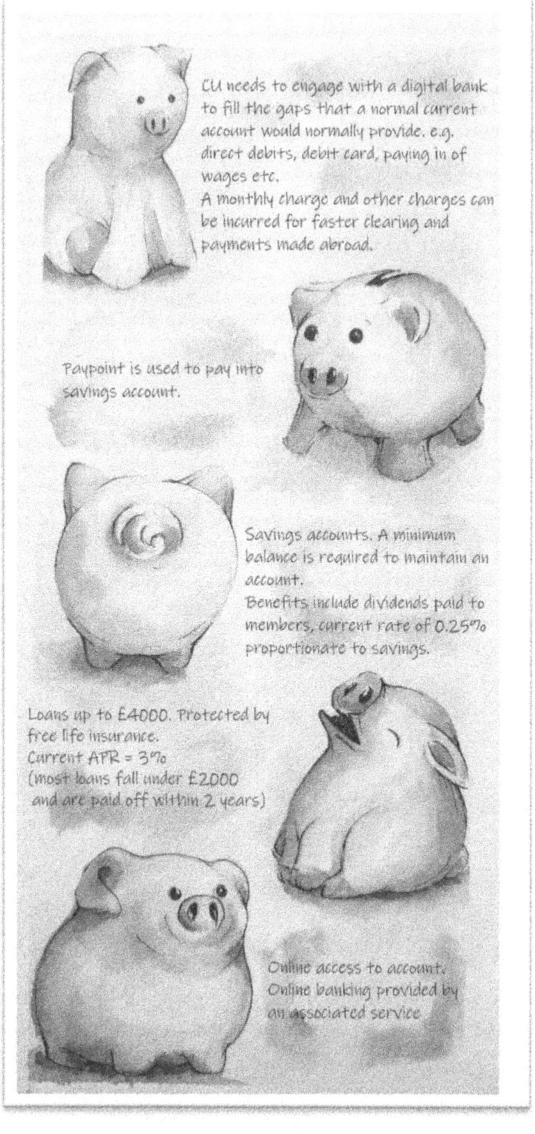

CU needs to engage with a digital bank to fill the gaps that a normal current account would normally provide. e.g. direct debits, debit card, paying in of wages etc.
A monthly charge and other charges can be incurred for faster clearing and payments made abroad.
Paypoint is used to pay into savings account.
Savings accounts. A minimum balance is required to maintain an account.
Benefits include dividends paid to members, current rate of 0.25% proportionate to savings.
Loans up to £4000. Protected by free life insurance.
Current APR = 3%
(most loans fall under £2000 and are paid off within 2 years)
Online access to account.
Online banking provided by an associated service

Functions of a Credit Union (CU)

The credit union service model can work well on a much smaller scale as I found when I visited my local mosque one Saturday.

18 April 2023. As I walk into my local town I am drawn to the pink flags hanging from certain buildings announcing Heritage Open Day. The brightly coloured bunting point people to historic monuments and buildings whose doors are normally closed to the public. Looking at the map to see which are open, I notice the town mosque had joined the scheme. It's been there for years but I've never stepped inside and am curious to visit.

Following a warm welcome and a full introduction to the history of the building by my guide, I ask why there are so many men coming and going despite there being no service. I notice that they arrive, embrace the host (and greet me), disappear around the back somewhere and then leave 10 minutes later. My host explains that his niece has died and members of the local community are paying their respects.

I express my own condolences and my admiration for the support he is receiving. He explains the mechanics of the Mosque's Bereavement Society which also serves 4 local villages. Like a credit union of sorts, each member (or represented family) of the Bereavement Society donates a nominal sum of money when a member suffers a death in the family. Each member is notified when there has been a death then the collected funds are awarded without delay. Donations can be as much as £7000. No questions are asked as to how the money will be spent as each member is trusted to make their own judgment.

A system like this works because it is small. Restricting it to an agreed geographical boundary keeps it personal and manageable. People know each other therefore each claim is significant and carries meaning and purpose.

Local Currencies

The town of Lewes in East Sussex launched its own currency in 2008. The printed notes represent Lewes pounds; each one is equivalent to the pound sterling. The banknotes are colourful and not dissimilar in layout representing local scenes and people who have contributed to the Lewes community, infrastructure and economy. As the currency can only be spent where establishments will receive it, local consumers are encouraged to purchase Lewes pounds and accept them as change so that they can spend them with local businesses. Lewes is one of the more successful schemes. Other areas have launched their own, but few have lasted beyond a few years.

Susan Murray of The Lewes Pound Community Interest Company kindly sent me a full promotional statement. Here is an excerpt:

'Why on earth do we think that Lewes needs its very own local currency. Does a sterling note or coin send a message beyond 'spend me'? It may denote national pride or power, but otherwise I think not. All our Lewes Pounds, however, bear a picture on the front of that great radical hero and one-time resident of Lewes, Tom Paine, along with his inspirational words – "We have it in our power to build the world anew." That is a rallying cry to live by! It has been said that money can recognise the price of everything, but the value of nothing. Can money (sterling) help us with recognising the true value of a thriving local community? Can money help us to celebrate what we cherish about our town and our local environment? Can money help us to determine the right things to do in face of the climate and biodiversity emergencies? Can money ensure that our local businesses flourish and continue to be part of the character of Lewes? The Lewes Pound says – yes! Spend Lewes Pounds and you can support all of those objectives!

'The Lewes Pound is MORE THAN JUST MONEY and this spending reflects values shared by business and customer alike, mostly relating to food that is local, healthy and organic. This in turn is underpinned by the desire to support and create a better environment that can be part of the struggle to control the climate and biodiversity emergencies and to help meet the UN Sustainable Development goals. It is almost impossible to believe that so much care and concern can be wrapped up in spending a sterling note or making a contactless payment. In the market recently a stall holder asked, "How come Lewes Pound notes are so much more beautiful than sterling notes?" The simple answer is that we care and want our notes to represent much more than just their monetary value – we wear our hearts on our notes.'

17 September 2022. I've arranged to meet one of the keepers at our local farmshop. He has agreed to give me some discarded feathers from some of the exotic birds kept on show, so I can add them to my collection. More than just a farm shop, Johnsons' of Oldhurst has been in business since 1899. From a very small village they operate a sustainable bakery, butchery, zoo, restaurant and coffee shop. As farmers, their 'carbon intake from the 12.5 acres of established woodland and 164 acres of permanent pasture, on which we graze our own herds of cattle, deer and buffalo surpasses the output of carbon from our business', which means they can call themselves a carbon neutral farm.

When I visit their modest zoo, I pay only £4 (£3 per child) to spend time with a variety of domestic and wild animals and witness firsthand their renowned contribution to the conservation of crocodiles. When I ask which of the animals is the most expensive to maintain I'm surprised to learn it is the macaws, as the birdseed has to be imported. All other animals are fed the leftovers from the shop and restaurant – there is no waste. After a traumatic rummage in the aviary, (I honestly wonder if I will come out in one piece), I triumphantly return with brightly coloured macaw and peacock feathers and a handful of porcupine quills. He invites me to return late November when they will be preparing bronze turkeys for Christmas.

I believe the best way to support a fairer economy is to buy local produce and materials from small suppliers. There are enough farm shops, market stalls, independent bakers and craft fairs to equip us with most of what we need, many of which can be delivered to our homes. I agree it may be time-consuming working with so many outlets and the initial outlay can exceed our customary budget, but once the account is open and the deliveries and communications become routine, efficiency will follow.

Reducing Debt

Logic tells me that if the infinite growth of the economy relies on continuous personal and professional debt, by reducing the amount we and businesses owe, the system should decelerate. Like playing the game in reverse; if you want to bring noise levels down, you speak more quietly, if you want to de-escalate conflict you communicate calmly, if you want a dog to come back to you, you run in the opposite direction (usually) and so it is with finance. Having established that debt drives the wedge between the *haves* and *have-nots*, by reducing debt the divide should weaken and a greater balance of power be reinstated, albeit marginal.

11 November 2022. I'm visiting one of our local larger museums to see the first exhibition of its kind - 'Defaced! Money, Conflict, Protest!' - 250 years of anger and frustration caused by the injustices of worldwide financial systems are unleashed on coins and notes. In case you're wondering, the Currency and Banknotes Act 1928 confirms: 'If any person prints or stamps, or by any like means impresses, on any bank note any words, letters or figures, he shall, in respect of each offence, be liable on summary conviction to a penalty'.[9]

Some of the exhibits defaced are crude, others are beautifully designed. A single word is added to an old one penny coin to read 'One Worthless Penny'. The word TRASH is printed boldly in red across a dollar bill. The image of Abe Lincoln becomes a green ninja turtle. Some more artistic displays show South American banknotes folded intricately to represent animals, and banknotes from Brixton have been redesigned to show contemporary heroes such as David Bowie. I wander to the room at the far end to see a three-dimensional display of a deconstructed van. Each piece is suspended from the ceiling whilst, against a wall, a video shows the vehicle exploding into pieces with banknotes floating down like ash. The story behind it goes:

'May 2019. In the shadow of the towers of London's financial centre, Canary Wharf, a golden Ford transit van explodes. With this single act, £1.2 million of high interest 'toxic debt' is cancelled in a London community. Influenced by the Strike Debt movement in the US that opened their eyes to the dark heart of the financial system, filmmaker and artist duo, Hilary Powell and Dan Edelstyn, set up a printing

---

9 Currency and Banknotes Act 1928 Section 12. 1928. Legislation.gov.uk

press in a disused bank in Walthamstow, East London. There they printed their own banknotes. The faces of local unsung heroes in their community replaced the traditional historical figures we are used to seeing on bank notes. When the notes were sold as Art, half the proceeds went to these local stalwarts and half for the purchase and destruction of local high interest debt.'[10]

Debt Jubilee - a clearance of debt from public
records across a wide sector or a nation

[Wikipedia]

'Jubilee 2000 was a global campaign that led ultimately to the cancellation of more than $100 billion of debt owed by 35 of the poorest countries.'[11] The campaign, led by Ann Pettifor and a coalition of famous and influential sympathisers and union movements, inspired a global petition signed by more than 21 million people – the aim was to write off debt owed by third world countries to their foreign creditors.

The practice of eliminating debt goes back to ancient history and evidenced in the first books of the Bible. 'At the end of every seven years you shall grant a release. And this is the manner of the release: every creditor shall release what he has lent to his neighbour' (Deutoronomy 15: verses 1-2).

Arguably an annulment of personal debt is morally attractive but not necessarily an economically sound decision. So long as there exists a monetary economy, the end of someone's debt may just lead to further loans in the future. For a person living in an unmanageable and intolerable situation with no change in sight, it most certainly can alleviate extreme stress that may otherwise result in absolute destitution or even suicide. Bankruptcy is an option but even this choice comes with an administrative cost of £680 that must be paid prior to application.

If debts are less than £30,000 a Debt Relief Order (DRO) is an alternative option and costs a single fee of £90 to initiate. 'A DRO normally lasts 12 months. If approved, you stop making payments towards the debts (and interest) listed in the DRO during that time. After the 12 months, you will not have to pay these debts anymore.'[12]

---

10 Bank Job. H. Powell & D. Edelstyn. 2020. Chelsea Green Publishing.

11 Jubilee 2000. A Pettifor, 2000. Advocacy International

12 How to get a Debt Relief Order (DRO). 2023. The Insolvency Service. GOV.UK

The National Economic Stabilization and Recovery Act (NESARA) as proposed by Dr. Harvey Barnard in the 1990's and published in a paper by R. Kingsley[13], has been dismissed by BBC's John Griffin as 'financial fantasy' and that if put into practice will ruin people's lives. It's a rather poisonous mocking attack which fails to acknowledge Barnard's purest of intentions, which is to create a fairer national and global society where currency is of equal value and life's necessities are readily accessible to all, and I applaud it.

Barnard's proposal stated that the US tax system was ill-equipped to counterbalance the problems of a rising deficit, trade imbalance, public debt and inflation. He therefore proposed a radical reformation which would overhaul tax systems and limit rates of interest. The proposition is noteworthy as it attempts to support the poorest in society and simplify a convoluted monetary system that creates more complications than it resolves. Whether or not this was Barnard's explicit plan, the essence of his proposals is simplified as follows:

- To abolish income tax
- To cancel all personal debt
- To introduce a flat rate of 14% tax on all non- essential items or services.
- Currency to be backed by gold, silver and other precious metals.

Unfortunately, the concept has been tainted by its strong connection to alleged religious groups and conspiracy theorists. The origins of this endorsement have been a deterrent for many, and the proposal has therefore not been given the earnest consideration it deserves.

If Barnard's key theory blames debt as the number one economic factor inhibiting the growth of the economy, then it's no surprise that his ideas have been ridiculed given that debt creates the greatest financial growth for those who have the most to lose.

13 The National Economic Stabilization and Recovery Act Dr. H. Barnard. 2005. The NESARA Institute

When the State Intervenes

"No penalty on earth will stop people from stealing, if it's their only way of getting food. You remind me of these incompetent schoolmasters, who prefer caning their pupils to teaching them. Instead of inflicting these horrible punishments, it would be far more to the point to provide everyone with some means of livelihood, so that nobody's under the frightful necessity of becoming, first a thief, and then a corpse."

[Utopia, Thomas More]

The Human Rights Act 1998 sets out 16 fundamental rights every individual is entitled to – these are known as articles. The second article is the Right to Life. Surprisingly it is not an absolute right, in other words there maybe exceptions. Article 3 of the Human Rights Act upholds 'Freedom from torture and inhuman or degrading treatment' and is an absolute right; there are no exceptions. The following excerpt is copied from the Equality and Human Rights Commission:

'Your right not to be tortured or treated in an inhuman or degrading way is absolute. This means it must never be limited or restricted in any way. For example, a public authority can never use lack of resources as a defence against an accusation that it has treated someone in an inhuman or degrading way.'

What about not being able to afford a home, or living with a constant fear of eviction? Is it not inhumane to expect a family of four or more to live in one room? What about not being able to afford to eat more than once a day? What about being cold - having to choose between heating a room or eating a hot meal? All of these point to a lack of resources, all of these infringe a person's rights under article 3.

'The effectiveness of the government has a major influence on human happiness of the people. The capacity of a state can be well-measured by - its fiscal capacity (ability to raise money) - its collective capacity (ability to deliver services) - its legal capacity (rule of law) Also crucial are - the avoidance of civil war, and - the avoidance of repression. Across countries, all these five measures are well correlated with the average life satisfaction of the people.'[14]

As a matter of interest, I asked a group 'if you could add to the list of articles in the Human Rights Act what would you propose?' See the illustration for their responses.

---

[14] World Happiness Report, Executive Summary. J. Helliwell et al. 2023

More Human Rights

Universal Basic Income

The principle of a Universal Basic Income (UBI) is to provide every adult with a monthly payment to cover their necessities such as food, energy, housing etc. This is not a means-tested plan and, unlike universal credit, it is given without conditions. Therefore each citizen receives a regular payment regardless of their employment, social or financial status. The income is substantial. Although distributed in a similar way to our national systems of child benefit or fuel allowance, the payments are considerably higher to ease the stress of living and to increase opportunities for the more deprived amongst us. To date, no country has fully implemented UBI, but many across the globe have trialled a scheme based on the UBI model.

Canada has trialled several Basic Income programmes and introduced the first in 1974 adopting the name Mincome. The programme 's purpose was to assess the impact on each family in the province of Manitoba on receiving a guaranteed and unconditional annual income of 16,000 Canadian Dollars. The chief concern being whether the obvious benefits of securing food, housing etc. would outweigh the potential risk of people not wanting to go to work. Although no official report was published, economist Evelyn Forget drew her own analytical conclusions: despite a very small drop in employment figures, particularly amongst women, there was evidence of an 8.5% reduction in hospital visits (including for mental health), and an increase in adolescents completing high school.[15]

---

[15] The Town with No Poverty: The Health Effects of a Canadian Guaranteed Annual Income Field Experiment. E. Forget. 2011. Community Health Sciences University of Manitoba.

There have been further pilot projects that followed. But when posed the question 'why isn't it happening?' Senator Bellemare voiced her reservations; "A basic income would be an unfair, complicated, and a costly way to eliminate poverty." In response Zhao and Whitehead put forward a compelling argument outlining how a national UBI strategy is not only affordable to the nation's economy, but will improve health, education, social cohesion and productivity. They conclude, 'Poverty touches us all — it is everyone's tragedy, which is absurd because poverty can be affordably reduced. Hopefully, one day future Canadians will look back to 2022 and ask how a just society could ever have tolerated such needless suffering'[16]

In the UK, Wales has taken up the mantle and is currently piloting a UBI scheme amongst a small group of young care leavers. 'From 1 July 2022, more than 500 people leaving care in Wales will be offered £1600 each month (before tax) for two years to support them as they make the transition to adult life.' This 'radical approach' is placing 'trust, autonomy and respect' at its centre.[17]

The pilot is cautious in its introduction but admirable in where it places its values. Seen as an investment in the future of Wales' younger population, the scheme costing £20 million will be regularly evaluated to measure its success. Advice and support will be available on how each recipient can plan their chosen future. 'This will be just the first step in what could be a journey that benefits generations to come.'[18]

When asked to comment on the prospects of having a national UBI, the Department for Work and Pensions (DWP) spokesperson said, "we have no plans to introduce a universal basic income. It would not incentivise work, target those most in need in society, or work for those who need more support, such as disabled people and those with caring responsibilities".[19] I find these comments a sad reflection of how the government distrusts and refuses to acknowledge a nation full of responsible and fair-minded adults.

---

16 Guaranteed basic income could end poverty, so why isn't it happening? J.Zhao., L.Whitehead. 2022. The University of British Columbia.

17 Basic income pilot for care leavers: overview of the scheme. 2022. GOV. WALES

18 Basic income pilot for care leavers: overview of the scheme. 2022. GOV. WALES

19 Cornwall universal basic income suggested to reduce poverty. 2022. BBC News

Furlough

14.5 million living in poverty
in the world's fifth largest economy
until a global pandemic forced our chancellor
to spend £69 billion on a word
none of us had ever heard of.

When the first unconditional money
hit mum's bank account she cried
with eyes that could now see a future.

[Harula Ladd, 2022. Turn on the Tap]

Did we ever really know the meaning of this word prior to 2020? The government may readily dismiss a UBI but during the time of lockdown the Furlough scheme provided similar support. Agreed, it was issued because people couldn't work but the purpose had the same effect as voiced in the first few lines of a poem by Harula Ladd. In total 1.7 million jobs were furloughed in the UK, at the cost of approximately £70 billion.

At its peak around May 2020, 8.9 million grateful individuals were receiving financial help of up to 80% of their normal weekly pay. The levels of support then fluctuated with the introduction of second and third lockdowns. On 1st July 2020, the government continued to offer support by the introduction of a flexible furlough scheme, whereby businesses were given the option to invite employees back to work on a part time basis. Any unworked hours were reimbursed by the usual payment i.e. 80% of salaries.

'By late October, it was estimated that 87% of furloughed employees returned to work, 3 % were made permanently redundant, 3% voluntarily left their role and 8% were classified as "other".'[20] Although there were many industries that did not receive the same benefits (at least not immediately) furlough kept employment figures high in times of extreme crisis. Those that received it were able to live out the lockdown without worrying about how they were going to pay to live.

---

20 Examining the end of the furlough scheme. H.Clark. 2021. House of Commons Library, UK Parliament.

Furlough has its critics. Some say it went on for far too long and should have ended after the first lockdown. 'We hoped it was just a three or four-week emergency and afterwards everything would get back to the way it was before. By the time of the second lockdown, it was clear that businesses were adjusting, that the way we all worked was changing, and it was no longer necessary. Even worse, it prevented the market from working. Lots of furloughed staff won't get their jobs back, but, given the shortages elsewhere, they could easily switch to something better paid. Most furloughed staff from the autumn onwards were concentrated in low-skilled, low-paid professions such as hospitality. Many of those people could have moved into booming sectors such as logistics and food production where employers are struggling to fill all their vacancies. But while they were paid to stay at home, there was no incentive to do so'.[21]

Furlough helped but it did not prevent the fallout of so much economic inactivity. On a recent visit to the City of Peterborough I was shocked at the number of major department stores that had closed, deserting a once thriving centre of retail. John Lewis, often considered to be the jewel in the crown of department stores, closed its doors to the city's public after 39 years, leaving a vacuum in the city that has yet to be filled.

My point about Furlough is that when the nation's need is great, the money will be found. It will be printed and distributed, and the national debt will increase in response to the demand. No-one will worry about the financial burden placed on the government, no one will care about the long-term effects, no-one will care about the who, how or what, so long as the tap stays open.

My own personal relationship with money is changing. I'm not sure whether I can attribute the change to my age or my circumstances, but I have certainly recognised that in writing this book I am re-examining my values in earnest. I've seen money disappear as if a sudden storm had blown it away and left me standing in a puddle of penury. I've seen the expectations of riches evaporate with no hope of recovery. Yet here I am, warm, fed and clothed and content. Money is energy, it simply needs to go where it is needed best and can do the most.

It is useful, it is essential, but it is not the only tool for exchange, it is not the only means of investment. It may have served the past, but I do not believe it will determine the future. Our treasures are far more accessible than we think.

---

21 Was furlough the worst £70 billion ever spent? M.Lynn. 2021. The Spectator.

PART FOUR
Financial Freedom

Chapter Thirteen

(Everybody needs)

Good Neighbours

Working with Nature

Give me spots on my apples but leave me the birds and the bees

[Song 'Yellow Taxi' by Joni Mitchell]

Man said to God, "We don't need you anymore. We've worked out how to clone and replicate human intelligence. We've mastered your craft. You are no longer needed."

God listened with intrigue and replied; "Well just to be sure, why don't we have a man-making contest and let's do this the original way, like I did at the beginning."

Man said, "Sure, no problem, we can do that", and he bent down and picked up a handful of dirt.

God intervened, "No, no, no! You get your own dirt!"

Everything comes from the earth and nothing leaves the earth. The wind, sun and the rain, the forests, fields and the oceans, the plants and the animals, the soil, rocks and minerals. The earth and the elements are all we have. This is our home. We can use what nature gives us in its natural form to feed, heal and sustain our bodies and nourish our soul. Or we can mix, manipulate and distort nature, claim it as intellectual property and make money from selling the concoctions to those who are suffering, or to fulfil our frivolous desires.

2 October 2023. Today on my walk I came across a man who had no name (out of choice, it's a long story and potentially another book). He was skilfully collecting seeds from nettle plants, with the aim of turning them into oil. By first mixing them with an alcohol solution and leaving the alcohol to evaporate, the remaining liquid is the oil that can be used for a multitude of ailments. He advised eating a leaf of the feverfew plant to remedy a headache – I tried one when I got home. It was extremely bitter to taste but gave me some relief for a few hours.

'Nettle leaves are abundant in fibre, minerals, vitamins, as well as antioxidant compounds like polyphenols and carotenoids. Stinging nettle has antiproliferative, anti-inflammatory, antioxidant, analgesic, anti-infectious, hypotensive, and antiulcer characteristics, as well as the ability to prevent cardiovascular disease, in all parts of the plant (leaves, stems, roots, and seeds)'.[1] To most of us nettles are just a nuisance and a

---

1 Nutritional and pharmacological importance of stinging nettle: A review. KK Bhusal et al. 2022. National Library of Medicine.

physical pain should we brush up against them. We are not encouraged to make use of them as a free resource. I now drink a cup of nettle tea most afternoons.

Last Christmas one of the gifts I received was a book on foraging; a guide to what we can pick directly from its natural source and use for food or medicine. Many are already known to us and sold in commercial establishments. Chamomile tea soothes and relaxes, it is particularly beneficial for upset stomachs. For those who have trouble sleeping the root of valerian can be purchased in pill form from most pharmacists and health food outlets. Aspirin is extracted from the bark of Willow and amongst other uses, thins the blood to manage heart conditions. Poppies provide opium, a very strong and addictive pain killer. You may recall the scene in the Wizard of Oz where the Wicked Witch of the West manifests a field of poppies to send Dorothy and her friends to sleep. Most recently turmeric and ginger have become popular as natural anti-inflammatory treatments. It is not unusual now to see viola flowers garnishing salads and lavender used to flavour cakes and confectionaries.

These are just a few of the most well-known and popular choices, there are many more. Before you pick, pluck and eat at random, I recommend researching the plant as some can cause reactions and a few are poisonous.

Mycelium

2 November 2023. They keeping cutting down the trees where I live and I've yet to see one replaced. Some are diseased, others lopsided and in danger of falling. We had a single larch of a modest size whose cones were small and dainty some of which still adorn my fireplace. Sadly it didn't survive the prolonged freezing temperatures we endured one winter and there is none of its type to replace it. I miss seeing it on my walks. We also had a tree that I nicknamed *Merlin's Tree* after a painting by Burne Jones.[2] It stood less than 7 foot high and its two main boughs curved sensually in opposite directions. I don't think the trunk was able to sustain the distribution of weight and one of the boughs fell off. It was not long after that the whole tree was cut to a stump. As I take Wynter on a walk I notice it has turned orange and assume it has been the victim of Halloween antics the night before. When I look closely, I see that I am mistaken. It has become home to a brightly coloured lichen in the formation of exquisite luminous circles.

In the dismal damp climate of the UK we are blessed with a huge variety of fungi and lichen. They appear as fairy like circles in grass, on the bark of trees and on tree

2 The Beguiling of Merlin (Merlin and Vivien). 1870 – 1874. Edward Burne-Jones. Lady Lever Art Gallery, Port Sunlight, UK

stumps. White, green, yellow, orange, some dimpled, some shaggy. They curve like laced petticoats, protrude like small suckers on an octopus, or lean like tiny parasols. A report by the Royal Botanic Gardens, Kew estimate that there are 2,500,500 species worldwide, of which almost 90% have yet to be named. They are the second largest living group after invertebrate animals. If you pick up a handful of soil, they will be there.

'Plants… provide us with food, materials, medicines and more. They regulate important planetary cycles that provide us with the air we breathe and water we drink, and contribute to our overall well-being ……..Fungi underpin nearly all life on Earth, being vitally important to land plants, how ecosystems function and ultimately the whole of humanity.'

'Current threats to fungal species largely mirror those faced by animals and plants. The main threat comes from land-use changes that modify natural systems, such as conversion to forestry, agriculture or residential and commercial development. For example, in parts of Europe, declining areas of older natural forest and expanded timber production are leading to less deadwood and fewer old trees being available for fungi to populate.'[3]

5 November 2023. On my walk with Wynter I take my camera to *Merlin's Stump* to capture and share an image of the beautiful lichen I spotted a few days ago. But the stump is no more. It has been chopped and ground to a pulp leaving nothing but a scattering of sawdust. No trace is left of the tree or the lichen. It's as if it never existed. It seems when one part of our ecosystem is under threat the rest are too.

Cycles and Seasons

Now and again I play a game with myself. I imagine I have landed on earth not knowing the month and I have to guess. I look around me for clues. I look to the fields to see which crops are growing and they height they have reached. I look at the wayside flowers, different species appear at different times of year. By August there is very little regrowth and everything (including my own garden) is looking scruffy. I look to the trees, the colour of the leaves and if the fruit is swelling, ripe or fallen. During the warmer months between April and September, I recognise the butterflies that emerge first and those that appear much later. The call of the cuckoo is unmistakable in late spring, whilst the birds are much quieter once the season of rearing their young comes to a close. There is an abundance of moths and spiders in late summer. The big ones enter our homes in September looking for a mate. Why

3 State of the World's Plants and Fungi 2023. Royal Botanic Gardens, Kew.

they assume they will find one in my laundry basket remains a mystery. The winter months are a little harder to detect, but the night sky provides vital clues. In December Jupiter is the brightest star at sunrise, and in early January evenings the constellation of Orion sits directly outside my door.

The seasons rarely change. The temperatures may fluctuate but I've noticed that there is a balance in the long run. A couple of wet months will usually be followed by a long dry spell. The season and the cycles are our constants. For me they bring a feeling of stability and security more than any bank balance. I have felt much more gratitude when the sun has risen and when the clouds have brought rain. A pay packet may bring relief, but sunshine always brings a smile.

Working and living in relationship to nature is the foundation for permaculture - a permanent culture that applies a deep sense of gratitude and appreciation for what is naturally available. It applies natural intelligence and wisdom to build sustainable communities.

'The discipline of permaculture design is based on observing what makes natural systems endure; establishing simple yet effective principles and using them to mirror nature in whatever we choose to design. This can be gardens, farms, buildings, woodlands, communities, businesses, even towns and cities. Permaculture is essentially about creating beneficial relationships between individual elements and making sure energy is captured in, rather than lost from, a system. Its application is only as limited as our imaginations.'[4]

Disturbing and manipulating nature's perfect chaos comes at a cost, often one we are unable to control. We risk the loss of vital wildlife that pollinate our food sources and feed on those that might damage our crops. We provoke extreme weather

4 What is Permaculture: Part 1 – Ethics. M. Harland. Permaculture.

conditions and increase the likelihood of ill health. We need all of nature, in its original quantity and design, nothing less will sustain us in the long term.

The Human Landscape

Is man a shaper or a distorter? What about exploiter and decimator? What has man accomplished in the last 50 years?

The WWF Living Planet Report confirms, 'an average 68% decrease in population sizes of mammals, birds, amphibians, reptiles and fish between 1970 and 2016. The tropical subregions of the Americas [showing] the largest fall observed in any part of the world. Since the industrial revolution, human activities have increasingly destroyed and degraded forests, grasslands, wetlands and other important ecosystems, threatening human well-being; 75% of the Earth's ice-free land surface has already been significantly altered, most of the oceans are polluted, and more than 85% of the area of wetlands has been lost.'

The report attributes the loss to 'an explosion in global trade, consumption and human population growth, as well as an enormous move towards urbanisation. To feed and fuel our 21st century lifestyles, we are overusing the Earth's biocapacity by at least 56%. Loss of biodiversity hurts the poorest people who depend on it, further exacerbating an already inequitable world; and it is a moral issue because we humans should not destroy the living planet.'[5]

2 November 2023. I am watching a Channel 4 production called 'Is it time to break the law?' - you may have seen it aired on 20th September 2023. Chris Packham, best known for his passionate promotion of wildlife is challenging his own conscience, questioning whether he is doing enough to halt the decimation of wildlife across the world. He wonders whether he should be taking a more radical approach to alert those in high office of the imminent catastrophe we all face if their policies continue at the pace of a snail.

I find myself becoming more and more exasperated. No amount of protests, regardless of how destructive the actions, will change anything within the powers of any national government. Anyone holding an office of influence will be manipulated by the few who hold the real power – those who stand to benefit financially from the continued sale of fossil fuels and rape of the environment.

---

5 Living Planet Report 2020 - Bending the curve of biodiversity loss. R. Almond et al. 2020. World Wildlife Fund.

But we are powerful –we are consumers, we are the payers. Our money is our weapon and our choices are the strategies for change. We just need to make better decisions. We can collapse a damaging system by simply not engaging with it.

I go to Chris Packham's website to give him this message, but find I have to tweet it. Now I have to learn how to use twitter (sigh).

The Splat Test

As a child with a vivid imagination, when I heard people say, 'insects will rule the world', I imagined ants and all kinds of species with numerous legs crawling everywhere in sight, under and above ground. Although the insect population has not been mentioned in the opening paragraphs of the WWF report, it has been the subject of a recent parliamentary select committee commencing 12 July 2023. Professor Lynn Dicks, lead of the Agroecology Research Group at the University of Cambridge observed that 'our protected areas are not enough to reverse the insect declines that we are seeing. We are looking after our rare species reasonably well; we are not looking after our common species.' Evidence confirms that the number of flying insects in the UK has plummeted by nearly 60% within the last 20 years. Whilst the more popular and appealing species such as birds and mammals receive the greatest attention and resources for preservation and revival, an assessment of the abundance of insects and invertebrates may have been neglected. The Bugs Matter report (2021) reminds us that the consequences of global declines in insect abundance (quantity, not necessarily diversity) is potentially catastrophic. 'Invertebrates are critical to ecosystem functions and services, and without them life on earth would collapse'.

It is both alarming and amusing to observe 'the anecdotal observation that people tend to find fewer insects squashed on the windscreens of their cars now, compared to in the past'. This observation is referred to as the Windscreen Phenomenon or the Splat Test. The report details the research undertaken to count the numbers of squashed insects drivers encountered on their vehicle number plates following a journey. I confess that I have given no thought to the fewer occasions I have cleaned my windscreen or number plate on account of dead bugs. And if I had, I may have assumed that the rain (there has been no shortage of recent downpours) simply washed them clean. In any case, 'the results show that the number of insects sampled on vehicle number plates in the UK decreased by 58.5% between 2004 and 2021, and that these differences were statistically significant'.[6]

6 The Bugs Matter Citizen Science Survey. Ball et al. 2021. Kent Wildlife Trust & Buglife.

On a good point, Professor Dicks has confirmed that our insect population that live in rivers and ponds have benefited from the national drive to clean up our waterways. They have since thrived in numbers since improvements have been made. I can vouch for this. When I joined a bat watch late one evening, the guide shone a torch on the surface of the backwater we were sailing through. The astonishing number of small insects we saw prompted everyone on board to zip their coats to their chins and firmly close their mouths.

THE NORTHERN FARMER **26th January 2023**

Government brings forward Sustainable Farming Incentive subsidies

Farmers will be paid to plant wildflowers and winter bird food on their farms from this year in new expedited sustainable agriculture plans unveiled by the Government.

The subsidies, which have been brought forward by a year as part of the Sustainable Farming Incentive (SFI), give farmers payments for implementing environmentally friendly agricultural practices.

We may be seeing more fields of wildflowers interspersed between those of crops, following a new government initiative and the withdrawal of European subsidies.

"Farmers are at the heart of our economy – producing the food on our tables as well as being the custodians of the land it comes from. These two roles go hand-in-hand, and we are speeding up the rollout of our farming schemes so that everyone can be financially supported as they protect the planet while producing food more sustainably."[7]

Insects matter. About 75% of the crops we grow rely on insect pollination. Insects break down and feed on animal excrement and carcasses. They feed our bats, reptiles, amphibians, fish and birds. They devour other insects that would otherwise decimate our crops. They aerate the soil by building tunnels to direct oxygen, water and nutrients to roots.[8]

7 Thérèse Coffey: Farmers central to food production and environmental action. 2023. Department for Environment, Food & Rural Affairs and Rural Payments Agency. GOV. UK

8 Why should we care about insects? T.Hibbert. 2020. Devon Wildlife Trust

'Life has vanished since I've loved it.'

[Chris Packham. 2023.]

Everyone needs good neighbours which is why I have decided to make friends with bugs. I have been insensitive to their importance and neglected their beauty. Like many gardeners I have considered them a pest and it's fair to say I have lost plants because of them. But I feel as a reward I have been blessed with visits from numerous species including a Garden Tiger Moth and a Hummingbird Hawkmoth. For the last 3 consecutive years a Red Admiral butterfly has landed on my person, and I have felt deeply privileged.

Our loss of wildlife worries me. When we first moved to this small community I recall seeing or hearing up to 15 species of bird on a single walk. Now I'm lucky if I see more than 5. Greenfinches regularly visited the garden, once a great spotted woodpecker took peanuts from the bird feeder, but no more. It's been years since I have seen lapwings in a field.

Communities

Communities, not communes, unless of course you like them.

22 September 23. For the first time in over 5 years I have returned to Spain to visit my family and celebrate my niece's wedding. I was born in Gibraltar where my father served in the Royal Air Force and met my mother who lived across the border in the port of Algeciras. My native Spanish family is immense. Although on this occasion I have reunited with over 30 relatives, there are as many again that I was not able to visit. The reunion is warm, sincere and exuberant. The authentic love and kindness shown to me and my family is overwhelming and I sometimes wonder why I am still living in the UK. I am staying with my cousin, his wife, daughter, her husband, their two children and 3 dogs. There is a peaceful synchrony of movement and activity that supports the lives and needs of each individual.

Early in the morning my cousin and I drive into the mountains with the dogs and then return to take the children to school with his daughter. There are no mealtimes. Someone buys the bread in the morning and it doesn't matter who. Everyone contributes to the cooking and leaves the food out for whoever wants to eat it and when it should suit them. A pot of soup is prepared and left on the stove with another of cooked chicken. There are cold meats, slices of Spanish omelette and plates of fruit for anyone to help themselves. A brother-in-law comes to clean their patios, back and front and helps himself to bread and coffee. All play their part in cleaning up, even the children.

I recall an occasion, whereby I was invited to a meal at another cousin's home. At 8pm we were picked up and taken to a beach. When I asked why we were there, they promptly responded 'if you want to eat, first we must catch the food.' After a short dive for mussels, followed by a very long discourse about everything and anything, we finally ate around 10.30pm. We joke that the Spanish timetable consists of one word, *mañana* - meaning either *tomorrow* or *morning*, but I personally think it's a reflection of our rigidity and how we chain ourselves to the clock. The responsibilities of daily living are the same everywhere, but people function and intermingle freely, openly, supportively, seemingly with ease and with less regard to time, which after all, never ceases.

We say the world is getting smaller because we can see from one end of it to the other. The corporations that sustain us are global, but in their enormity they are faceless leaving us feeling insignificant and powerless. We converse with machines not people, and in doing so we disassociate ourselves with any outcome. 'Proximity is how close we are to the action and that affects the way in which we assess, relate and respond to it.'[9] Our sense of responsibility fades the further we are from the source of decision and provision.

Permanent and successful change starts small. We should consider devolving power and responsibility to smaller communities, to ensure the results of collaboration and unification of systems are seen and felt. Intimate arrangements with those that we know and see, regularly increase our responsibility and accountability for the welfare of each other.

How small is small? A village, a town? Certainly a small community working cohesively can provide virtually all that is needed to sustain its members. The responsibilities will be shared according to the skills and passions of those contributing. Resources that can be shared include:

- Produce – fresh food that is seasonal or preserved by natural means. This can also include livestock where there are those willing to rear and slaughter them.
- transport – shared where practical to conserve energy, but not obligatory. The designation of one or two larger vehicles for the carriage of individuals and the distribution of goods.
- Childcare – operating much the same way as nurseries do now, to support those working but at no cost
- Care of the elderly or vulnerable – including those in the community to safeguard against loneliness and isolation.

---

9 The Social Distance Between Us. D. McGarvey. 2022. Ebury Publishing

- Education for all ages – the sharing of knowledge to manage relationships and to build skills to support and develop shared services and resources.

Functioning on a local scale, the allocation and distribution of labour, produce and assistance will be more manageable. Certain local planning laws will need to be abolished or at the very least allow more leniency in favour of practicality and widening the scope of amenities. If someone wants to convert an outhouse into a library then they should be encouraged and supported to do so. Certain aspects of daily living will be met on a county scale such as the maintenance of roads, management of waste and support of acute health conditions (hospitals and health centres).

Where there are local communities, there is a risk of territoriality. There is as much scope for conflict as there is for collaboration. Where for example, will a community draw its boundaries? Will they be geographic or demographic? What will be the degree of flexibility, and will it depend on eligibility or availability of resources? For example, an empty house should not remain unoccupied. A surplus of resources should not be hoarded but shared or traded with other communities. This again depends on altruistic coordination. Drawing on other chapters, I remind myself that we are charitable, we are caring, creative and we like to communicate. We can overcome any obstacles when we realise we each have enough.

6 September 2023. Whilst taking Wynter for a walk around the village, I marvel at the ideas people have to decorate their gardens. One has converted an open canoe into a pond of sorts with a cascading water feature, plants and a discreet yellow rubber duck - enchanting. Another has used old rusty, ornate metal bed posts as a garden fence – ingenious. Someone has grown sunflowers, poppies and cosmos in a piece of wasteland that belongs to no individual. Vegetation that has escaped the boundaries of a garden has now grown into a flourishing pumpkin patch. The village copse is now a fairy wood with miniature doors and ornaments adorning the base of tree trunks – magical.

My friend and I often contemplate taking early retirement. We ask ourselves why not? why wait? We talk about all the things we could do to survive if money got really tight, like growing our own food, buying from charity shops, renovating old bits of furniture or adapting utensils to serve a different use. We agree we've made it this far, we haven't starved, we've never been homeless – we have our pensions, our homes, our families and our friends and each other– what's to stop us? We have everything we need, and we don't need as much as we think we do.

The conversation ends on a dream and the dream fades with the daylight. Perhaps we'll edge a little closer to it on our next walk.

Chapter Fourteen

Enough for Everyone

Food

Last year I took the plunge and moved from growing herbs to producing small vegetables. Having a small garden I was limited to containers so the choice of produce was limited too. The crops were modest but fruitful (pardon the pun). I successfully reaped a satisfying harvest of spring onions and radishes. The radishes were a good size with plenty of heat, and the spring onions proved tasty tossed in a salad. Remembering my junior school experiments, I also grew my own cress from a very large packet of seeds on a wet paper towel on the kitchen windowsill. This year I have progressed to growing tomatoes and (small) green peppers. An old potato stuffed in a pot has yielded several small ones and 4 cloves of garlic have sprouted within a couple of weeks. The slugs seem to be avoiding them, so I will certainly consider garlic as a deterrent for next year's harvest. Even though the produce is little to speak of (I doubt it would fill a single dinner plate), it is giving me immense enjoyment. It is a beginning and I am learning.

Our experts assure us that there is enough food on this planet to feed everyone, yet world hunger is on the rise. Where there is poverty there is hunger. Where there is conflict there is also hunger. Where climates no longer support the growing of crops or feeding of livestock, hunger persists. Food is available, but for many it is either unaffordable or inaccessible.

Action Against Hunger confirms that 783 million people suffer from hunger around the world - that's equivalent to one person in ten.[1] You don't have to look for hunger in a third world country suffering from drought and in the midst of civil unrest, you can find it in our own country, ostensibly at peace and considered affluent compared to many. The Food Foundation commissioned to assess the impact of household food insecurity across the UK, confirm that 9.7 million adults and 4 million children have experienced what they term as *food insecurity*. This means they are unsure of how they will afford their weekly meals, or that they have eaten less or skipped meals to keep within a tight allowance.[2]

How is it then that we face an epidemic of obesity? Is it simply a case of not being able to afford good nutrition? Over 12 million obese adults in England have a body mass index (BMI) measuring over 30+ that puts them at severe risk of ill health and shortened lives. When you've worked a full day, it's quicker to open a ready meal or buy a take-away than it is to prepare a wholesome meal for the family. It is estimated

---

1 783 Million People Face Hunger Globally. 2023. Action Against Hunger.

2 The Broken Plate, 2023. The state of the Nation's food system. The Food Foundation.

that 20% of our most deprived citizens would have to part with half of their disposable income to meet what the government regards as a healthy diet.

We know our diet needs to improve. Thanks to the likes of Jamie Oliver, Hugh Fearnley-Whittingstall, and countless others whose lives are dedicated to the promotion of nutritional health we know about the risks we face every time we make a cheap choice.

The National Food Strategy 2021 lists several recommendations to begin a long-term shift in our culture and attitude towards better eating habits. It includes imposing taxes on sugar and salt and using the funds to buy fresh food for the disadvantaged. It includes educating the public, particularly children and new mums, supporting farmers to make best use of their land and collating data to monitor targets and regulate changes in legislation[3]. Yet with all the will and passion in the world, so long as there is a commercial industry that relies on sugar and other addictive additives to sell their products, the problem will continue.

Where there is no money there is no commercial incentive to produce food products for profit. We could see an end to ready-meals, fast food outlets and a processed diet. We could see a return to natural raw produce and all of the beneficial nutrients that would normally be lost in mass production. The adjustment may seem daunting, but it all depends on your starting point. Creating a cereal breakfast from oats, nuts, dried fruit and sweetened with honey and spiced with cinnamon can be easily prepared in bulk quantities to last a week or more. It may take a little more thought and preparation, but it is easily achievable given the time. Last night's meal was put together in just 30 minutes. I served a salad of spinach leaves, cress, cucumber, tomatoes (homegrown), beetroot, spring onion, alongside chicken breast and roasted sweet potato – a perfect meal for one of the hottest days of the year. Tonight's will be jacket potato with cheese, tuna and salad. In winter, there is nothing to beat a bowl of homemade hot soup made of seasonal root vegetables flavoured with garlic, black pepper and cheese.

With money out of the equation, we will have so much to gain in health, vitality, firsthand knowledge of nature's bounty and the skills to use it to our advantage. Remember that we will have extra time to make our own pastry, cakes, sauces, dressings and pickles. We already have labour saving machines to create yogurts, ice creams and ones that bake bread. We also have kits to make wine, cheese and boxes in which to grow mushrooms. It doesn't just have to stop at food. Recently I have noticed an increase in adverts that show us how to use natural products in other ways.

---

3 The National Food Strategy, the Plan 2021. nationalfoodstrategy.org.

Chopped up banana skin left in water becomes a fertilizer for plants; white vinegar and baking soda cleans through grease and clears drains. Many diligent gardeners grow fruit, vegetables, herbs in gardens and allotments and some keep livestock. They share their produce with friends and neighbours or in some cases leave the surplus outside their house labelled 'please take me home.'

Will this mean we no longer visit pubs and restaurants? Not necessarily, it may depend on the interests of the local community. Perhaps pub meals will become *bring and share events*.

Energy

Energy is a hot topic. The Climate Change Act 2008 commits the government in power to 'reduce greenhouse gas emissions by at least 100% of 1990 levels (net zero) by 2050'.[4] This entails a strategy to replace fossil fuels such as coal, gas etc with cleaner renewable energy sources – electricity. Our planet provides many natural resources such as the sun, the wind, waves and even microbes in the soil. In fact, we are surrounded by energy all of the time, and the higher we go into the atmosphere the more powerful it becomes.

> 'Here we sit in 2012 with the earth still burning oil and gas and coal when we have had technologies, sciences and all the information we need to have had a completely new civilisation.'
>
> [Dr Steven Greer, 2012.]

According to those who describe the feats of Nichola Tesla, we could all have free energy. We have the technology, we have the resources and we have the information, we just lack the commercial and political power. Were it not a threat for the capitalist dominions, we could all implement Tesla's theories and pay nothing for this essential resource. Energy is everywhere and there are vast amounts of it. His vision for an ideal world included the building of large towers that produce and transfer electrical currents over many miles, wirelessly. He believed that the Earth had fluid electrical charges running beneath its surface, that when interrupted by a series of electrical discharges at repeated set intervals, would create a limitless power supply by generating low-frequency electrical waves.

---

4 The Climate Change Act 2008. What is Climate Change? A Legal Duty to Act. Climate Change Committee

The option for individual sustainable homes is currently unaffordable for many despite the long-term financial benefits. If the government is committed to promoting clean affordable energy, why can't new houses be built for energy sustainability? The cost of energy to the consumer is the manpower required for harness, storage and distribution, therefore Installing the solar panels and batteries as a necessity will move the nation closer to its agreed target.

An alternative to solar power is the installation of an air source heat pump which 'transfers heat from the outside air to water, which heats your rooms via radiators or underfloor heating. It can also heat water stored in a hot water cylinder for your hot taps, showers and baths'.[5] As this is adjoined to the home, there needs to be sufficient space and adequate access to air flow. Those preferring to live in smaller tight-knit communities could use natural waste (including human excrement) to power their tools and devices. If sufficient land is available wind turbines are also a feasible alternative.

On the horizon, Hydrogen is looking to become a more attractive option for heating our homes and running our vehicles, hopefully finally eliminating the need for fossil fuels. Available locally and with no toxic waste or by products, Hydrogen is a breakthrough for the energy industry. 'Hydrogen is the most abundant molecule in the universe, but it isn't present on Earth in its free form. We must first produce it. That can be done cleanly by splitting water into hydrogen and oxygen using renewable electricity from solar and wind power. But the cheaper and more prevalent method is to extract it from natural gas or coal, which emits carbon dioxide and locks us into further exploitation of fossil fuels.'[6] The world's first hydrogen fuelled double decker bus was launched in Scotland in 2021. The inbuilt Hydrogen Fuel Cell and battery pack provides sufficient energy to travel 280 miles taking only 8 minutes to refuel. If the first production electric car was built as early as 1884, let's hope we don't have to wait another century before clean cars become available to all.

Shelter.

In a world where everyone has somewhere they can call their home, there is no room for second residences. Just short of 10% of the UK population own a second home, many of which sit in the popular picturesque counties like Cornwall and counties in Wales and NE England. Those that purchase holiday homes deny local residents the opportunity to buy. They also raise the value of property beyond affordable.

---

5 Heating Your Home. Air source heat pumps. 2023. Energy Saving Trust.

6 Hydrogen has a dirty secret – let's not think it's always a green fuel. 2021. New Scientist.

DAILY MAIL **3rd October 2023**

Another picturesque coastal community has imposed a ban on second homes

To prevent their towns being swamped with outsiders

'Britain today has a backlog of 4.3 million homes that are missing from the national housing market as they were never built. This housing deficit would take at least half a century to fill even if the Government's current target to build 300,000 homes a year is reached.'[7]

Does the government need to build more homes? 'Government data shows around 250,000 properties in England have stood empty for more than six months; another 200,000 empty homes are covered by exemptions and do not pay any council tax. Officially the total vacancy now stands at over 676,000. This figure excludes a further 257,000 so-called 'second homes' or 'furnished empties' and over 70,000 second homes flipped to paying business rates as permanent short-lets'.[8] This equates to almost one million homes in this country which stand empty and have no one living in them.

If you also count industrial building and business complexes that remain unoccupied there are enough buildings that are either readily habitable or can be converted into domestic dwellings for the entire population. With the withdrawal of businesses that would no longer operate following dissolution of a monetary system, (no money, no gain, therefore no point in trading), the number of vacant structures will increase further. Current housing law that currently restricts their usage would need to change.

Technology

'The application of knowledge for achieving practical goals in a reproducible way…can also mean the products resulting from such efforts, including both tangible tools such as utensils or machines, and intangible ones such as software' (Wikipedia).

---

7 The housebuilding crisis: The UK's 4 million missing homes. S. Watling & A. Breach. 2023. Centre for Cities.

8 National Empty Homes Week 2023 sees call for action on One Million homes nobody lives in. 2023. Action on Empty Homes.

Who or what is going to do all the jobs we hate – the backbreaking, boring ones, the mucky ones we feel are below us and the ones we avoid or pay others to do for us? When technology ceases to be in competition with itself, practical labour-saving solutions can be developed to support a comfortable standard of living for all. Imagination and innovation will not end just because no one makes any money out of it.

From 1972 to 1974, Friday nights were stressful. After a hard week's work my parents would take over the tiny kitchen to wash the week's dirty laundry in one go. A small top loader machine did the washing, and the sopping wet clothes were put through a mangle. The garments, bedlinen and towels dried overnight on numerous clothes horses or were hung out the next day if the weather was warm and fine. They saved hard to purchase a spin dryer which made a difference to time and energy (and marital harmony) and after a few years were able to buy a standard front loader model, the one we are all familiar with. If there is one device I would never be without, it's a washing machine.

THE GUARDIAN **23rd October 2023**

UK officials use AI to decide on issues from benefits to marriage licences

Government officials are using artificial intelligence and complex algorithms to help decide everything from who gets benefits to who should have their marriage licence approved, according to Guardian investigation. The findings shed light on the haphazard and often uncontrolled way that cutting-edge technology is being used across Whitehall.

Technology enables us to keep in touch with one another every minute wherever we are, cook food in less than five minutes, and keep us entertained 24 hours a day if we choose. It has lifted the limitations of having to be in a certain place at a certain time, we can pick and choose what we want to do at a time that suits us best. But if we believe current technology has made our lives easier, we are mistaken. Devices have simply increased our capacity for more work. Just because our automated machines are doing our manual work and our computers are resolving our challenges, does this mean we are sitting back and enjoying the benefits? On the contrary, we are chained to desks and screens for longer hours. And if all our responsibilities were being met by automated means, in our current system most of us would be unemployed.

In a moneyless world, technology will be essential. It will help us to connect and to communicate. It will enable us to organise, coordinate and allocate tasks and resources. It will store information for when we need it and it will monitor and evaluate our activities. Where there is no competition, technology will be more streamlined and there will be compatibility between operating systems and software. Speed, functionality and fairness should prevail.

Artificial intelligence (AI

14 May 2023. BBC Sunday programme. Craig Jackson, CEO for Octopus Energy describes efficient use of AI: 'During the energy crisis, there was an increased time spent talking to customers to help them through. One way we've done that is augmenting teams with artificial intelligence doing the equivalent of 250 people's work, answering emails. The interesting fact is emails written by AI achieve a higher satisfaction rate than ones written by humans. That's 34% of all our emails delivered by AI in just six weeks. Governments need to understand the pace at which this economic dislocation could occur'.[9]

AI is inevitable, it is happening, and it will be a part of our lives – just like the washing machine, the internet and the mobile phone. We will become accustomed to it and eventually we will embrace it and use it to our advantage. Our relationship with AI will be interdependent. AI will also be misused, unlike the washing machine, but very much like the internet and the mobile phone. 'AI basically refers to a machine that can simulate human cognitive abilities, whether that's problem-solving or learning. A human has to program the machine to perform these tasks, such as a chess-playing AI. In other words, AI performs pre-programmed functions.'[10]

What is concerning governments and the public, is the development of Artificial General Intelligence (AGI) which describes technology that has the capability to perform human tasks that it has not been programmed for. AGI can think and act without the need for human intervention; it will function and evolve independently.

We assume AGI will be developed to serve the people, to save labour and to help us manage our lives with more efficiency and accuracy, but will it not simply expand the motives of whoever controls it, so long as it remains controllable? Just like money, AGI will work for the few and against the many. Where no wealth is to be made from the sale of AGI, the likelihood of danger to individuals and civilisation should diminish or at the very least, reduce negative impact. Taking away the need

---

9 Will It Be Hard to Make a Living for Years to Come? Sunday with Laura Kueunssberg, 2023. BBC Programmes.

10 AI vs AGI – what's the difference between these artificial intelligences? R.Cotta. 2023. Videogamer.

for money however does not necessarily eradicate a person's need for power. The development of AGI to assert authority over a group or a population is still a threat. 'The most important question we have to ask ourselves at this point in history and requires no technical knowledge is- what sort of future society do we want to create with all this technology we are making? What do we want the role of humans to be in this world?'[11]

This is a valid concern - what will be our role? When all the work is done for us, what will our lives look like, what will be our primary function, our incentives and our motivation? I believe that no amount of labour-saving technology will extinguish our instinctive need for relationships, for self expression and improvement; we will still take pride in what we are able to accomplish ourselves – we will always be seeking purpose in our lives and therein lies our choices. We can and should consciously choose what we agree to adopt and to make use of. We should ask ourselves does this device (and let's keep calling it a device to ensure we feel in control of it) serve my body, my family, my way of living? What skills will I lose if I come to depend on it?

Just in case you are wondering, AI has not been used to write any part of this book. All wording (that is not referenced) is my own.

Stuff

I have too much stuff, we all have too much stuff, but we still like to have our own stuff; containers, furniture, linen, bits of ribbon and tape, cables, kitchenware, soft toys and useless but treasured ornaments.

Once a year my friend and I save up all our surplus stuff and take it to a local car boot sale. We don't expect to make much money, we mainly do it because we can't bear to see good things go to waste, and because we enjoy the experience and the time together. We play at shopkeepers for a few hours, with only the weather to dampen the fun. The public barter because they can, and as the morning progresses we drop the prices till eventually we give items away, not wishing to take them back home. We leave with maybe £60 in our pockets – the cost of a week's groceries. Occasionally we return home with a little of someone else's stuff for which we too have successfully haggled.

When my brother pays me a visit we scour the local charity shops for stuff. He looks for obscure DVD's and packs of stamps, and I for blank canvasses or boards on which to paint. I often wonder how long we, the public, could survive on all the stuff

---

11 ihuman Storyville Documentary. 2019. Aired on BBC 29 August 2023.

that is in circulation if no new hardware was produced. How long before we run out of glass bottles, plates, clothes, toys and all the things we use, discard and replace with no real need?

Car boot sales and charity shops are popular. They are always busy. There is a sense of the unexpected, the curious, not knowing what we will find and when we do find something of interest, paying very little for it. We not only buy from them, we stock them too. I see the future of shops in a similar vein. When we need stuff we will go to the appropriate *exchange*, take what is useful to us and give back what isn't, with just the obligation of ensuring items are clean and in good repair.

There will be the repairers, the restorers and renovators who will work with items such as furniture and domestic machinery– production will only be necessary when essential items are no longer available. Given the length of time hardware takes to decompose I doubt there will be much that will wear out – perhaps soft textiles and smaller appliances.

Ownership

The phrase 'you will own nothing and be happy' has been circulated widely and perceived from different perspectives. It was first written in 2016, by Ida Auken in an essay published for the World Economic Forum titled 'Welcome to 2030. I own nothing, have no privacy, and life has never been better', later retitled 'Here's how life could change in my city by the year 2030'. It describes an imagined life in which a person owns nothing but instead relies on shared services to meet all their daily needs. It's a paradoxical predicament. What does it matter if we own nothing so long as we are happy? But it we don't own anything, who does? Who owns our house, our cars, our treasures? Who acquires and who maintains it? Moreover, who has control over its lease – and more importantly, who or what has the power to remove it and under what circumstances?

The concept is not utopian and only implies a perfect world; one of clean air and waters and numerous green spaces. A world where consumerism is obsolete and free time is plentiful. There is no ownership; "everything you considered a product has now become a service. We have access to transportation, accommodation, food and all the things we need in our daily lives. We don't pay any rent because someone else is using our free space or whenever we do not need it; my living room is used for business meetings when I am not there." If this hasn't got you worrying the final words of the essay are a clue to the conditions for living in a progressive society: "Once in a while I get annoyed about the fact that I have no real privacy. Nowhere I can go and not be registered. I know that somewhere everything I do, think and dream of is recorded. I just hope that nobody will use it against me."

I do not advocate the complete surrender of ownership. I don't think we are ready for that. Ownership can be reviewed as a form of custody or guardianship. If I own a house or a car, it should always be mine until such time that I no longer have a use for it. Never should it be taken from me. When I, or the belonging expires, or when I willingly give it up, only then should it be reallocated. Nobody should ever have to give up their home and their belongings prematurely and without consent. We must feel secure to trust each other and our communities; we must feel confident to be able to live peaceably and with whatever certainty exists for us at any given time.

It doesn't have to be perfect, but it could be far more simple, peaceful and rewarding. We just might become healthier, in our bodies and in our minds. We could have more time for our families and our interests. We could become more skilled. We may rescue our planet's natural resources – we just might find our true purpose.

Chapter Fifteen

It doesn't have to be perfect

'You are erratic, conflicted, disorganised, every decision is debated; every action questioned, every individual entitled to their own small opinion.

[Seven of Nine; Star Trek Voyager series 4 episode 1.]

Yesterday, during the course of my waking hours, I witnessed a sick world come crashing down on the shoulders of defenceless victims and I despaired. On my TV screen I watched a deluded patriarchy stubbornly hold on to the selfish belief that it can control a population with guns and fear. In conversation, I witnessed the consequences of an outdated ideology that believes if you make people work harder and longer you will reap greater profits. I patiently listened to an incompetent leadership that knows no better than to punish its subordinates through its own ignorance and fear. I held a solitary individual hopelessly fighting to reclaim a piece of their life that had been ripped from their control. What I saw was a dispirited world a million miles away from me, in my workplace and then arriving in my very home. In just one day and from many angles I saw conflict propelled by a consuming fear of lack. Why are we so frightened? What are we so frightened of losing?

To expect a perfectly fair and harmonious society in a moneyless world is unreasonable. We are a planet of 8.1 billion individuals; that equates to 8.1 billion unique representations of humanity, each with its own experience, opinions and preferred way of living.

A new system, an equitable model doesn't have to be perfect, but for the majority of people it can be better. If according to many sources the world is on the brink of financial collapse, what do we have to lose? We could be healed and restored, we could enjoy balance and fairness, we could be returned to the earth, to ourselves and to each other.

"Your scientific beliefs tell you that your entire world happened accidentally. Your religions tell you that man is sinful, the body is not to be trusted and the senses can lead you astray. In this maze of beliefs you have largely lost a sense of your own worth and purpose. A generalised fear and suspicion is generated, and life too often becomes stripped of any heroic qualities."[1]

Imagine that - we have all been endowed with heroic qualities. We have innate superpowers that we have been taught to doubt and suppress and an inner knowing that we distrust and dismiss. Everything we want, we already are. Our error is believing

1 The Individual and the Nature of Mass Events: A Seth Book. J. Roberts. 1982. Amber Allen Publishing.

that everything we want to be, can only be accomplished by purchasing, adding and accumulating, when in fact the more we subtract from ourselves the greater and more powerful we become. It is as though the goods, the experiences and the status we seek to strengthen our position in the world, just add further veils of illusion and dependency until we can no longer see or trust who we really are.

Our Intuition

I've had headaches since I was a child. They are not migraines. I do not need to lay in a dark room, in fact resting my head increases the pain. Standard painkillers usually help and most of the time the pressure eases and the pain subsides. I was referred to every clinic the GP could think of and all found nothing. I then realised at a late age, that my body was simply responding to changes in atmospheric pressure. How is that no medical professional told me that. The GP checked bloods and wanted to prescribe anti-depressants, the consultants checked ears, eyes, facial muscles and scanned my brain for abnormalities or at least a cause. Each clinician focussed on their area of discipline and expertise and found nothing within their medical parameters. Nevertheless, the pain persisted. After I met someone who described how an imminent storm brought on a headache, I started to monitor my own physical reactions. I sat with the pain, what does it feel like? Sometimes piercing in the left or right temple, sometimes as though a clamp had been placed about my head. What intensifies and what relieves it? What should I avoid and how should I care for myself?

How many of us manage our own conditions by simply monitoring the pattern of our symptoms, noticing the foods that cause us discomfort, the postures that create pain in our joints, the motion that is going to give us nausea, the situations that increase our anxiety or withhold our sleep. We are each 100% unique and we know ourselves better than anyone else can. Countless times I have heard women speak of being dismissed by doctors as being overanxious, worrying too much, being told to expect certain symptoms and not having their concerns taken seriously. Maybe it's the same for men too.

How often do we listen to our intuition? That small voice of knowing that is linked to neither logic, nor memory; the voice we hear first but dismiss quickly – who am I to know that? How can I believe what is just a feeling? I must be wrong. And when our intuition proves valid, we are surprised - I knew that! I was right! Why didn't I speak up? Why didn't I trust myself? On how many occasions have we surprised ourselves by our inner wisdom, intelligence, our foresight?

That small voice can barely be heard over the blare of expertise, the blast of authority and the chatter of persuasive rhetoric. We have become accustomed to placing all our concerns and our decisions in the hands of the professionals, the experts whom we believe know best. Anyone who has followed any major public enquiry such as Mid Staffordshire NHS, Grenfell and now COVID, will see that experts do not always make good judgements, that they frequently make assumptions. They hesitate, they stubbornly follow a path that blinds them to risk, and we just let them. Even though our intuition screams at us, we ignore it because we assume someone else knows better.

The Law of Attraction

"Everything is energy and that is all there is to it. Match the frequency of the reality you want, and you cannot help but get that reality. It can be no other way. This is not philosophy."

[Albert Einstein.]

Not only do we have innate knowledge, but we also have the physical means to create what we want. There are different ways of approaching the law of attraction and I will leave you to investigate this phenomenon for yourself. You can look at it from a physical perspective, take a spiritual approach, or you can simply see it as exercising a muscle you didn't know you had.

Put in basic terms, the law of attraction endorses the principle of what you give, you receive. Whatever you give your energy and attention to, is what you can expect in return. If you exude a fear of lack, then you will live frugally and accumulate little. If you project an energy of gratitude and abundance, then this is what you will experience. It's like viewing the world as a mirror. What you give your energy to is reflected back to you. I have heard people use the law of attraction both flippantly and effectively when they summon the *Parking Angel.* They firmly believe that if they say aloud that there will be a parking space waiting for them at the end of their journey then one will be available. They are adamant that it never fails, and I believe them. If it works for parking, then it can work for other things too.

After a long time searching for a bottle of squash in a garage and finding none, I paused. Standing still I closed my eyes and focussed on the item intently. I calmed my breathing and placed all my energy in the visualisation of a bottle of Robinson's Orange Barley Water. In less than half a minute, I looked again, turned a corner and there I saw it on the shelf that I had already passed several times, looking as though it had been there all along. Funnily, I left without making the purchase as it was far more than I wanted to pay. When needed to, I have generated nail brushes, powdered milk and body spray. There are things I have not been able to retrieve such as lost items or the health of my dog, but I also believe that there is a reason for everything.

Manifestation requires focus, our full attention with no distractions, and a force that is directed to a single outcome. When my dog did not stop coughing for over 24 hours, I told him with full vigour and with no uncertainty, aloud so that the energy would carry, "that is your last cough!". He coughed once more and then ceased. He didn't cough again. Recently I showed a friend how to rid himself of a pesky wasp by simply telling it to leave. To his surprise the wasp immediately flew away and did not return.

When it comes to money, I maintain 'I always have enough'. My friend's mantra is "I love money and money loves me." She drives a Jaguar and takes several holidays a year, I drive a standard Citroën and manage a couple of weekend breaks. We can attribute results to coincidences and so consequently deny ourselves the opportunity to create the life we want. In doing so we deny ourselves our power and once again, resign ourselves to the hand (we think or believe) life has dealt us. Is it magic? Only if you want to call it that. It's physics. As Einstein says, everything is energy, and we align ourselves with the energy we want to experience. If everything is energy, energy is everywhere, we share it, we absorb it, we influence and we in turn can be affected by the energies of others. In this respect we are all connected. It therefore stands to reason that if two or more combine their energies these will be amplified, hence the power of like-minded groups, cohesive communities, protesting crowds and fussy monkeys.

Healing Energies

If our thoughts and emotions are energy we can transmit these to others to heal, to comfort, to calm and to inspire. I perfected the technique of telepathically soothing my dog Chip when he was having a bad dream at night. He slept on his own bed at the foot of mine and like dogs often do, he whimpered when dreaming. The whimpering usually increased until it woke up him and me both. Because I couldn't bear to leave a warm bed, when I started to hear him whimper I imagined calmly stroking his fur just under his ear and then gently down his side. In my mind I could feel his softness and his body heat and very soon he quietened without waking. As we both became more accustomed to this method of soothing he relaxed more quickly each time. I have instilled calm in people but not so easily. People have to be open and receptive or even oblivious to what you are doing. Animals offer no resistance, there is no ego, no need for self-preservation nor need for scientific evidence - they simply respond.

Thankfully the practice of meditation and mindfulness are becoming more popular and acceptable to the public, both encouraged in the workplace and in schools. Like anything, it needs to be practised but the efforts are well worth the rewards. Studies have shown that children with attention-deficit hyperactivity disorder (ADHD) respond favourably to short regular periods of meditation or exercise by increasing attention span and reducing their hyperactivity - surely a far better method of helping them than relying solely on the effects and side effects of potent medication.[2]

Medicinal drugs still play a vital role in how we manage our physiology and will do for a long time to come. I relied on them as a child to manage epileptic seizures. My eldest son would have died without them. I was grateful for them during childbirth, dental extraction and I rely on them now for immediate neurological or muscular pain relief, but they need not be the only means of treatment to the exclusion of others. Local therapy centres are becoming increasingly popular and diverse with the choice of treatments they can offer. Some such as acupuncture, aromatherapy and even Reiki are now being offered by the NHS as a supplement to support main treatment, but there are a still a multitude of healing practices that go unacknowledged or are not taken seriously.

'Some Complementary and Alternative Medicines (CAM) treatments are based on principles and an evidence base, not recognised by the majority of independent scientists. Others have been proven to work for a limited number of health conditions When a person uses any health treatment, including CAM, and experiences an improvement, this may be due to the placebo effect.'[3] A survey examining the use of CAM amongst the UK population noted an increase particularly for those wishing to relieve musculoskeletal and mental health problems. Those able to access and benefit from alternative treatment were generally better off financially and therefore able to fund the treatment themselves. 'People most commonly visited CAM practitioners for manual therapies (massage, osteopathy, chiropractic) and acupuncture, as well as yoga, Pilates, reflexology, and mindfulness or meditation. Women, people with higher socioeconomic status and those in south England were more likely to access CAM.'[4]

These findings are not surprising. Several of my family members, friends and colleagues choose to pay for private treatment. I have personally elected to privately pay for a course of acupuncture for tendonitis (tennis elbow). I did approach the NHS first but was not examined. I was seen in the waiting room, given a strap and a sheet of exercises with no explanation of how to apply either. The consultation took less than 2 minutes. This is no reflection of expertise, but more of resources. When

---

2 Exercise and Meditation Help Kids with ADHD in Just 10 Minutes. J. Sweet. 2021. Very Well Mind.

3 Complimentary and Alternative Medicine. NHS.UK

4 Complementary medicine use, views, and experiences: a national survey in England. D. Sharp et al. 2018. British Journal of General Practice.

I saw a private acupuncturist I underwent a non-intrusive holistic consultation that asked about all aspects of my health. I was healed within 6 weeks.

Traditional Chinese Medicines base the treatment of acupuncture on the acknowledgement of Qi, an energy that follows specific pathways or meridians through the body. The body has 12 meridians, which house two energies – Yin and Yang. Yin moves outwards whilst Yang moves inwards towards our core. Where there is an imbalance or blockage an ailment is sure to arise. Acupuncturists use very fine needles to unblock the path of energy and in doing so, relieve the ailment. Since the success of the acupuncture, I have preferred to pay for private chiropractic treatment and osteopathy. I have even experienced significant pain relief after a session of sound therapy.

Why are we still taking a blinkered approach to our body by simply focussing on one part of it as the problem? Why are we not making the connection between our thoughts and beliefs, and the impact this has on our health? I can't help but wonder if no money was to be made from pharmaceuticals, would this finally open the door for a greater acceptance of non-invasive effective treatment. Increasing numbers of individuals are seeking a more holistic method of treating and healing themselves, recognising that body, spirit and mind are of one and the same, and that each has an impact on the other. Could we make more use of yoga, hypnosis, light, sound or crystals as primary sources of remedy? The more I understand energies the more I am convinced that they are the gateway to our future health and wellbeing.

A Holistic Approach

I have now watched several interviews with John White, an inventor from New Zealand with a background in Electrical Engineering, Physics, and Computer Sciences. John's research of pulsed electromagnetic field (PEMF) therapy has led him to design and manufacture Rife machines that are based on the original theories of Royal Raymond Rife.

'PEMF therapy effectively can realign the electricity in your cells. When a cell is stimulated, it allows positive charges to enter a cell in an open ION channel. The inside of this cell becomes positively charged, which will trigger other electrical currents, turning into pulses. This can positively influence movement, healing, and sending of signals. Any disruption in electrical currents can lead to dysfunction or illness. PEMF therapy helps restore this disruption in electrical current to the normal state, which promotes overall wellness.'[5]

---

5 What are the benefits of PULSE PEMF Therapy? Dr. C Williams 2021. Interventional Orthpaedics of Atlanta.

By applying the treatment as a gentle pulse, the energy of cells can be restored in a safe way at a safe pace; treatment therefore acts in a holistic fashion as well as a targeted one. This is not medical treatment that must be paid for, the purchase of Rife machines is available to anyone. It is also regarded not just as a treatment for illness but for the maintenance of good health.

Not only does our body, mind and spirit function as one, we should also remember that we are connected and affected by our planet Earth, the phases of our moon and the galactic activities beyond both, such as solar flares. I have recently come to learn about the Schumann Resonances, natural electromagnetic fields that surround our planet often known as the earth's heartbeat.

'At any given moment about 2,000 thunderstorms roll over Earth, producing some 50 flashes of lightning every second. Each lightning burst creates electromagnetic waves that begin to circle around Earth captured between Earth's surface and a boundary about 60 miles up. Some of the waves – if they have just the right wavelength – combine, increasing in strength, to create a repeating atmospheric heartbeat known as Schumann resonance.'[6]

The Schumann resonance which normally resonates at a frequency of 7.83 Hz is said to positively affect human health and well-being including brain function, sleep patterns, our heart, nervous systems, cells, proteins and DNA. For a full explanation I recommend watching YouTube videos by Stefan Burns.[7]

Our bodies are our own, we understand them best, we know what affects us and how. We can be in charge of the controls if we allow ourselves to be.

Anything is Possible.

I invite you to draw a large circle and imagine it represents everything there is to know, everything that is possible, everything both solid and intangible that exists in the universe. Within the circle draw a smaller one that represents everything we do know or have managed to prove, without doubt. How would the two compare? What size would the inner one be in contrast to the outer – a fraction for sure. Would it measure a tenth, a hundredth, maybe just a pinprick? Would it expand with time or just change shape, after all how many times did we believe something to be true only to discover we were wrong, recalculated and then found we misjudged yet again.

6 Schuman resonance. Dr. K Bhattacharyya. 2023. The Times of India.

7 Schumann resonances basics, biology, & bioelectricity. S Burns. 2023. www.youtube.com

What happens to all that space in between? Does it cease to exist because we cannot comprehend, believe or evidence what lies therein? Try drawing another circle beyond the smallest one, that represents all that has been seen, heard and experienced but not yet proven. How much bigger would it be? Two, three, ten times the size?

You can complete the same exercise and relate it to your life. If your most fulfilling life possible is the largest circle, and your current life is the smallest circle, what is the scale of difference? What are the limitations, the barriers, the assumptions and the fears that prevent you from expanding? And if you could expand the smallest circle of reality to include what you believe to be desirable, feasible and achievable, how much would it grow?

Who is telling us it cannot be done? What is limiting our imagination, and dampening our aspirations? And for what purpose? Or is this it - is this the best we can expect?

I believe certain powers, perhaps beyond governments, have technologies so advanced that it could resolve many of the world's problems should they choose to apply them. I believe there is much out there that we either don't know about or we refuse to believe exists. Those brave enough to speak out about such knowledge face risk of ridicule or harm to themselves and their families. Look for it and you will find it.

> 'Keep people fat, keep them happy, keep them diverted and keep them entertained with drivel and shock and nonsense. That unfortunately is the sort of thing that has taken the place of news and information.'
>
> [Dr Steven Greer, 2012]

I believe we are being denied resources that would resolve the issues around health, travel, energy, environmental deterioration, communication, defence and a whole host of other concerns. I believe it serves the interests of a few to keep us in a constant state of separation, lack, fear, even illness so that we might continue to consume, comply and to compete. Consumption keeps us spending and therefore borrowing. Fear keeps us dependent on government direction. Competition keeps us apart from each other. Is there any easier way to control a population?

There are many revelations appearing more openly and frequently, on channels less known and in some cases, in national papers that can no longer ignore them. There are public enquiries that are holding our elected officials to account. There is increasing evidence of failures that have been hidden or denied leaving a nation bewildered and uncertain of who to trust and in doing so denying their own power as a citizen, a voter and a consumer. We've been looking for hope and guidance in the wrong places.

There is a shift, I can feel it. Never have I encountered so much despondency and dissatisfaction amongst individuals who are trying for something better. Sometimes they don't know what it is they want, but they do know what it isn't – and that's more of the same.

We don't need money. We need the love of our families and the support of our friends and communities.

We don't need debt. We need the generosity of nature and emotional intelligence to respect and preserve it. We are everything we need.

We have the ability to think and act independently and trust our instincts. We need to reclaim our fundamental entitlement to a life of comfort, security and abundance.

It is our birthright.

A New Beginning

2 December 2023. My parents have safely moved into their new care residence. It's a weight off my mind and brings my brother and I peace to know they are being looked after by compassionate staff in a clean and comfortable home. As we drive away, passing a busy junction, something I spot compels us to pull over to the side of the road.

When we look across the landscape, to my amazement we see a flock of lapwings wading in a waterlogged field. I think back to a couple of months ago when I saw, for the first time in many years, a horse chestnut tree's leaves turn yellow in Autumn. They don't usually make it past September. I dare to hope we have turned a corner.

My life is its own definition,
so is yours.
Let us leave the priests
to their hells and heavens
and confine the scientists
to their dying universe
with its accidentally created stars.
Let us each dare
to open our dream's door
and explore
the unofficial thresholds,
where we begin.

A Psychic Manifesto by Jane Roberts

A Final Note

A merrier Christmas Bob, my good
fellow, than I have given you for
many a year. I'll raise your
salary and endeavour to assist
your struggling family."
"Make up the fires and buy
another Coal-Scuttle before you
dot another i, Bob Cratchit!"

Yesterday I was clever, so I wanted to change the world.
Today I am wise, so I am changing myself
[Rumi]

24 December 2023

The book may be finished, but the stories continue. A new hospital was approved and so were improvements to the Kings residence. The US government has been bailed out yet again, I've no doubt it won't be long before it crawls back to the Federal Reserve, cap in hand.

The Body Shop closed 75 stores but was rescued from administration and on the horizon are two elections (UK and USA) that are likely to have a significant impact on our future.

Camp Beagle achieved over 100,000 signatures thanks to the support of a couple of celebrities; and claimed their day in parliament. Marshall BioResources (MBR) published accounts for 2022 declaring a loss of £798, 808. Even though it has halved its number of employers (since 2017) the number of puppies bred for experiments, has increased. Their youngest and most fervent protester publicly stated:

'Our petition spoke the words of the people and was sadly ignored. we need to make them hear our noise even more now. This is not over and we will never ever give up. Our government is failing this country yet again and not listening to who know best. Non-animal methods need to be started immediately and MBR acres needs to be closed down. Please stay positive and keep the faith as we will see the end to his torturous evil place. You heard the debate, you heard so many MP's saying what we need them to be saying. They are hearing us. Home Office wake up! you need to care and stop the greed on torturing animals for the horror of so-called science. it's time for change and it needs to happen now, not a phase out of many years. I feel you have just pushed our petition away and ignored the people of this country. We will not go away!'

I am certain there will be no let-up of efforts to increase production of unnecessary goods and services, the drive for economic growth is relentless. The corporations and governments will encourage more spending which will result in more waste and more debt. The economy and the earth will groan and subside under the weight of the few whose greed and near sightedness is costing us all dear. Our monetary system will continue to serve the 1% and slowly kill our only home.

Even if no one reads this book, there has nevertheless been a change. I have changed. My relationship to money has changed. Money is energy; it comes and it goes, moves and flows to wherever, whenever and to whomever needs it most. it will not dominate my decisions or my choices. It is a factor but it is not my ruler. I am everything I need.

I owe this book to many.

To Nicola and Heather whose initial question; 'what do you mean, we don't need money?' prompted me to write it – thank you.

To the research participants who willingly contributed their opinions and experiences – thank you.

To Bob and Carol for sharing their memories and their literature so that the work of Ebyon continues to inspire– thank you.

To my family, friends and colleagues who have provided encouragement and support not to mention valuable stories – thank you.

To Allan for his gracious criticisms and tireless proofreading – thank you.

To Sherile, for showing me how to write a better book - thank you

To Chip, Wynter and Ronnie. If you have a dog you will know how much they fill your heart and soothe your pain – thank you.

To all those sharing their words, their actions and their light to bring in a better world

thank you.

Together we will reach critical mass.

Books

M. Boyle. 2010. The Money-less Man – A year of free economic living. Oneworld Publications

D. Boyle. 2013. Broke – who killed the middle classes? Fourth Estate.

D.Evans. 2015. The Utopia Experiment. Picador Books.

D.R.Hawkins. 2005. Truth vs Falsehood: How to Tell the Difference. Veritas Publishing

F.Herzberg, B.Mausner & B.Snyderman. 1959. The Motivation to Work. New York: Wiley.

A.Jackson, B.Dyson. 2012. Modernising Money; Why our monetary system is broken and how it can be fixed. Positive Money.

J. Mackey & R. Sisodia. 2014. Conscious Capitalism; Liberating the Heroic Spirit of Business. Havard Business Review Press

D.McGarvey. 2022. The Social Distance Between Us. Ebury Publishing

B Mezrich. 2019. Bitcoin Billionaires. A True story of genius, betrayal and redemption. Little Brown Book Group

R.Patel. 2009. The Value of Nothing: how to reshape market society and redefine democracy. Portobello Books

J. Piper. 2022. The Rubbish Book: A Complete Guide to Recycling. Unbound.

H. Powell & D. Edelstyn. 2020 . Bank Job Chelsea Green Publishing.

D.Price. 2021. Laziness Does Not Exist. Atria Books

J. Roberts. 1982. The Individual and the Nature of Mass Events: A Seth Book. Amber Allen Publishing.

B.Sanders. 2023. It's OK to be Angry About Capitalism. Allen lane (Penguin Group).

P.Selig. 2013. the Book of Knowing and Worth. TarcherPerigee (Penguin Group).

M.Slater. 2018. The National Debt A short history. C.Hurst & Co. publishers

M.Thomas. 2020. 99% How We've Been Screwed, and How to Fight Back. Apollo.

R. Van de Weyer. 2005. Zen Economics . Third Eye (an imprint of Bhavana Books)

R.Wax. 2020. And Now for the Good News. Penguin Books.

R.Webb. 2019. The Economics of Star Trek: the Proto – Post-Scarcity Economy. Pipertext

R. Winn. 2018. The Salt Path. Penguin Books

www.ingramcontent.com/pod-product-compliance
Lightning Source LLC
Chambersburg PA
CBHW031122020426
42333CB00012B/190
* 9 7 8 1 8 3 5 3 8 7 1 0 8 *